Vanguards of tl

A Romance of the Old S.......

Margaret Hill McCarter

Alpha Editions

This edition published in 2024

ISBN : 9789362925947

Design and Setting By
Alpha Editions
www.alphaedis.com
Email - info@alphaedis.com

Contents

FOREWORD

Westward, along the level prairies of a kingdom yet to be, my memory runs, with a clear vision of the days when romance died not and strong hearts never failed. The glamour of the plains is before my eyes; the tingle of courage, danger-born, is in my pulse-beat; the soft hand of love is touching my hand. I live again the drama of life wherein there are no idle actors, no stale, unmeaning lines. And beyond the action, this way *up* the years, there runs also the forward-gazing vision toward a new Hesperides:

Through the veins
Of whose vast Empire flows, in strength'ning tides,
Trade, the calm health of nations.

* * * * *

And sometimes I would doubt
If statesmen, rocked and dandled into power,
Could leave such legacies to kings.

I

CLEARING THE TRAIL
VANGUARDS OF THE PLAINS
A ROMANCE OF THE SANTA FÉ TRAIL

I

THE BEGINNINGS OF A PLAINSMAN

There came a time in the law of life
When over the nursing sod
The shadows broke, and the soul awoke
In a strange, dim dream of God.
--LANGDON SMITH.

It might have been but yesterday that I saw it all: the glinting sunlight on
the yellow Missouri boiling endlessly along at the foot of the bluff; the
flood-washed sands across the river; the tangle of tall, coarse weeds fringing
them, edged by the scrubby underbrush. And beyond that the big trees of
the Missouri woodland, so level against the eastern horizon that I used to
wonder if I might not walk upon their solid-looking tops if I could only
reach them. I wondered, too, why the trees on our side of the river should
vary so in height when those in the eastern distance were so evenly grown.
One day I had asked Jondo the reason for this, and had learned that it was
because of the level ground on the farther side of the valley. I began then to
love the level places of the earth. I love them still. And, always excepting
that one titanic rift, where the world stands edgewise, with the sublimity of
the Almighty shimmering through its far depths, I love them more than any
other thing that nature has yet offered to me.

But to come back to that picture of yesterday: old Fort Leavenworth on the
bluff; the little and big ravines that billow the landscape about it; the faint
lines of trails winding along the hillsides toward the southwest; the
unclouded skies so everlastingly big and intensely blue; and, hanging like a
spray of glorious blossoms flung high above me, the swaying folds of the
wind-caressed flag, now drooping on its tall staff, now swelling full and
free, straight from its gripping halyards.

Between me and the fort many people were passing to and fro, some of
whom were to walk with me down the long trail of years. Evermore that
April day stands out as the beginning of things for me. Dim are the days
behind it, a jumble of happy childish hours, each keen enough as the things
of childhood go; but from that one day to the present hour the unforgotten
deeds of busy years run clearly in my memory as I lift my pen to write
somewhat of their dramatic record.

And that this may not seem all a backward gaze, let me face about and look forward from the beginning--a stretch of canvas, lurid sometimes, sometimes in glorious tinting, sometimes intensely dark, with rifts of lightning cleaving through its blackness. But nowhere dull, nowhere without design in every brush-stroke.

I had gone out on the bluff to watch for the big fish that Bill Banney, a young Kentuckian over at the fort, had told me were to be seen only on those April days when the Missouri was running north instead of south. And that when little boys kept very still, the fish would come out of the water and play leap-frog on the sand-bars.

If I failed to see them this morning, I meant to run back to the parade-ground and play leap-frog myself with my cousin Beverly, who wanted proof for most of Bill Banney's stories. Beverly was growing wise and lanky for his age. I was still chubby, and in most things innocent, and inclined to believe all that I heard, or I should not have been taken in by that fish story.

We were orphans with no recollection of any other home than the log house near the fort. We had been fathered and mothered by our uncle, Esmond Clarenden, owner of the little store across the square from our house, and a larger establishment down at Independence on the Missouri River.

Always a wonderful man to me was that Esmond Clarenden, product of one of the large old New England colleges. He found time to guard our young years with the same diplomatic system by which he controlled all of his business affairs. He laid his plans carefully and never swerved from carrying them through afterward; he insisted on order in everything; he rendered value for value in his contracts; he chose his employees carefully, and trusted them fully; he had a keen sense of humor, a genial spirit of good-will, and he loved little children. Fitted as he was by culture and genius to have entered into the greater opportunities of the Eastern States, he gave himself to the real up-building of the West, and in the larger comfort and prosperity and peace of the Kansas prairies of to-day his soul goes marching on.

The waters, as I watched them, were all running south toward that vague, down-stream world shut off by trees at a bend of the course. I waited a long time there for the current to shift to the north, wondering meanwhile about those level-topped forests, and what I might see beyond them if I were sitting on their flat crests. And, as I wondered, the first dim sense of being *shut in* came filtering through my childish consciousness. I could not cross the river. Big as my playground had always been, I had never been out of sight of the fort's flagstaff up-stream, nor down-stream. The wooded ravines blocked me on the southwest. What lay beyond these limits I had tried to picture again and again. I had been a dreamer all of my short life, and this new feeling of being shut in, held back, from something slipped upon me easily.

As I sat on the bluff in the April sunshine, I turned my face toward the west and stretched out my chubby arms for larger freedom. I wanted to *see the open level places*, wanted till it hurt me. I could cry easily enough for some things. I could not cry for this. It was too deep for tears to reach. Moreover, this new longing seemed to drop down on me suddenly and overwhelm me, until I felt almost as if I were caught in a net.

As I stared with half-seeing eyes toward the wooded ravines beyond the fort, suddenly through the budding branches I caught sight of a horseman riding down a half-marked trail into a deep hollow. Horsemen were common enough to forget in a moment, but when this one reappeared on the hither side of the ravine, I saw that the rider's face was very dark, that his dress, from the sombrero to the spurred heel, was Mexican, and that he was heavily armed, even for a plainsman. When he reached the top of the bluff he made straight across the square toward my uncle Esmond Clarenden's little storehouse, and I lost sight of him.

Something about him seemed familiar to me, for the gift of remembering faces was mine, even then. A fleeting childish memory called up such a face and dress somewhere back in the dim days of babyhood, with the haunting sound of a low, musical voice, speaking in the soft Castilian tongue.

But the memory vanished and I sat a long time gazing at the wooded west that hid the open West of my day-dreams.

Suddenly Jondo came riding up on his big black horse to the very edge of the bluff.

"You are such a little mite, I nearly forgot to see you," he called, cheerily. "Your Uncle Esmond wants you right away. Mat Nivers, or somebody else, sent me to run you down," he added, leaning over to lift me up to a seat on the horse behind him.

Few handsomer men ever graced a saddle. Big, broad-shouldered, muscular, yet agile, a head set like a Greek statue, and a face--nobody could ever make a picture of Jondo's face for me--the curling brown hair, soft as a girl's, the broad forehead, deep-set blue eyes, heavy dark brow, cheeks always ruddy through the plain's tan, strong white teeth, firm square chin, and a smile like sunshine on the gray prairies. Eyes, lips, teeth--aye, the big heart behind them--all made that smile. No grander prince of men ever rode the trails or dared the dangers of the untamed West. I did not know his story for many years. I wish I might never have known it. But as he began with me, so he ended--brave, beloved old Jondo!

Down on the parade-ground Beverly Clarenden and Mat Nivers were sitting with their feet crossed under them, tailor fashion, facing each other and talking earnestly. Over by the fort, Esmond Clarenden stood under a big elm-tree. A round little, stout little man he was, whose sturdy strength and grace of bearing made up for his lack of height. Like a great green tent the boughs of the elm, just budding into leaf, drooped over him. A young army officer on a cavalry horse was talking with him as we came up.

"Run over there to Beverly now. Gail," my uncle said, with a wave of his hand.

I was always in awe of shoulder-straps, so I scampered away toward the children. But not until, child-like, I had stared at the three men long enough to take a child's lasting estimate of things.

I carry still the keen impression of that moment when I took, unconsciously, the measure of the three: the mounted army man, commander of the fort, big in his official authority and force; Jondo on his great black horse, to me the heroic type of chivalric courage; and between the two, Esmond Clarenden, unmounted, with feet firmly planted, suggesting nothing heroic, nothing autocratic. And yet, as he stood there, square-built, solid, certain, he seemed in some dim way to be the real man of whom the other two were but shadows. It took a quarter of a century for me to put into words what I learned with one glance that day in my childhood.

As I came running toward the parade-ground Beverly Clarenden called out:

"Come here, Gail! Shut your little mouth and open your big ears, and I'll tell you something. Maybe I'd better not tell you all at once, though. It might make you dizzy," he added, teasingly.

"And maybe you better had," Mat Nivers said, calmly.

"Maybe you'd better tell him yourself, if you feel that way," Beverly retorted.

"I guess I'll do that," Mat began, with a twinkle in her big gray eyes; but my cousin interrupted her.

Beverly loved to tease Mat through me, but he never got far, for I relied on her to curb him; and she was not one to be ruffled by trifles. Mat was an orphan and, like ourselves, a ward of Esmond Clarenden, but there were no ties of kinship between us. She was three years older than Beverly, and although she was no taller than he, she seemed like a woman to me, a keen-witted, good-natured child-woman, neat, cleanly, and contented. I wonder if many women get more out of life in these days of luxurious comforts than she found in the days of frontier hardships.

"Well, it's this way, Gail. Mat doesn't know the straight of it," Beverly began, dramatically. "There's going to be a war, or something, in Mexico, or somewhere, and a lot of soldiers are coming here to drill, and drill, and drill. And then--"

The boy paused for effect.

"And then, and then, *and* then--or some time," Mat Nivers mimicked, jumping into the pause. "Why, they'll go to Mexico, or somewhere. And what Bev is really trying to tell hasn't anything to do with it--not directly, anyhow," she added, wisely. "The only new thing is that Uncle Esmond is going to Santa Fé right away. You know he has bought goods of the Santa Fé traders since we couldn't remember. And now he's going down there himself, and he's going to take you boys with him. That's what Bev is trying to get out, or keep back."

"Whoopee-diddle-dee!" Beverly shouted, throwing himself backward and kicking up his heels.

I jumped up and capered about in glee at the thought of such a journey. But my heart-throb of childish delight was checked, mid-beat.

"Won't Mat go, too?" I asked, with a sudden pain at my throat. Mat Nivers was a part of life to me.

The smile fell away from the girl's lips. Her big, sunshiny gray eyes and her laughing good nature always made her beautiful to Beverly and me.

"I don't want to go and leave Mat," I insisted.

"Oh, I do," Beverly declared, boastingly. "It would be real nice and jolly without her. And what could a little girl do 'way out on the prairies, and no mother to take care of her, while we were shooting Indians?"

He sprang up and took aim at the fort with an imaginary bow and arrow. But there was a hollow note in his voice as if it covered a sob.

"She can shoot Indians as good as you can, Beverly Clarenden, and, besides, there isn't anybody to mother her here but Jondo, and I reckon he'll go with us, won't he?" I urged.

Mothering was not in my stock of memories. The heart-hunger of the orphan child had been eased by the gentleness of Jondo, the championship of Mat Nivers, and the sure defense of Esmond Clarenden, who said little to children, and was instinctively trusted by all of them.

With Beverly's banter the smile came back quickly to Mat's eyes. It was never lost from them long at a time.

"Beverly Clarenden, you keep *your* little mouth shut and *your* big ears open," she began, laughingly. "I know the whole sheboodle better 'n any of you, and I'm not teasing and whimpering both at the same time, neither. Bev doesn't know anything except what I've told him, and I wasn't through when you got here, Gail. There is going to be a big war in Texas, and our soldiers are going to go, and to win, too. Just look up at that flag there, and remember now, boys, that wherever the Stars and Stripes go they *stay*."

"Who told you all that?" Beverly inquired.

"The stars up in the sky told me that last night," Mat replied, pulling down the corners of her mouth solemnly. "But Uncle Esmond hasn't anything to do with the war, nor soldiers, only like he has been doing here," the girl went on. "He's a store-man, a merchant, and I guess he's just about as good as a general--a colonel, anyhow. But he's too short to fight, and too fat to run."

"He isn't any coward," Beverly objected.

"Who said he was?" Mat inquired. "He's one of them usefulest men that keeps things going everywhere."

"I saw a real Mexican come up out of the ravine awhile ago and go straight over toward Uncle Esmond's store. What do you suppose he came here for? Is he a soldier from down there?" I asked.

"Oh, just one Mexican don't mean anything anywhere, but the war in Mexico has something to do with our going to Santa Fé, even if Uncle Esmond is just a nice little store-man. That's all a girl knows about things," Beverly insisted.

Mat opened her big eyes wide and looked straight at the boy.

"I don't pretend to know what I don't know, but I'll bet a million billion dollars there is something else besides just all this war stuff. I can't tell it, I just feel it. Anyhow, I'm to stay here with Aunty Boone till you come back. Girls can be trusted anywhere, but it may take the whole Army of the West, yet, to follow up and look after two little runty boys. And let me tell *you* something, Bev, something I heard Aunty Boone say this morning." She said: "Taint goin' to be more 'n a minnit now till them boys grows up an' grows together, same size, same age. They been little and big, long as they goin' to be. Now you know what you're coming to."

Mat was digging in the ground with a stick, and she flipped a clod at Beverly with the last words. Both of us had once expected to marry her when we grew up, unless Jondo should carry her away as his bride before that time. He was a dozen years older than Mat, who was only fourteen and small for her age. A flush always came to her cheeks when we talked of Jondo in that way. We didn't know why.

We sat silent for a little while. A vague sense of desolateness, of the turning-places of life, as real to children as to older folk, seemed to press suddenly down upon all three of us. Ours was not the ordinary child-life even of that day. And that was a time when children had no world of their own as they have to-day. Whatever developed men and women became a part of the younger life training as well. And while we were ignorant of much that many children then learned early, for we had lived mostly beside the fort on the edge of the wilderness, we were alert, and self-dependent, fearless and far-seeing. We could use tools readily: we could build fires and prepare game for cooking; we could climb trees, set traps, swim in the creek, and ride horses. Moreover, we were bound to one another by the force of isolation and need for playmates. Our imagination supplied much that our surroundings denied us. So we felt more deeply, maybe, than many city-bred children who would have paled with fear at dangers that we only laughed over.

No ripple in the even tenor of our days, however, had given any hint of the coming of this sudden tense oppression on our young souls, and we were stunned by what we could neither express nor understand.

"Whatever comes or doesn't come," Beverly said at last, stretching himself at full length, stomach downward, on the bare ground, "whatever happens to us, we three will stand by each other always and always, won't we, Mat?"

He lifted his face to the girl's. Oh, Beverly! I saw him again one day down the years, stretched out on the ground like this, lifting again a pleading face. But that belongs--down the years.

"Yes, always and always," Mat replied, and then because she had a Spartan spirit, she added: "But let's don't say any more that way. Let's think of what you are going to see--the plains, the Santa Fé Trail, the mountains, and maybe bad Indians. And even old Santa Fé town itself. You are in for 'the big shift,' as Aunty Boone says, and you've got to be little men and take whatever comes. It will come fast enough, you can bet on that."

Yesterday I might have sobbed on her shoulder. I did not know then that out on the bluff an hour ago I had come to the first turn in my life-trail, and that I could not look back now. I did know that I *wanted to go with Uncle Esmond.* I looked away from Mat's gray eyes, and Beverly's head dropped on his arms, face downward--looked at nothing but blue sky, and a graceful drooping flag; nothing but a half-sleepy, half-active fort; nothing but the yellow April floods far up-stream, between wooded banks tenderly gray-green in the spring sunshine. But I did not see any of these things then. Before my eyes there stretched a vast level prairie, with dim mountain heights beyond them. And marching toward them westward, westward, past lurking danger, Indians here and wild beasts there, went three men: the officer on his cavalry mount; Jondo on his big black horse; Esmond Clarenden, neither mounted nor on foot, it seemed, but going forward somehow. And between these three and the misty mountain peaks there was a face--not Mat Nivers's, for the first time in all my day-dreams--a sweet face with dark eyes looking straight into mine. And plainly then, just as plainly as I have heard it many times since then, came a call--the first clear bugle-note of the child-soul--a call to service, to patriotism, and to love.

All that afternoon while Mat Nivers sang about her tasks Beverly and I tried to play together among the elm and cottonwood trees about our little home, but evening found us wide awake and moping. Instead of the two tired little sleepy-heads that could barely finish supper, awake, when night came, we lay in our trundle-bed, whispering softly to each other and staring at the dark with tear-wet eyes--our spiritual barometers warning us of a coming change. Something must have happened to us that night which only the retrospect of years revealed. In that hour Beverly Clarenden lost a year of his life and I gained one. From that time we were no longer little and big to each other--we were comrades.

It must have been nearly midnight when I crept out of bed and slipped into the big room where Uncle Esmond and Jondo sat by the fireplace, talking together.

"Hello, little night-hawk! Come here and roost," Jondo said, opening his arms to me.

I slid into their embrace and snuggled my head against his broad shoulder, listening to all that was said. Three months later the little boy had become a little man, and my cuddling days had given place to the self-reliance of the fearless youngster of the trail.

"Why do you make this trip now, Esmond?" Jondo asked at length, looking straight into my uncle's face.

"I want to get down there right now because I want to get a grip on trade conditions. I can do better after the war if I do. It won't last long, and we are sure to take over a big piece of ground there when it is over. And when that is settled commerce must do the real building-up of the country. I want to be a part of that thing and grow with it. Why do you go with me?"

My uncle looked directly at Jondo, although he asked the question carelessly.

"To help you cross the plains. You know the redskins get worse every trip," Jondo answered, lightly.

I stared at both of them until Jondo said, laughingly:

"You little owl, what are you thinking about?"

"I think you are telling each other stories," I replied, frankly.

For somehow their faces made me think of Beverly's face out on the parade-ground that morning, when he had lifted it and looked at Mat Nivers; and their voices, deep bass as they were, sounded like Beverly's voice whispering between his sobs, before he went to sleep.

Both men smiled and said nothing. But when I went to my bed again Jondo tucked the covers about me and Uncle Esmond came and bade me good night.

"I guess you have the makings of a plainsman," he said, with a smile, as he patted me on the head.

"The beginnings, anyhow," Jondo added. "He can see pretty far already."

For a long time I lay awake, thinking of all that Uncle Esmond and Jondo had said to me. It is no wonder that I remember that April day as if it were but yesterday. Such days come only to childhood, and oftentimes when no one of older years can see clearly enough to understand the bigness of their meaning to the child who lives through them.

All of my life I had heard stories of the East, of New York and St. Louis, where there were big houses and wonderful stores. And of Washington, where there was a President, and a Congress, and a strange power that could fill and empty Fort Leavenworth at will. I had heard of the Great Lakes, and of cotton-fields, and tobacco-plantations, and sugar-camps, and ships, and steam-cars. I had pictured these things a thousand times in my busy imagination and had longed to see them. But from that day they went out of my life-dreams. Henceforth I belonged to the prairies of the West. No one but myself took account of this, nor guessed that a life-trend had had its commencement in the small events of one unimportant day.

———————————————————————

II

A DAUGHTER OF CANAAN

One stone the more swings to her place
In that dread Temple of Thy worth;
It is enough that through Thy grace
I saw naught common on Thy earth.

The next morning I was wakened by the soft voice of Aunty Boone, our
cook, saying:

"You better get up! Revilly blow over at the fort long time ago. Wonder it
didn't blow your batter-cakes clear away. Mat and Beverly been up since
'fore sunup."

Aunty Boone was the biggest woman I have ever seen. Not the tallest,
maybe--although she measured up to a height of six feet and two inches--
not the fattest, but a woman with the biggest human frame, overlaid with
steel-hard muscles. Yet she was not, in her way, clumsy or awkward. She
walked with a free stride, and her every motion showed a powerful
muscular control. Her face was jet-black, with keen shining eyes, and
glittering white teeth. In my little child-world she was the strangest creature
I had ever known. In the larger world whither the years of my manhood
have led me she holds the same place.

She had been born a princess of royal blood, heir to a queenship in her
tribe in a far-away African kingdom. In her young womanhood, so the tale
ran, the slave-hunter had found her and driven her aboard a slave-ship
bound for the American coast. He never drove another slave toward any
coast. In Virginia her first purchaser had sold her quickly to a Georgia
planter whose *heirs* sent her on to Mississippi. Thence she soon found her
way to the Louisiana rice-fields. Nobody came to take her back to any place
she had quitted. "Safety first," is not a recent practice. She had enormous
strength and capacity for endurance, she learned rapidly, kept her own
counsel, obeyed no command unless she chose to do so, and feared
nothing in the Lord's universe. The people of her own race had little in
common with her. They never understood her and so they feared her. And
being as it were outcast by them, she came to know more of the ways and
customs, and even the thoughts, of the white people better than of her
own. Being quick to imitate, she spoke in the correcter language of those
whom she knew best, rather than the soft, ungrammatical dialect of the
plantation slave or the grunt and mumble of the isolated African. Realizing

that service was to be her lot, she elected to render that service where and to whom she herself might choose.

One day she had walked into New Orleans and boarded a Mississippi steamer bound for St. Louis. It took three men to eject her bodily from the deck into a deep and dangerous portion of the stream. She swam ashore, and when the steamer made its next stop she walked aboard again. The three men being under the care of a physician, and the remainder of the crew burdened with other tasks, she was not again disturbed. Some time later she appeared at the landing below Fort Leavenworth, and strode up the slope to the deserted square where Esmond Clarenden stood before his little store alone in the deepening twilight.

I have heard that she had had a way of appearing suddenly, like a beast of prey, in the dusk of the evening, and that few men cared to meet her at that time alone.

My uncle was a snug-built man, sixty-two inches high, with small, shapely hands and feet. Towering above him stood this great, strange creature, barefooted, ragged, half tiger, half sphinx.

"I'm hungry. I'll eat or I kill. I'm nobody's slave!"

The soft voice was full of menace, the glare of famine and fury was in the burning eyes, and the supple cruelty of the wild beast was in the clenched hands.

Esmond Clarenden looked up at her with interest. Then pointing toward our house he said, calmly:

"Neither are you anybody's master. Go over there to the kitchen and get your supper. If you can cook good meals, I'll pay you well. If you can't, you'll leave here."

Possibly it was the first time in her strange and varied career that she had taken a command kindly, and obeyed because she must. And so the savage African princess, the terror of the terrible slave-ship, the untamed plantation scourge, with a record for deeds that belong to another age and social code, became the great, silent, faithful, fearless servant of the plains; with us, but never of us, in all the years that followed. But she fitted the condition of her day, and in her place she stood, where the beloved black mammy of a gentler mold would have fallen.

She announced that her name was Daniel Boone, which Uncle Esmond considered well enough for one of such a westward-roving nature. But Jondo declared that the "Daniel" belonged to her because, like unto the Bible Daniel, no lion, nor whole den of lions, would ever dine at her expense. To us she became Aunty Boone. With us she was always gentle-- docile, rather; and one day we came to know her real measure, and--we never forgot her.

I bounced out of bed at her call this morning, and bounced my breakfast into a healthy, good-natured stomach. The sunny April of yesterday had whirled into a chilly rain, whipped along by a raw wind. The skies were black and all the spring verdure was turned to a sickish gray-green.

"Weather always fit the times," Aunty Boone commented as she heaped my plate with the fat buckwheat cakes that only she could ever turn off a griddle. "You packin' up for somepin' now. What you goin' to get is fo'casted in this here nasty day."

"Why, we *are* going away!" I cried, suddenly recalling the day before. "I wish, though, that Mat could go. Wouldn't you like to go, too, Aunty? Only, Bev says there's deserts, where there's just rocks and sand and everything, and no water sometimes. You and Mat couldn't stand that 'cause you are women-folks."

I stiffened with importance and clutched my knife and fork hard.

"Couldn't!" Aunty Boone gave a scornful grunt. "Women-folks stands double more 'n men. You'll see when you get older. I know about you freightin' off to Santy Fee. *You* don't know what desset is. *You* never *see sand*. You never *feel* what it is to *want watah*. Only folks 'cross the ocean in the real desset knows that. Whoo-ee!"

I remembered the weird tales she had told us of her girlhood--tales that had thrilled me with wonder--told sometimes in the twilight, sometimes by the kitchen fire on winter nights, sometimes on long, still, midsummer afternoons when the air quivered with heat and the Missouri hung about hot sand-bars, half asleep.

"What do you know about this trip, Aunty Boone?" I asked, eagerly; for although she could neither read nor write, she had a sponge-like absorbing power for keeping posted on all that happened at the fort.

"Cla'n'den"--the woman never called my uncle by any other name--"he's goin' to Santy Fee, an' you boys with him, 'cause--"

She paused and her shining eyes grew dull as they had a way of doing in her thoughtful or prophetic moments.

"He knows what for--him an' Jondo. One of 'em's storekeeper an' t'other a plainsman, but they tote together always--an' they totin' now. You can't see what, but they totin', they totin', just the same. Now run out to the store. Things is stirrin'. Things is stirrin'."

I bolted my cakes, sodden with maple syrup, drank my mug of milk, and hurried out toward the storehouse.

Fort Leavenworth in the middle '40's was sometimes an indolent place, and sometimes a very busy one, depending upon the activity of the Western frontier. On this raw April morning everything was fairly ajerk with life and motion. And I knew from child-experience that a body of soldiers must be coming up the river soon. Horses were rushed to-day where yesterday they had been leisurely led. Orders were shouted now that had been half sung a week ago. Military discipline took the place of fatigue attitudes. There was a banging of doors, a swinging of brooms, a clatter of tin, and a clanging of iron things. And everywhere went that slapping wind. And every shallow place in the ground held a chilly puddle. The government buildings always seemed big and bare and cold to me. And this morning they seemed drearier than ever, beaten upon by the fitful swish of the rain.

In contrast with these were my uncle's snug quarters, for warmth was a part of Esmond Clarenden's creed. I used to think that the little storeroom, filled with such things as a frontier fort could find use for, was the biggest emporium in America, and the owner thereof suffered nothing, in my eyes, in comparison with A.T. Stewart, the opulent New York merchant of his day.

As I ran, bareheaded and coatless, across the wide wet space between our home and the storehouse a soldier came dashing by on horseback. I dodged behind him only to fall sprawling in a slippery pool under the very feet of another horseman, riding swiftly toward the boat-landing.

Neither man paid any attention to me as I slowly picked myself up and started toward the store. The soldier had not seen me at all. The other man's face was dark, and he wore the dress of the Mexican. It was only by his alertness and skill that his horse missed me, but as he hurried away he gave no more heed to me than if I had been a stone in his path.

I had turned my ankle in the fall and I could only limp to the storehouse and drop down inside. I would not cry out, but I could not hold back the sobs as I tried to stand, and fell again in a heap at Jondo's feet.

"Things were stirrin'" there, as Aunty Boone had said, but withal there was no disorder. Esmond Clarenden never did business in that way. No loose ends flapped about his rigging, and when a piece of work was finished with him, there was nothing left to clear away. Bill Banney, the big grown-up boy from Kentucky, who, out of love of adventure, had recently come to the fort, was helping Jondo with the packing of certain goods. Mat and Beverly were perched on the counter, watching all that was being done and hearing all that was said.

"What's the matter, little plainsman?" Jondo cried, catching me up and setting me on the counter. "Got a thorn in your shoe, or a stone-bruise, or a chilblain?"

"I slipped out there behind a soldier on horseback, right in front of a little old Mexican who was just whirling off to the river," I said, the tears blinding my eyes.

"Why, he's turned his ankle! Looks like it was swelling already," Mat Nivers declared, as she slid from the counter and ran toward me.

"It's a bad job," Jondo declared. "Just when we want to get off, too."

"Can't I go with you to Santa Fé, Uncle Esmond?" I wailed.

"Yes, Gail, we'll fix you up all right," my uncle said, but his face was grave as he examined my ankle.

It was a bad job, much worse than any of us had thought at first. And as they all gathered round me I suddenly noticed the same Mexican standing in the doorway, and I heard some one, I think it was Uncle Esmond, say:

"Jondo, you'd better take Gail over to the surgeon right away--" His voice trailed off somewhere and all was blank nothingness to me. But my last impression was that my uncle stayed behind with the strange Mexican.

In the excitement everybody forgot that I had on neither hat nor coat as they carried me through the raw wet air to the army surgeon's quarters beyond the soldiers' barracks.

A chill and fever followed, and for a week there was only pain and trouble for me. Nothing else hurt quite so deeply, however, as the fear of being left behind when the Clarendens should start for Santa Fé. I would ask no questions, and nobody mentioned the trip, for which everything was preparing. I began at last to have a dread of being left in the night, of wakening some morning to find only Mat and myself with Aunty Boone in the little log house. Uncle Esmond had already been away for three days, but nobody told me where he had gone, nor why he went, nor when he would come back. It kept me awake at night, and the loss of sleep made me nervous and feverish.

One afternoon about a week after my accident, when Beverly and Mat were putting the room in order and chattering like a couple of squirrels, Beverly said, carelessly:

"Gail, it's been a half a week since Uncle Esmond went down to our other store in Independence, and we are going to start on our trip just as soon as he gets back, unless he sends for me and Jondo."

I knew that he was trying to tell me that they meant to go without me, for he hurried out with the last words. No boy wants to talk to a disappointed boy, and I had to clinch my teeth hard to keep back the tears.

"I want to get well quicker, Mat. I want to go to Santa Fé with Beverly," I wailed, making a desperate effort to get out of bed.

"You cuddle right down there, Gail Clarenden, if you want to get well at all. If you're real careful you'll be all right in a day or two. Let's wait for Uncle Esmond to come home before we start any worries."

It was in her voice, girl or woman, that comforting note that could always soothe me.

"Mat, won't you try to get them to let me go?" I pleaded.

She made no promises, but busied herself with getting my foot into its place again, singing softly to herself all the while. Then she read me stories from our few story-books till I fell asleep.

It was twilight when I wakened. Where I lay I could hear Esmond Clarenden and Aunty Boone talking in the kitchen, and I listened eagerly to all they said.

"But it's no place for a woman," my uncle was urging, gravely.

"I ain't a woman, I'm a cook. You want cooks if you eats. Mat ain't a woman, she's a girl. But she's stronger 'n Beverly. If you can't leave him, how can you leave her? An' Gail never get well if he's left here, Cla'n'den, now he's got the goin' fever. Never! An' if you never got back--"

"I don't believe he would get well, either." Then Uncle Esmond spoke lower and I could not hear any more.

Pretty soon Mat and Beverly burst open the door and came dancing in together, the sweet air of the warm April evening coming in with them, and life grew rose-colored for me in a moment.

"We are all going to Santa Fé over the long trail. Every last gun of us. Aunty Boone, and Mat, and you, and me, and Jondo, and Uncle Esmond, rag-tag and bobtail. Whoop-ee-diddle-dee!" Beverly threw up his cap, and, catching Mat by the arms, they whirled around the room together.

"Who says so, Bev?" I asked, eagerly.

"Them as knows and bosses everything in this world. Jondo told me, and he's just the boss's shadow. Now guess who," Beverly replied.

"It's all true, Gail," Mat assured me. "Esmond Clarenden *is* going to Santa Fé in spite of 'war, pestilence, famine, and sword,' as my *History of the World* says, and he *is* going to take son Beverly, and son Gail to watch son Beverly; and Miss Mat Nivers to watch both of them and shoo Indians away; and Aunt Daniel Boone to scare the Mexicans into the Gulf of California, if they act ugly, see!"

She capered about the room, and as she passed me she stooped and patted me on the forehead. I didn't want her to do that. I had taken a long jump away from little-boy-dom a week ago, but I was supremely content now that all of us were to take the long trail together.

That evening while Mat and Beverly went to look after some fishing-lines they had set--Mat and Bev were always going fishing--and Jondo was down at the store, the officer in command of the fort came in. He paid no attention to me lying there, all eyes and ears whenever shoulder-straps were present.

"What did you decide to do about the trip to Santa Fé?" he asked, as he tipped back in his chair and settled down to cigars and an evening chat.

"We shall be leaving on the boat in the morning," my uncle replied.

The colonel's chair came down with a crack. "You don't mean it!" he exclaimed.

"I told you a week ago that I would be starting as soon as possible," Esmond Clarenden said, quietly.

"But, man, the war is raging, simply raging, down in Mexico right now. Our division will be here to commence drill in a few weeks, and we start for the border in a few months. You are mad to take such a risk." The commander's voice rose.

"We must go, that's all!" my uncle insisted.

"We? We? Who the devil are 'we'? None of my companies mutinied, I hope."

The words did not sound like a joke, and there was little humor in the grim face.

"'We' means Jondo, Banney, a young fellow from Kentucky--" Uncle Esmond began.

"Humph! Banney's father carried a gun at Fort Dearborn in 1812. I thought that young fellow came here for military service," the colonel commented, testily.

"Rather say he came for adventure," Esmond Clarenden suggested.

"He'll get a deuced lot of it in a hurry, if you persuade him off with you."

A flush swept over Esmond Clarenden's face, but his good-natured smile did not fail as he replied:

"I don't persuade anybody. The rest of the company are my two nephews and the little girl, my ward, with our cook, Daniel Boone, as commander-in-chief of the pots and pans and any Indian meat foolish enough to fall in her way."

Then came the explosion. Powder would have cost less than the energy blown off there. The colonel stamped and swore, and sprang to his feet in opposition, and flung himself down in disgust.

"Women and children!" he gasped. "Why do you sacrifice helpless innocent ones?"

Just then Aunty Boone strode in carrying a log of wood as big as a man's body, which she deftly threw on the fire. As the flame blazed high she gave one look at the young officer sitting before it, and then walked out as silently and sturdily as she had entered. It was such a look as a Great Dane dog full of superiority and indifference might have given to a terrier puppy, and from where I lay I thought the military man's face took on a very strange expression.

"I 'sacrifice my innocent ones,'" my uncle answered the query, "because they will be safer with me than anywhere else. Young as they are, there are some forces against them already."

"Well, you are going to a perilous place, over a most perilous trail, in a most perilous time of national affairs, to meet such treacherously villainous men as New Mexico offers in her market-places right now? And all for the sake of the commerce of the plains? Why do you take such chances to do business with such people, Clarenden?"

Esmond Clarenden had been staring at the burning logs in the big fireplace during this conversation. He turned now and faced the young army officer squarely as he said in that level tone that we children had learned long ago was final:

"Colonel, I'd go straight to hell and do business with the devil himself if I had any business dealings with him."

The colonel's face fell. Slowly he relighted his cigar, and leaned back again in his chair, and with that diplomacy that covers a skilful retreat he said, smilingly:

"If any man west of the Missouri River ever could do that it would be you, Clarenden. By the holy Jerusalem, the military lost one grand commander when you chose a college instead of West Point, and the East lost one well-bred gentleman from its circles of commerce and culture when you elected to do business on the old Santa Fé Trail instead of Broadway. But I reckon the West will need just such men as you long after the frontier fort has become a central point in the country's civilized area. And, blast you, Clarenden, blast your very picture! No man can help liking you. Not even the devil if he had the chance. Not one man in ten thousand would dare to make that trip right now. You've got the courage of a colonel and the judgment of a judge. Go to Santa Fé! We may meet you coming back. If we do, and you need us, command us!"

He gave a courteous salute, and the two began to talk of other things; among them the purposes that were bringing young men westward.

"So Banney, right out of old blue-grassy Kentucky, is going to back out of here and go with you," the colonel remarked.

"I've hired him to drive one team. It's a lark for him, but the army would be a lark just the same," Esmond Clarenden declared. "He says he is to kill rattlesnakes and Mexicans, while Jondo kills Indians and I sit tight on top of the bales of goods to keep the wind from blowing them away. And the boys are to be made bridle-wise, *plains-broke* for future freighting. That's all that life means to him right now."

I do not know what else was said, nor what I heard and what I dreamed after that. If this journey meant a lark to a grown-up boy, it meant a pilgrimage through fairyland to a young boy like myself.

And so the new life opened to us; and if the way was fraught with hardship and danger, it also taught us courage and endurance. Nor must we be measured by the boy life of to-day. Children lived the grown-up life then. It was all there was for them to live.

The yellow Missouri boiled endlessly along by the foot of the bluff. The flag flapped broadly in the strong breeze that blew in from the west; the square log house--the only home we had ever known--looked forlornly after us, with its two front windows with blinds half drawn, like two half-closed, watching eyes; the cottonwoods and elms, the tiny storehouse--everything--grew suddenly very dear to us. The fort buildings throwing long shadows in the early morning, the level-topped forests east of the Missouri River, and the budding woodland that overdraped the ravines to the west, even in their silence, seemed like sentient things, loving us, as we loved them.

We children had gone all over the place before sunrise and touched everything, in token of good-by; from some instinct tarrying longest at the flagpole, where we threw kisses to the great, beautiful banner high above us. Now, at the moment of leaving all these familiar things of all our years, a choking pain came to our throats. Mat's eyes filled with tears and she looked resolutely forward. Beverly and I clutched hands and shut our teeth together, determined to overcome this home-grip on our hearts. Aunty Boone sat in a corner of the deck as the boat swung out into the stream, her eyes dull and unseeing. She never spoke of her thoughts, but I have wondered often, since that big day of my young years, if she might not have recalled other voyages: the slave-ship putting out to sea with the African shores fading behind her; and the big river steamer at the New Orleans dock where brutal hands had hurled her from the deck into the dangerous floods of the Mississippi. This was her third voyage, a brief run from Fort Leavenworth to Independence. She was apart from her fellow-passengers as in the other two, but now nobody gave her a curse, nor a blow.

III

THE WIDENING HORIZON

Whose furthest footsteps never strayed
Beyond the village of his birth,
Is but a lodger for the night
In this old Wayside Inn of Earth.

The broad green prairies of the West roll back in huge billows from the
Missouri bluffs, and ripple gently on, to melt at last into the level grassy
plains sloping away to the foothills of the Rocky Mountains. Up and down
these land-waves, and across these ripples, the old Santa Fé Trail, the
slender pathway of a wilderness-bridging commerce, led out toward the
great Southwest--a thousand weary miles--to end at last, where the narrow
thoroughfare reached the primitive hostelry at the corner of the plaza in the
heart of the capital of a Spanish-Mexican demesne.

It was a strange old highway, tying the western frontier of a new, self-reliant
American civilization to the eastern limit of an autocratic European
offshoot, grafted upon an ancient Indian stock of the Western Hemisphere.
In language, nationality, social code, political faith, and prevailing spiritual
creed, the terminals of this highway were as unlike as their geographical
naming. For the trail began at *Independence*, in Missouri, and ended at Santa
Fé, the "*City of the Holy Faith*," in New Mexico.

The little trading town of Independence was a busy place in the frontier
years of the Middle West. Ungentle and unlovely as it was, it was the great
gateway between the river traffic on the one side, and the plains commerce
of the far Southwest on the other. At the wharf at Westport, only a few
miles away, the steamers left their cargoes of flour and bacon, coffee and
calicoes, jewelry and sugar--whatever might have a market value to
merchants beyond the desert lands. And here these same steamers took on
furs, and silver bullion, and such other produce of the mountains and
mines and open plains as the opulently laden caravans had toiled through
long days, overland, to bring to the river's wharf.

To-day the same old gateway stands as of yore. But it may be given only to
men who have seen what I have seen, to know how that our Kansas City,
the Beautiful, could grow up from that old wilderness outpost of commerce

threescore and more years ago.

The Clarenden store was the busiest spot in the center of this busy little town. Goods from both lines of trade entered and cleared here. In front of the building three Conestoga wagons with stout mule teams stood ready. A fourth wagon, the Dearborn carriage of that time, filled mostly with bedding, clothing, and the few luxuries a long camping-out journey may indulge in, waited only for a team, and we would be off to the plains.

Jondo and Bill Banney were busy with the last things to be done before we started. Aunty Boone sat on a pile of pelts inside the store, smoking her pipe. Beverly and Mat stood waiting in the big doorway, while I sat on a barrel outside, because my ankle was still a bit stiff. A crowd had gathered before the store to see us off. It was not such a company as the soldier-men at the fort. The outlaw, the loafer, the drunkard, the ruffian, the gambler, and the trickster far outnumbered the stern-faced men of affairs. When the balance turns the other way the frontier disappears. Mingling with these was a pale-faced invalid now and then, with the well-appointed new arrivals from the East.

"What are we waiting for, Bev?" I asked, as the street filled with men.

"Got to get another span of moolies for our baby-cart. Uncle Esmond hadn't counted on the nurse and the cook going, you know, but he rigged this littler wagon out in a twinkle."

"That's the family carriage, drawn by spirited steeds. Us children are to ride in it, with Daniel Boone to help with the driving," Mat added.

Just then Esmond Clarenden appeared at the door.

"How soon do you start, Clarenden?" some one in the crowd inquired.

"Just as soon as I can get a pair of well-broken mules," he replied. "I'm looking for the man who has them to sell quick. I'm in a hurry."

"What's your great rush?" a well-dressed stranger asked. "They tell me things look squally out West."

"All the more reason for my being in a hurry then," Uncle Esmond returned.

"They ain't but three men of you, is they? What do you want of more mules?" put in an inquisitive idler of the trouble-loving class who sooner or later turn arguments into bitter brawls.

"These three children and the cook in there have this wagon. They are all fair drivers, if I can get the right mules," my uncle said.

Women and children did not cross the plains in those days, nor could public welfare allow that so valuable a piece of property as Aunty Boone would be in the slave-market should be lost to commerce, and the storm of protest that followed would have overcome a less determined man. It was not on account of sympathy for the weak and defenseless that called out all this abuse, but the lawless spirit that stirs up a mob on the slightest excuse.

I slid away to the door, where, with Mat and Beverly, I watched Esmond Clarenden, who was listening with his good-natured smile to all of that loud street talk.

"No man's life is insurable in these troublesome times, with our troops right now down in Mexico," a suave Southern trader urged. "Better sell your slave and put that nice little gal in a boardin'-school somewhere in the South."

"I'll give you a mighty good bargain for that wench, Clarenden. She might be worth a clare fortune in New Orleans. What d'ye say to a cool thousand?" another man declared, with a slow. Southern drawl.

Aunty Boone took the pipe from her lips and looked at the stranger.

"Y'would!" she grunted, stretching her big right hand across her lap, like a huge paw with claws ready underneath.

"Them plains Injuns never was more *hostile* than they air right now. I just got in from the mountains an' I know. An' they're bein' set on by more *hostile* Mexican devils, and political *intrigs*," a bearded mountaineer trapper argued.

"'Sides all that," interposed the suave Southern gentleman, "it's too early in the spring. Freightin's bound to be delayed by rains--and a nice little gal with only a nigger--" He was not quite himself, and he did not try to say more.

"Seems like some of these gentlemen consider you are some sort of a fool," a tall, lean Yankee youth observed, as he listened to the babble.

I had climbed back on the barrel again to see the crowd better, and I stared at the last speaker. His voice was not unpleasant, but he appeared pale and weak and spiritless in that company of tanned, rugged men. Evidently he was an invalid in search of health. We children had seen many invalids, from time to time, at the fort harmless folk, who came to fuss, and stayed to flourish, in our gracious land of the open air.

"You are a dam' fool," roared a big drunken loafer from the edge of the crowd. "An' I'd lick you in a minnit if you das step into the middle of the street onct. Ornery sneak, to take innocent children into such perils. Come on out here, I tell ye!"

A growl followed these words. Many men in that company were less than half sober, and utterly irresponsible.

"Le's jes' hang the fool storekeepin' gent right now; an' make a free-fur-all holiday. I'll begin," the drunken ruffian bawled. He was of the sort that always leads a mob.

The growl deepened, for blood-lust and drunkenness go together.

Terrified for my uncle's safety, I stood breathless, staring at the evil-faced crowd of men going suddenly mad, without excuse. At the farthest edge of the insipient mob, sitting on his horse and watching my uncle's face intently, was the very Mexican whom I had twice seen at Fort Leavenworth. At the drunken rowdy's challenge, I thought that he half-lifted a threatening hand. But Esmond Clarenden only smiled, with a mere turn of his head as if in disapproval. In that minute I learned my first lesson in handling ruffians. I knew that my uncle was not afraid, and because of that my faith in his power to take care of himself came back.

"I want to leave here in half an hour. If you have any good plains-broke mules you will sell for cash, I can do business with you right now. If not, the sooner you leave this place the better."

He lifted his small, shapely hand unclenched, his good-natured smile and gentlemanly bearing unchanged, but his low voice was stronger than all the growls of the crowd that fell back like whipped dogs.

As he spoke a horse-dealer, seeing the gathering before the store, came galloping up.

"I'm your man. Money talks so I can understand it. Wait five minutes and ten seconds and I'll bring a whole strand of mules."

A rattling of wagons and roar of voices at the far end of the street told of the arrival of a company coming in from the wharf at Westport, and the crowd whirled about and made haste toward the next scene of interest.

Only two men remained behind, the tall New England youth and the Mexican on the farther side of the street sitting motionless on his horse. A moment later he was gone, and the street was empty save for the pale-faced invalid who had come over to the doorway where Mat and Beverly and I waited together.

"Why don't you youngsters stay home with your mother, or is she going with you?" he asked, a gleam of interest lighting his dull face as he looked at Mat Nivers.

"We haven't any of us got a mother," Mat replied, timidly, lifting her gray eyes to his.

"Mother! Ain't you all one family?" the young man questioned in surprise.

"No, we are three orphan children that Uncle Esmond has adopted all our lives, I guess." Beverly informed him.

A wave of sympathy swept over his face.

"You poor, lonely, unhappy cubs! You've never had a mother to love you!" he exclaimed, in kindly pity.

"We aren't poor nor lonely nor unhappy. We have always had Uncle Esmond and we didn't need a mother," I exclaimed, earnestly.

The young man stared at me as I spoke. "What's he, a bachelor or married man?" he inquired.

"He couldn't be married and keep us, I reckon, and he's taking us with him so nothing will happen to us while he's gone. He's really truly Bev's uncle and mine, but he's just the same as uncle to Mat, who hasn't anybody else," I declared, enthusiastically. Uncle Esmond was my pride, and I meant that he should be fully appreciated.

The Yankee gazed at all three of us, his eyes resting longest on Mat's bright face. The listlessness left his own that minute and a new light shone on his countenance. But when he turned to my uncle the seeming lack of all interest in living returned to his face again.

"Say," he drawled, looking down at the stubborn little merchant from his slim six feet of altitude, "you are such a dam' fool as our friend, the tipsy one, says, that I believe I'll go along 'cross the plains with you, if you'll let me. I've not got a darned thing to lose out there but a sick carcass that I'm pretty tired of looking after," he went on, wearily. "I reckon I might as well see the fun through if I never set a hoof on old Plymouth Rock again. My granddaddy was a minute-man at Lexington. Say"--he paused, and his sober face turned sad--"if all the bean-eaters who claim their grandpas were minute-men tell the truth, there wasn't no glory in winning at Lexington, there was such a tremendous sight of 'em. I've heard about eight million men myself make the same claim. But my granddad was the real article in the minute-men business. And I've always admired his grit most of any man in the world. He was about your shape, I reckon, from his picture that old man Copley got out. But, man! he wasn't a patchin' on your coat-sleeve. You are the preposterous-est unlawful-est infamous-est man I ever saw. It's just straight murder and suicide you are bent on, takin' this awful chance of plungin' into a warrin', snake-eatin' country like New Mexico, and I like you for it. Will you take me as an added burden? If you will, I'll deposit the price of my state-room right now. I've got only a little wad of money to get well on or die on. I can spend it either way--not much difference which. My name is Krane, Rex Krane, and in spite of such a floopsy name I hail from Boston, U.S.A."

There was a hopeless sagging about the young man's mouth, redeemed only by the twinkle in his eye.

Esmond Clarenden gave him a steady measuring look. He estimated men easily, and rarely failed to estimate truly.

"I'll take you on your face value," he answered, "and if you want to turn back there will be a chance to do it out a hundred miles or more on the trail. You can try it that far and see how you like it. I'll furnish you your board. There are always plenty of bedrooms on the ground floor and in one of the wagons on rainy nights. You can take a shift driving a team now and then, and every able-bodied man has to do guard duty some of the time. You understand the dangers of the situation by this time. Here comes my man," he added, as the horse-dealer appeared, leading a string of mules up the street.

"Here's your critters. Take your choice," the dealer urged.

"I'll take the brown one," my uncle replied, promptly. And the bargain was closed.

Mat and Beverly and I had already climbed into our wagon, and Aunty Boone appeared now at the store door, ready to join us.

"You takin' that nigger?" the trader asked.

"Yes. Lead out your best offer now. I want another mule," Esmond Clarenden replied.

But the horse-merchant proved to be harder to deal with than the crowd had been. The foolish risk of losing so valuable a piece of property as Daniel Boone ought to be in the slave-market taxed his powers of understanding, profanity, and abuse.

"Cussin' solid, an' in streaks," Aunty Boone chuckled, softly, as she listened to him unmoved.

Equally unmoved was Esmond Clarenden. But his genial smile and diplomatic power of keeping still did not prevent him from being as set as the everlasting hills in his own purpose.

"This here critter is all I'll sell you," the trader declared at last, pulling a big white-eyed dun animal out of the group. "An' nobody's goin' to drive her easy."

"I'll take it," Uncle Esmond said, promptly, and the vicious-looking beast was brought to where Aunty Boone stood beside the wagon-tongue.

It was a clear case of hate at first sight, for the mule began to plunge and squeal the instant it saw her. The woman hesitated not a minute, but lifting her big ham-like foot, she gave it one broadside kick that it must have mistaken for a thunderbolt, and in that low purr of hers, that might frighten a jungle tiger, she laid down the law of the journey.

"You tote me to Santy Fee, or be a dead mule. Take yo' choice right now! Git up!"

For fifty days the one dependable, docile servant of the Clarendens was the big dun mule, as gentle and kitten-like as a mule can be.

And so, in spite of opposing conditions and rabble protest and doleful prophecy and the assurance of certain perils, we turned our faces toward the unfriendly land of the sunset skies, the open West of my childish day-dreams.

* * * * *

The prairies were splashed with showers and the warm black soil was fecund with growths as our little company followed the windings of the old trail in that wondrous springtime of my own life's spring. There were eight of us: Clarenden, the merchant; Jondo, the big plainsman; Bill Banney, whom love of adventure had lured from the blue grass of Kentucky to the prairie-grass of the West; Rex Krane, the devil-may-care invalid from Boston; and the quartet of us in the "baby cab," as Beverly had christened the family wagon. Uncle Esmond had added three swift ponies to our equipment, which Jondo and Bill found time to tame for riding as we went along.

We met wagon-trains, scouts, and solitary trappers going east, but so far as we knew our little company was the only westward-facing one on all the big prairies.

"It's just like living in a fairy-story, isn't it, Gail?" Beverly said to me one evening, as we rounded a low hill and followed a deep little creek down to a shallow fording-place. "All we want is a real princess and a real giant. Look at these big trees all you can, for Jondo says pretty soon we won't see trees at all."

"Maybe we'll have Indians instead of giants," I suggested. "When do you suppose we'll begin to see the real *bad* Indians; not just Osages and Kaws and sneaky little Otoes and Pot'wat'mies like we've seen all our lives?"

"Sooner than we expect," Beverly replied. "Could Mat Nivers ever be a real princess, do you reckon?"

"I know she won't," I said, firmly, the vision of that fateful day at Fort Leavenworth coming back as I spoke--the vision of level green prairies, with gray rocks and misty mountain peaks beyond. And somewhere, between green prairies and misty peaks, a sweet child face with big dark eyes looking straight into mine. I must have been a dreamer. And in my young years I wondered often why things should be so real to me that nobody else could ever understand.

"I used to think long ago at the fort that I'd marry Mat some day," Beverly said, reminiscently, as if he were looking across a lapse of years instead of days.

"So did I," I declared. "But I don't want to now. Maybe our princess will be at the end of the trail, Bev, a real princess. Still, I love Mat just as if she were my sister," I hastened to add.

"So do I," Beverly responded, heartily.

A little grain of pity for her loss of prestige was mingling with our subconscious feeling of a need for her help in the day of the giant, if not in the reign of the princess.

We were trudging along behind our wagon toward the camping-place for the night, which lay beyond the crossing of the stream. We had lived much out of doors at Fort Leavenworth, but the real out of doors of this journey was telling on us already in our sturdy, up-leaping strength, to match each new hardship. We ate like wolves, slept like dead things, and forgot what it meant to be tired. And as our muscles hardened our minds expanded. We were no longer little children. Youth had set its seal upon us on the day when our company had started out from Independence toward the great plains of the Middle West. Little care had we for the responsibility and perils of such a journey; and because our thoughts were buoyant our bodies were vigorous.

Our camp that night was under wide-spreading elm-trees whose roots struck deep in the deep black loam. After supper Mat and Beverly went down to fish in the muddy creek. Fishing was Beverly's sport and solace everywhere. I was to follow them as soon as I had finished my little chores. The men were scattered about the valley and the camp was deserted. Something in the woodsy greenness of the quiet spot made it seem like home to me--the log house among the elms and cottonwoods at the fort. As I finished my task I wondered how a big, fine house such as I had seen in pictures would look nestled among these beautiful trees. I wanted a home here some day, a real home. It was such a pleasant place even in its loneliness.

To the west the ground sloped up gently toward the horizon-line, shutting off the track of the trail beyond the ridge. A sudden longing came over me to see what to-morrow's journey would offer, bringing back the sense of being *shut in* that had made me lose interest in fishes that wouldn't play leap-frog on the sand-bars. And with it came a longing to be alone.

Instead of following Mat and Beverly to the creek I went out to the top of the swell and stood long in the April twilight, looking beyond the rim of the valley toward the darkening prairies with the great splendor of the sunset's afterglow deepening to richest crimson above the purpling shadows.

Oh, many a time since that night have I looked upon the Kansas plains and watched the grandeur of coloring that only the Almighty artist ever paints for human eyes. And always I come back, in memory, to that April evening. The soul of a man must have looked out through the little boy's eyes on that night, and a new mile-stone was set there, making a landmark in my life trail. For when I turned toward the darkening east and the shadowy camp where the evening fires gleamed redly in the dusk, I knew then, as well as I know now, if I could only have put it into words, that I was not the same little boy who had run up the long slope to see what lay next in to-morrow's journey.

I walked slowly back to the camp and sat down beside Esmond Clarenden.

"What are you thinking about, Gail?" he asked, as I stared at the fire.

"I wish I knew what would happen next," I replied.

Jondo was lying at full length on the grass, his elbow bent, and his hand supporting his head. What a wonderful head it was with its crown of softly curling brown hair!

"I wonder if we have done wrong by the children, Clarenden," the big plainsman said, slowly.

Uncle Esmond shook his head as he replied:

"I can't believe it. They may not be safe with us, but we know they would not have been safe without us."

Just then Beverly and Mat came racing up from the creek bank.

"Let us stay up awhile," Mat pleaded. "Maybe we'll be less trouble some of these days if we hear you talk about what's coming."

"They are right, Jondo. Gail here wants to know what is coming next, and Mat wants a share in our councils. What do you want, Beverly?"

"I want to practise shooting on horseback. I can hit a mark now standing still. I want to do it on the run," Beverly replied.

I can see now the earnest look in Esmond Clarenden's eyes as he listened. I've seen it in a mother's eyes more than once since then, as she kissed her eldest-born and watched it toddle off alone on its first day of school; or held her peace, when, breaking home ties, the son of her heart bade her good-by to begin life for himself in the world outside.

The last light of day was lost over the western ridge. The moon was beginning to swell big and yellow through the trees. Twilight was darkening into night. Bill Banney and Rex Krane had joined us now, for every hour we were learning to keep closer together. Jondo threw more wood on the fire, and we nestled about it in snug, homey fashion as if we were to listen to a fairy-tale--three children slipping fast out of childhood into the stern, hard plains life that tried men's souls. As we listened, the older men told of the perils as well as the fascinating adventures of trail life, that we might understand what lay before us in the unknown days. And then they told us stories of the plains, and of the quaint historic things of Santa Fé; of El Palacio, home of all the Governors of New Mexico; an Indian pueblo first, it may have been standing there when William the Norman conquered Harold of the Saxon dynasty of England; or further back when Charlemagne was hanging heathen by the great great gross to make good Christians of them; or even when old Julius Cæsar came and saw and conquered, on either side of the Rubicon, this same old structure may have sheltered rulers in a world unknown. They told us of the old, old church of San Miguel, a citadel for safety from the savage foes of Spain, a sanctuary ever for the sinful and sorrowing ones. And of the Plaza--sacred ground whereon by ceremonial form had been established deeds that should change the destinies of tribes and shape the trend of national pride and power in a new continent. And of La Garita, place of execution, facing whose blind wall the victims of the Spanish rule made their last stand, and, helpless, fell pierced by the bullets of the Spanish soldiery.

And we children looked into the dying camp-fire and builded there our own castles in Spain, and hoped that that old flag to which we had thrown good-by kisses such a little while ago would one day really wave above old Santa Fé and make it ours to keep. For, young as we were, the flag already symbolized to us the protecting power of a nation strong and gentle and generous.

"The first and last law of the trail is to 'hold fast,'" Jondo said, as we broke up the circle about the camp-fire.

"If you can keep that law we will take you into full partnership to-night," Esmond Clarenden added, and we knew that he meant what he said.

IV

THE MAN IN THE DARK

A stone's throw from either hand,
From that well-ordered road we tread,
And all the world is wide and strange.
--KIPLING

"We shall come to the parting of the ways to night if we make good time,
Krane," Esmond Clarenden said to the young Bostonian, as we rested at
noon beside the trait. "To-night we camp at Council Grove and from there
on there is no turning back. I had hoped to find a big crowd waiting to start
off from that place. But everybody we have met coming in says that there
are no freighters going west now. Usually there is no risk in coming alone
from Council Grove to the Missouri River, and there is always opportunity
for company at this end of the trail."

We were sitting in a circle under the thin shade of some cottonwood-trees
beside a little stream; the air of noon, hot above our heads, was tempered
with a light breeze from the southwest. As my uncle spoke, Rex glanced
over at Mat Nivers, sitting beside him, and then gazed out thoughtfully
across the stream. I had never thought her pretty before. But now her face,
tanned by the sun and wind, had a richer glow on cheek and lip. Her damp
hair lay in little wavelets about her temples, and her big, sunny, gray eyes
were always her best feature.

Girls made their own dresses on the frontier, and I suppose that anywhere
else Mat would have appeared old-fashioned in the neat, comfortable little
gowns of durable gingham and soft woolen stuffs that she made for herself.
But somehow in all that long journey she was the least travel-soiled of the
whole party.

At my uncle's words she looked up questioningly and I saw the bloom
deepen on her cheek as she met the young man's eyes. Somebody else saw
that shadow of a blush--Bill Banney lying on the ground beside me, and
although he pulled his hat cautiously over his face, I thought he was
listening for the answer.

The young New-Englander stared long at the green prairie before he spoke.
I never knew whether it was ignorance, or a lack of energy, that was
responsible for his bad grammar in those early days, for Rex Krane was no

sham invalid. The lines on his young face told of suffering, and the thin, bony hands showed bodily weakness. At length he turned to my uncle.

"I started out sort of reckless on this trip," he said, slowly. "I'm nearly twenty and never been worth a dang to anybody anywhere on God's earth; so I thought I might as well be where things looked interestin'. But"--he hesitated--"I'm gettin' a lot stronger every day, a whole lot stronger. Mebby I'd be of some use afterwhile--I don't know, though. I reckon I'd better wait till we get to that Council Grove place. Sounds like a nice locality to rest and think in. Are you goin' on, anyhow, Clarenden, crowd or no crowd?"

"Though the heavens fall," my uncle answered, simply.

Jondo had turned quickly to hear this reply and a great light leaped into his deep-set blue eyes. I glanced over at Aunty Boone, sitting apart from us, as she ever chose to do, her own eyes dull, as they always were when she saw keenest; and I remembered how, back at Fort Leavenworth, she had commented on this journey, saying: "They tote together always, an' they're totin' now." Child though I was, I felt that a something more than the cargo of goods was leading my uncle to Santa Fé. What I did not understand was his motive for taking Beverly and Mat and me with him. I had been satisfied before just to go, but now I wanted very much to know why I was going.

Council Grove by the Neosho River was the end of civilization for the freighter. Beyond it the wilderness spread its untamed lengths, and excepting Bent's Fort far up the Arkansas River on the line of the first old trail, rarely followed now, it held not a sign of civilization for the traveler until he should reach the first outposts of the Mexican almost in the shadow of Santa Fé. It is no wonder that wagon-trains mobilized here, waiting for an increase in numbers before they dared to start on westward. And now there were no trains waiting for our coming. Only a gripping necessity could have led a man like Esmond Clarenden to take the trail alone in the certain perils of the plains during the middle '40's. I did not know until long afterward how brave was the loving heart that beat in that little merchant's bosom. A devotee of ease and refinement, he walked the prairie trails unafraid, and made the desert serve his will.

The dusk of evening had fallen long before we pitched camp that night under the big oak-trees in the Neosho River valley outside of the little trading-post. Up in the village a light or two gleamed faintly. From somewhere in the darkness came the sound of a violin, mingling with loud talking and boisterous laughter in a distant drinking-den. It would be some time until moon-rise, and the shadowy places thickened to blackness.

In fair weather all of us except Mat Nivers slept in the open. On stormy nights the younger men occupied one of the wagons, Jondo and Beverly another, and my uncle and myself the third. Mat had the "baby-cab" as Beverly called it, with Aunty Boone underneath it. The ground was Aunty Boone's kingdom. She sat upon it, ate from it, slept on it, and seemed no more soiled than a snake would be by the contact with it.

"Some day I goes plop under it, and be ground myself," she used to say. "Good black soil I make, too," she always added, with her low chuckle.

To-night we were all in the wagons, for the spring rains had made the Neosho valley damp and muddy. I was just on the edge of dreamless slumber when a low voice that seemed to cut the darkness caught my ear.

"Cla'nden! Cla'nden!" it hissed, softly.

My uncle slipped noiselessly out to where Aunty Boone stood, her head so near to the canvas wagon-cover inside of which I lay that I could hear all that was said.

She was always a night prowler. What other women learn now from the evening newspaper or from neighborly gossip she, being created without a sense of fear, went forth in her time and gathered at first hand.

"I been prospectin' up 'round the saloon, Cla'nden. They's a nasty mess of Mexicans in town, all gettin' drunk."

Then I heard a faint rustle of the bushes and I knew that the woman was slipping away to her place under the wagon. I remembered the Mexican whom I had last seen across the street from the Clarenden store in Independence. These were bad Mexicans, as Aunty Boone had said, and that man had seemed in a silent way a friend of my uncle. I wondered what would happen next. It soon happened. My uncle Esmond came inside the wagon and called, softly:

"Gail, wake up."

"I'm awake," I replied, in a half-whisper, as alert as a mystery-loving boy could be.

"Slip over to Jondo and tell him there are Mexicans in town, and I'm going across the river to see what's up. Tell him to wake up everybody and have them stay in the wagons till I get back."

He slid away and the shadows ate him. I followed as far as Jondo's wagon, and gave my message. As I came back something seemed to slip away before me and disappear somewhere. I dived into our wagon and crouched down, waiting with beating heart for Uncle Esmond to come back. Once I thought I heard the sound of a horse's feet on the trail to the eastward, but I was not sure.

All was still and black in the little camp for a long time, and then Esmond Clarenden and Rex Krane crept into the wagon and dropped the flap behind them.

"Krane, have you decided about this trip yet?" Uncle Esmond asked. "If not, you'd better get right up into town and forget us. You can't be too quick about it, either."

"Ain't we going to stay here a few days? Why do you want to know to-night?"

Rex Krane, Yankee-like, met the query with a query.

"Because there's a pretty strong party of Mexican desperadoes here who are going on east, and they mean trouble for somebody. I shouldn't care to meet them with our strength alone. They are all pretty drunk now and getting wilder every minute. Listen to that!"

A yell across the river broke the night stillness.

"There is no telling how soon they may be over here, hunting for us. We must get by them some way, for I cannot risk a fight with them here. Which chance will you choose, the possibility of being overtaken by that Mexican gang going east, or the perils of the plains and the hostility of New Mexico right now? It's about as broad one way as the other for safety, with staying here for a time as the only middle course at present. But that is a perfectly safe one for you."

"I am going on with you," Rex Krane said, with his slow Yankee drawl. "When danger gets close, then I scatter. There's more chance in seven hundred miles to miss somethin' than there is in a hundred and fifty. And even a half-invalid might be of some use. Say, Clarenden, how'd you get hold of this information? You turned in before I did."

"Daniel Boone went out on scout duty--self-elected. You know she considers that the earth was made for her to walk on when she chooses to use it that way. She spied trouble ahead and came back, and gave me the key to the west door of Council Grove so I could get out early," my uncle replied.

"I reckoned as much," Rex declared.

In the dark I could feel Esmond Clarenden give a start.

"What do you mean?" he inquired.

"Oh, I saw the fat lady start out, so I followed her, but I located the nest of Mexicans before she did, and got a good deal out of their drunken jargon. And then I cat-footed it back after a snaky-looking, black Spaniard that seemed to be following her. There were three of us in a row, but the devil hasn't got the hindmost one, not yet--that's me."

"You saw some one follow Daniel into camp?" my uncle broke in, anxiously. But no threatening peril ever hurried Rex Krane's speech.

"Yes, and I also followed some one; but I lost him in this ink-well of a hole, and I was waitin' till he left so I could put the cat out, an' shut the door, when you cut across the river. I've been sittin' round now to see that nothin' broke loose till you got back. Meantime, the thing sort of faded away. I heard a horse gallopin' off east, too. Mebby they are outpostin' to surround our retreat. I didn't wake Bill. He's got no more imagination than Bev. If I had needed anybody I'd have stirred up Gail, here."

In the dark I fairly swelled with pride, and from that moment Rex Krane was added to my little list of heroes that had been made up, so far, of Esmond Clarenden and Jondo and any army officer above the rank of captain.

"Krane, you'll do. I thought I had your correct measure back in Independence," Uncle Esmond said, heartily. "As to the boys, I can risk them; they are Clarendens. My anxiety is for the little orphan girl. She is only a child. I couldn't leave her behind us, and I must not let a hair of her head be harmed."

"She's a right womanly little thing," Rex Krane said, carelessly; but I wondered if in the dark his eyes might not have had the same look they had had at noon when he turned to Mat sitting beside my uncle. Maybe back at Boston he had a little sister of his own like her. Anyhow, I decided then that men's words and faces do not always agree.

Again the roar of voices broke out, and we scrambled from the wagon and quickly gathered our company together.

"What did you find out?" Jondo asked.

"We must clear out of here right away and get through to the other side of town and be off by daylight without anybody knowing it. They are a gang of ugly Mexicans who would not let us cross the river if we should wait till morning. They have already sent a spy over here, and they are waiting for him to report."

"Where is he now?" Bill Banney broke in.

"They's two of him--I know there is," Rex Krane declared. "One of him went east, to cut us off I reckon; an' t'other faded into nothin' toward the river. Kind of a double deal, looks to me."

Both men looked doubtingly at the young man; but without further words, Jondo took command, and we knew that the big plainsman would put through whatever Esmond Clarenden had planned. For Aunty Boone was right when she said, "They tote together."

"We must snake these wagons through town, as though we didn't belong together, but we mustn't get too far apart, either. And remember now, Clarenden, if anybody has to stop and visit with 'em, I'll do it myself," Jondo said.

"Why can't we ride the ponies? We can go faster and scatter more," I urged, as we hastily broke camp.

"He is right, Esmond. They haven't been riding all their lives for nothing," Jondo agreed, as Esmond Clarenden turned hesitatingly toward Mat Nivers.

In the dim light her face seemed bright with courage. It is no wonder that we all trusted her. And trust was the large commodity of the plains in those days, when even as children we ran to meet danger with courageous daring.

"You must cross the river letting the ponies pick their own ford," Jondo commanded us. "Then go through to the ridge on the northwest side of town. Keep out of the light, and if anybody tries to stop you, ride like fury for the ridge."

"Lemme go first," Aunty Boone interposed. "Nobody lookin' for me this side of purgatory. 'Fore they gets over their surprise I'll be gone. Whoo-ee!"

The soft exclamation had a breath of bravery in it that stirred all of us.

"You are right, Daniel. Lead out. Keep to the shadows. If you must run make your mules do record time," Uncle Esmond said.

"You'll find me there when you stop," Rex Krane declared. No sick man ever took life less seriously. "I'm goin' ahead to John-the-Baptist this procession and air the parlor bedrooms."

"Krane, you are an invalid and a fool. You'd better ride in the wagon with me," Bill Banney urged.

"Mebby I am. Don't throw it up to me, but I'm no darned coward, and I'm foot-loose. It's my job to give the address of welcome over t'other side of this Mexican settlement."

The tall, thin young man slouched his cap carelessly on his head and strode away toward the river. Youth was reckless in those days, and the trail was the home of dramatic opportunity. But none of us had dreamed hitherto of Rex Krane's degree of daring and his stubborn will.

The big yellow moon was sailing up from the east; the Neosho glistened all jet and silver over its rough bed; the great shadowy oaks looked ominously after us as we moved out toward the threatening peril before us. Slowly, as though she had time to kill, Aunty Boone sent the brown mule and trusty dun down to the river's rock-bottom ford. Slowly and unconcernedly she climbed the slope and passed up the single street toward the saloon she had already "prospected." Pausing a full minute, she swung toward a far-off cabin light to the south, jogging over the rough ground noisily. The door of the drinking-den was filled with dark faces as the crowd jostled out. Just a lone wagon making its way somewhere about its own business, that was all.

As the crowd turned in again three ponies galloped up the street toward the slope leading out to the high level prairies beyond the Neosho valley. But who could guess how furiously three young hearts beat, and how tightly three pairs of young hands clutched the bridle reins as we surged forward, forgetting the advice to keep in the shadow.

Just after we had crossed the river, a man on horseback fell in behind us. We quickened our speed, but he gained on us. Before we reached the saloon he was almost even with us, keeping well in the shadow all the while. In the increasing moonlight, making everything clear to the eye, I gave one quick glance over my shoulder and saw that the horseman was a Mexican. I have lived a life so fraught with danger that I should hardly remember the feeling of fear but for the indelible imprint of that one terrified minute in the moonlit street of Council Grove.

Two ruffians on watch outside the saloon sprang up with yells. The door burst open and a gang of rowdies fairly spilled out around us. We three on our ponies had the instinctive security on horseback of children born to the saddle, else we should never have escaped from the half-drunken crew. I recall the dust of striking hoofs, the dark forms dodging everywhere, the Mexican rider keeping between us and the saloon door, and most of all I remember one glimpse of Mat Nivers's face with big, staring eyes, and firm-set mouth; and I remember my fleeting impression that she could take care of herself if we could; and over all a sudden shadow as the moon, in pity of our terror, hid its face behind a tiny cloud.

When it shone out again we were dashing by separate ways up the steep slope to the west ridge, but, strangely enough, the Mexican horseman with a follower or two had turned away from us and was chasing off somewhere out of sight.

Up on top of the bluff, with Rex Krane and Aunty Boone, we watched and waited. The wooded Neosho valley full of inky blackness seemed to us like a bottomless gorge of terror which no moonlight could penetrate. We strained our ears to catch the rattle of the wagons, but the noise from the saloon, coming faintly now and then, was all the sound we could hear save the voices of the night rising up from the river, and the whisperings of the open prairie to the west.

In that hour Rex Krane became our good angel.

"Keep the law, 'Hold fast'! You made a splendid race of it, and if Providence made that fellow lose you gettin' out, and led him and his gang sideways from you, I reckon she will keep on takin' care of you till Clarenden resumes control, so don't you worry."

But for his brave presence the terror of that lonely watch would have been harder than the peril of the street, for he seemed more like a gentle mother than the careless, scoffing invalid of the trail.

Midnight came, and the chill of midnight. We huddled together in our wagon and still we waited. Down in the village the lights still burned, and angry voices with curses came to our ears at intervals.

Meantime the three men across the river moved cautiously, hoping that we were safe on the bluff, and knowing that they dared not follow us too rapidly. The wagons creaked and the harness rattled noisily in the night stillness, as slowly, one by one, they lumbered through the darkness across the river and up the bank to the village street. Here they halted and grouped together.

"We must hide out and wait, Clarenden," Jondo counciled. "I hope the ponies and the wagon ahead are safe, but they stirred things up. If we go now we'll all be caught."

The three wagons fell apart and halted wide of the trail where the oak-trees made the blackest shade. The minutes dragged out like hours, and the anxiety for the unprotected group on the bluff made the three men frantic to hurry on. But Jondo's patience equaled his courage, and he always took the least risk. It was nearly midnight, and every noise was intensified. If a mule but moved it set up a clatter of harness chains that seemed to fill the valley.

At last a horseman, coming suddenly from somewhere, rode swiftly by each shadow-hidden wagon, half pausing at the sound of the mules stamping in their places, and then he hurried up the street.

"Three against the crowd. If we must fight, fight to kill," Jondo urged, as the ready firearms were placed for action.

In a minute or two the crew broke out of the saloon and filled the moonlit street, all talking and swearing in broken Spanish.

"Not come yet!"

"Pedro say they be here to-morrow night!" "We wait till to-morrow night!"

And with many wild yells they fell back for a last debauch in the drinking-den.

"I don't understand it," Jondo declared. "That fellow who rode by here ought to have located every son of us, but if they want to wait till to-morrow night it suits me."

An hour later, when the village was in a dead sleep, three wagons slowly pulled up the long street and joined the waiting group at the top, and the crossing over was complete.

Dawn was breaking as our four wagons, followed by the ponies, crept away in the misty light. As we trailed off into the unknown land, I looked back at the bluff below which nestled the last houses we were to see for seven hundred miles. And there, outlined against the horizon, a Mexican stood watching us. I had seen the same man one day riding up from the ravine southwest of Fort Leavenworth. I had seen him dashing toward the river the next day. I had watched him sitting across the street from the Clarenden store in Independence.

I wondered if it might have been this man who had hung about our camp the evening before, and if it might have been this same man who rode between us and the saloon mob, leading the crowd after him and losing us on the side of the bluff. And as we had eluded the Council Grove danger, I wondered what would come next, and if he would be in it.

V

WOMEN AND CHILDREN FIRST

"So I draw the world together, link by link."
--KIPLING.

Day after day we pushed into the unknown wilderness. No wagon-trains passed ours moving eastward. No moccasined track in the dust of the trail gave hint of any human presence near. Where to-day the Pullman car glides in smooth comfort, the old Santa Fé Trail lay like a narrow brown ribbon on the green desolation of Nature's unconquered domain. Out beyond the region of long-stemmed grasses, into the short-grass land, we pressed across a pathless field-of-the-cloth-of-green, gemmed with myriads of bright blossoms--broad acres on acres that the young years of a coming century should change into great wheat-fields to help fill the granaries of the world. How I reveled in it--that far-stretching plain of flower-starred verdure! It was my world--mine, unending, only softening out into lavender mists that rimmed it round in one unbroken fold of velvety vapor.

At last we came to the Arkansas River--flat-banked, sand-bottomed, wide, wandering, impossible thing--whose shallow waters followed aimlessly the line of least resistance, back and forth across its bed. Rivers had meant something to me. The big muddy Missouri for Independence and Fort Leavenworth, that its steamers might bring the soldiers, and my uncle's goods to their places. The little rivers that ran into the big ones, to feed their currents for down-stream service. The creeks, that boys might wade and swim and fish, else Beverly would have lived unhappily all his days. But here was a river that could neither fetch nor carry. Nobody lived near it, and it had no deep waters like our beloved, ugly old Missouri. I loved the level prairies, but I didn't like that river, somehow. I felt exposed on its blank, treeless borders, as if I stood naked and defenseless, with no haven of cover from the enemies of the savage plains.

The late afternoon was hot, the sky was dust-dimmed, the south wind feverish and strength-sapping. At dawn we had sighted a peak against the western horizon. We were approaching it now--a single low butte, its front a sheer stone bluff facing southward toward the river, it lifted its head high above the silent plains; and to the north it stretched in a long gentle slope back to a lateral rim along the landscape. The trail crept close about its base, as if it would cling lovingly to this one shadow-making thing amid all the open, blaring, sun-bound miles stretching out on either side of it.

As Beverly and I were riding in front of Mat's wagon, of which we had elected ourselves the special guardians, Rex Krane came up alongside Bill Banney's team in front of us. The young men were no such hard-and-fast friends as Beverly and I. For some reason they had little to say to each other.

"Is that what you call Pike's Peak, Bill?" Rex asked.

"No, the mountains are a month away. That's Pawnee Rock, and I'll breathe a lot freer when we get out of sight of that infernal thing," Bill replied.

"What's its offense?" Rex inquired.

"It's the peak of perdition, the bottomless pit turned inside out," Bill declared.

"I don't see the excuse for a rock sittin' out here, sayin' nothin', bein' called all manner of unpleasant names," the young Bostonian insisted.

"Well, I reckon you'd find one mighty quick if you ever heard the soldiers at Fort Leavenworth talk about it once. All the plainsmen dread it. Jondo says more men have been killed right around this old stone Sphinx than any other one spot in North America, outside of battle-fields."

"Happy thought! Do their ghosts rise up and walk at midnight? Tell me more," Rex urged.

"Nobody walks. Everybody runs. There was a terrible Indian fight here once; the Pawnees in the king-row, and all the hosts of the Midianites, and Hivites, and Jebusites, Kiowa, Comanche, and Kaw, rag-tag and bobtail, trying to get 'em out. I don't know who won, but the citadel got christened Pawnee Rock. It took a fountain filled with blood to do it, though."

Rex Krane gave a long whistle.

"I believe Bill is trying to scare him, Bev," I murmured.

"I believe he's just precious wasting time," Beverly replied.

"And so," Bill continued, "it came to be a sort of rock of execution where romances end and they die happily ever afterward. The Indians get up there and, being able to read fine print with ease as far away as either seacoast, they can watch any wagon-train from the time it leaves Council Grove over east to Bent's Fort on the Purgatoire Creek out west; and having counted the number of men, and the number of bullets in each man's pouch, they slip down and jump on the train as it goes by. If the men can make it to beat them to the top of the rock, as they do sometimes, they can keep the critters off, unless the Indians are strong enough to keep them up there and sit around and wait till they starve for water, and have to come down. It's a grim old fortress, and never needs a garrison. Indians or white men up there, sometimes they defend and sometimes they attack. But it's a bad place always, and on account of having our little girl along--" Bill paused. "A fellow gets to see a lot of country out here," he added.

"Banney, just why didn't you join the army? You'd have a chance to see a lot more of the country, if this Mexican War goes on," Rex Krane said, meditatively.

"I'd rather be my own captain and order myself to the front, and likewise command my rear-guard to retire, whenever I doggone please," Bill said. "It isn't the soldiers that'll do this country the most good. They are useful enough when they are useful, Lord knows. And we'll always need a decent few of 'em around to look after women and children, and invalids," he went on. "I tell you, Krane, it's men like Clarenden that's going to make these prairies worth something one of these days. The men who build up business, not them that shoot and run to or from. That's what the West's got to have. I'm through going crazy about army folks. One man that buys and sells, if he gives good weight and measure, is, himself, a whole regiment for civilization."

Just then Jondo halted the train, and we gathered about him.

"Clarenden, let's pitch camp at the rock. The horses are dead tired and this wind is making them nervous. There's a storm due as soon as it lays a bit, and we would be sort of protected here. A tornado's a giant out in this country, you know."

"This tavern doesn't have a very good name with the traveling public, does it, Clarenden?" Rex Krane suggested.

"Not very," my uncle replied. "But in case of trouble, the top of it isn't a bad place to shoot from."

"What if the other fellow gets there first?" Bill Banney inquired.

"We can run from here as easily as any other place," Jondo assured us. "I haven't seen a sign of Indians yet. But we've got to be careful. This point has a bad reputation, and I naturally begin to *feel* Indians in the air as soon as I come in sight of it. If we need the law of the trail anywhere, we need it here," he admonished.

Beverly and I drew close together. We were in the land of *bad* Indians, but nothing had happened to us yet, and we could not believe that any danger was near us now, although we were foolishly half hoping that there might be, for the excitement of it.

"There's no place in a million miles for anybody to hide, Bill. Where would Jondo's Indians be?" Beverly asked, as we were getting into camp order for the night.

Beverly's disposition to demand proof was as strong here as it had been in the matter of rivers turning their courses, and fishes playing leap-frog.

"They might be behind that ridge out north, and have a scout lying flat on the top of old Pawnee Rock, up there, lookin' benevolently down at us over the rim of his spectacles right now," Bill replied, as he pulled the corral ropes out of the wagon.

"What makes you think so?" I asked, eagerly.

"What Jondo said about his *feeling Indians*, I guess, but he reads these prairie trails as easy as Robinson Crusoe read Friday's footprints in the sand, and he hasn't read anything in 'em yet. Indians don't fight at night, anyhow. That's one good thing. Get hold of that rope, Bev, and pull her up tight," Bill replied.

Every night our four wagons in camp made a hollow square, with space enough allowed at the corners to enlarge the corral inside for the stock. These corners were securely roped across from wagon to wagon. To-night, however, the corral space was reduced and the quartet of vehicles huddled closer together.

At dusk the hot wind came sweeping in from the southwest, a wild, lashing fury, swirling the sand in great spirals from the river bed. Our fire was put out and the blackness of midnight fell upon us. The horses were restless and the mules squealed and stamped. All night the very spirit of fear seemed to fill the air.

Just before daybreak a huge black storm-cloud came boiling up out of the southwest, with a weird yellow band across the sky before it. Overhead the stars shed a dim light on the shadowy face of the plains. A sudden whisper thrilled the camp, chilling our hearts within us.

"Indians near!" We all knew it in a flash.

Jondo, on guard, had caught the sign first. Something creeping across the trail, not a coyote, for it stood upright a moment, then bent again, and was lost in the deep gloom. Jondo had shifted to another angle of the outlook, had seen it again, and again at a third point. It was encircling the camp. Then all of us, except Jondo, began to see moving shapes. He saw nothing for a long time, and our spirits rose again.

"You must have been mistaken, Jondo," Rex Krane ventured, as he stared into the black gloom. "Maybe it was just this infernal wind. It's one darned sea-breeze of a zephyr."

"I've crossed the plains before. I wasn't mistaken," the big plainsman replied. "If I had been, you'd still see it. The trouble is that it is watching now. Everybody lay low. It will come to life again. I hope there's only one of it."

We had hardly moved after the first alarm, except to peer about and fancy that dark objects were closing in upon us.

It did come to life again. This time on Jondo's side of the camp. Something creeping near, and nearer.

The air was motionless and hot above us, the upper heavens were beginning to be threshed across by clouds, and the silence hung like a weight upon us. Then suddenly, just beyond the camp, a form rose from the ground, stood upright, and stretched out both arms toward us. And a low cry, "Take me. I die," reached our ears.

Still Jondo commanded silence. Indians are shrewd to decoy their foes out of the security of the camp. The form came nearer--a little girl, no larger than our Mat--and again came the low call. The voice was Indian, the accent Spanish, but the words were English.

"Come to us!" Esmond Clarenden answered back in a clear, low tone; and slowly and noiselessly the girl approached the camp.

I can feel it all now, although that was many years ago: the soft starlight on the plains; the hot, still air holding its breath against the oncoming tornado; the group of wagons making a deeper shadow in the dull light; beyond us the bold front of old Pawnee Rock, huge and gray in the gloom; our little company standing close together, ready to hurl a shower of bullets if this proved but the decoy of a hidden foe; and the girl with light step drawing nearer. Clad in the picturesque garb of the Southwest Indian, her hair hanging in a great braid over each shoulder, her dark eyes fixed on us, she made a picture in that dusky setting that an artist might not have given to his brush twice in a lifetime on the plains.

A few feet from us she halted.

"Throw up your hands!" Jondo commanded.

The slim brown arms were flung above the girl's head, and I caught the glint of quaintly hammered silver bracelets, as she stepped forward with that ease of motion that generations of moccasined feet on sand and sod and stone can give.

"Take me," she cried, pleadingly. "The Mexicans steal me from my people and bring me far away. They meet Kiowa. Kiowa beat me; make me slave."

She held up her hands. They were lacerated and bleeding. She slipped the bright blanket from her brown shoulder. It was bruised and swollen.

"You go to Santa Fé? Take me. I do you good, not bad."

"What would these Kiowas do to us, then?"

It was Bill Banney who spoke.

"They follow you--kill you."

"Oh, cheerful! I wish you were twins," Rex Krane said, softly.

Jondo lifted his hand.

"Let me talk to her," he said.

Then in her own language he got her story.

"Here we are." He turned to us. "Stolen from her people by the Mexicans, probably the same ones we passed in Council Grove; traded to the Kiowas out here somewhere, beaten, and starved, and held for ransom, or trade to some other tribe. They are over there behind Pawnee Rock. They got sight of us somehow, but they don't intend to bother us. They are on the lookout for a bigger train. She has slipped away while they sleep. If we send her back she will be beaten and made a slave. If we keep her, they will follow us for a fight. They are fifty to our six. What shall we do?"

"We don't need any Indians to help us get into trouble. We are sure enough of it without that," Bill Banney declared. "And what's one Indian, anyhow? She's just--"

"Just a little orphan girl like Mat," Rex Krane finished his sentence.

Bill frowned, but made no reply.

The Indian girl was standing outside the corral, listening to all that was said, her face giving no sign of the struggle between hope and despair that must have striven within her.

"Uncle Esmond, let's take her, and take our chances." Beverly's boyish voice had a defiant tone, for the spirit of adventure was strong within him. The girl turned quickly and a great light leaped into her eyes at the boy's words.

"Save a life and lose ours. It's not the rule of the plains, but--there's a higher law like that somewhere, Clarenden," Jondo said, earnestly.

The girl came swiftly toward Uncle Esmond and stood upright before him.

"I will not hide the truth. I go back to Kiowas. They sell me for big treasure. They will not harm you," she said, "I stay with you, they say you steal me, and they come at the first bird's song and kill you every one. They are so many."

She stood motionless before him, the seal of grim despair on her young face.

"What's your name?" Esmond Clarenden asked. "Po-a-be. In your words, `Little Blue Flower,'" the girl said.

"Then, Little Blue Flower, you must stay with us."

She pointed toward the eastern sky where a faint light was beginning to show above the horizon. "See, the day comes!"

"Then we will break camp now," my uncle said.

"Not in the face of this storm, Clarenden," Jondo declared. "You can fight an Indian. You can't do a thing but 'hold fast' in one of these hurricanes."

The air was still and hot. The black cloud swept swiftly onward, with the weird yellow glow before it. In the solitude of the plains the trail showed like a ghostly pathway of peril. Before us loomed that grim rock bluff, behind whose crest lay the sleeping band of Kiowas. It was only because they slept that Little Blue Flower could steal away in hope of rescue.

Hotter grew the air and darker the swiftly rolling clouds; black and awful stood old Pawnee Rock with the silent menace of its sleeping enemy. In the stillness of the pause before the storm burst we heard Jondo's voice commanding us. With our first care for the frightened stock, we grouped ourselves together as he ordered close under the bluff.

Suddenly an angry wind leaped out of the sky, beating back the hot dead air with gigantic flails of fury. Then the storm broke with tornado rage and cloudburst floods, and in its track terror reigned. Beverly and I clung together, and, holding a hand of each, Mat Nivers crouched beside us, herself strong in this second test of courage as she had been in the camp that night at Council Grove.

I have never been afraid of storms and I can never understand why timid folk should speak of them as of a living, self-directing force bent purposely on human destruction. I love the splendor of the lightning and the thunder's peal. From our earliest years, Beverly and Mat and I had watched the flood-waters of the Missouri sweep over the bottomlands, and we had heard the winds rave, and the cannonading of the angry heavens. But this mad blast of the prairie storm was like nothing we had ever seen or heard before. A yellow glare filled the sky, a half-illumined, evil glow, as if to hide what lay beyond it. One breathed in fine sand, and tasted the desert dust. Behind it, all copper-green, a broad, lurid band swept up toward the zenith. Under its weird, unearthly light, the prairies, and everything upon them, took on a ghastly hue. Then came the inky-black storm-cloud--long, funnel-shaped, pendulous--and in its deafening roar and the thick darkness that could be felt, and the awful sweep of its all-engulfing embrace, the senses failed and the very breath of life seemed beaten away. The floods fell in streams, hot, then suddenly cold. And then a fusillade of hail bombarded the flat prairies, defenseless beneath the munitions of the heavens. But in all the wild, mad blackness, in the shriek and crash of maniac winds, in the swirl of many waters, and chill and fury of the threshing hail, the law of the trail failed not: "Hold fast." And with our hands gripped in one another's, we children kept the law.

Just at the moment when destruction seemed upon us, the long swinging cloud--funnel lifted. We heard it passing high above us. Then it dropped against the face of old Pawnee Rock, that must have held the trail law through all the centuries of storms that have beaten against its bold, stern front. One tremendous blast, one crashing boom, as if the foundations of the earth were broken loose, and the thing had left us far behind.

Daylight burst upon us in a moment, and the blue heavens smiled down on the clean-washed prairies. No homes, no crops, no orchards were left in ruins in those days to mark the cyclone's wrath on wilderness trails. As the darkness lifted we gathered ourselves together to take hold of life again and to defend ourselves from our human enemy.

A shower of arrows from the top of the bluff might rain upon us at any moment, yelling warriors might rush upon us, or a ring of riders encircle us. It was in times like this that I learned how quickly men can get the mastery.

Jondo and Esmond Clarenden did not delay a minute in protecting the camp and setting it in order, taking inventory of the lost and searching for the missing. Three of our number, with one of the ponies, were missing.

Aunty Boone had crouched in a protected angle at the base of the bluff, and when we found her she was calmly smoking her pipe.

"Yo' skeered of this little puff?" she queried. "Yo' bettah see a simoon on the desset, then. This here--just a racket. What's come of that little redskin?"

She was not to be found. Nor was there any trace of Rex Krane anywhere. In consternation we scanned the prairies far and wide, but only level green distances were about us, holding no sign of life. We lived hours in those watching minutes.

Suddenly Beverly gave a shout, and we saw Little Blue Flower running swiftly from the sloping side of the bluff toward the camp. Behind her stalked the young New-Englander.

"I went up to see what she was in such a hurry for to see," he explained, simply. "I calculated it would be as interestin' to me as to her, and if anything was about to cut loose"--he laid a hand carelessly on his revolver-- "why, I'd help it along. The little pink pansy, it seems, went to look after our friends, the enemy," Rex went on. "The hail nearly busted that old rock open. I thought once it had. The ponies are scattered and likewise the Kiowas. Gone helter-skelter, like the--tornado. The thing hit hard up there. Some ponies dead, and mebby an Indian or two. I didn't hunt 'em up. I can't use 'em that way," he added. "So I just said, 'Pax vobiscum!' and a lot of it, and came kittering back."

Little Blue Flower's eyes glistened.

"Gone, all gone. The rain god drove them away. Now I know I may go with you. The rain god loves you."

It was to Beverly, and not to my uncle, that her eyes turned as she spoke, but he was not even listening to her. To him she was merely an Indian. She seemed more than that to me, and therein lay the difference between us.

If she had been interesting under the starlight, in the light of day she became picturesque, a beautiful type of her race, silent, alert of countenance, with big, expressive, black eyes, and long, heavy braids of black hair. With her brilliant blanket about her shoulders, a turquoise pendant on a leather band at her throat, silver bracelets on her brown arms, she was as pleasing as an Indian maiden could be--adding a touch of picturesque life to that wonderful journey westward from Pawnee Rock to Santa Fé. Aunty Boone alone resented her presence among us.

"You can trust a nigger," she growled, "'cause you know they none of 'em no 'count. But you can't tell about this Injun, whether she's good or bad. I lets that sort of fish alone."

Little Blue Flower looked up at her with steady gaze and made no reply.

Out of that morning's events I learned a lasting lesson, and I know now that the influence of Rex Krane on my life began that day, as I recalled how he had followed Aunty Boone about the dark corners of the little trading-post on the Neosho; and how he had looked at Mat Nivers once when Uncle Esmond had suggested his turning back to Independence; and how he had gone before all of us, the vanguard, to the top of the bluff west of Council Grove; and now he had followed this Indian girl. From that time I knew in my boy heart that this tall, careless Boston youth had a zealous care for the safety of women and children. How much care, events would run swiftly on to show me. But welded into my life from that hour was the meaning of a man's high, chivalric duty. And among all the lessons that the old trail taught to me, none served me more than this one that came to me on that sweet May morning beneath the shadow of Pawnee Rock.

———————————————————

VI

SPYING OUT THE LAND

City of the Holy Faith,
In thy streets so dim with age,
Do I read not Faith's decay,
But the Future's heritage.
-LILIAN WHITING.

Day was passing and the shadows were already beginning to grow purple in the valleys, long before the golden light had left the opal-crowned peaks of the Sangre-de-Christo Mountains beyond them.

On the wide crest of a rocky ridge our wagons halted. Behind us the long trail stretched back, past mountain height and cañon wall, past barren slope and rolling green prairie, on to where the wooded ravines hem in the Missouri's yellow floods.

Before us lay a level plain, edged round with high mesas, over which snowy-topped mountain peaks kept watch. A sandy plain, checkered across by verdant-banded arroyos, and splotched with little clumps of trees and little fields of corn. In the heart of it all was Santa Fé, a mere group of dust-brown adobe blocks--silent, unsmiling, expressionless--the city of the Spanish Mexican, centuries old and centuries primitive.

As our tired mules slackened their traces and drooped to rest after the long up-climb, Esmond Clarenden called out:

"Come here, children. Yonder is the end of the trail."

We gathered eagerly about him, a picture in ourselves, maybe, in an age of picturesque things; four men, bronzed and bearded; two sturdy boys; Mat Nivers, no longer a little girl, it seemed now, with the bloom of health on her tanned cheeks, and the smile of good nature in wide gray eyes; beside her, the Indian maiden, Little Blue Flower, slim, brown, lithe of motion, brief of speech; and towering back of all, the glistening black face of the big, silent African woman.

So we stood looking out toward that northwest plain where the trail lost itself among the low adobe huts huddled together beside the glistening waters of the Santa Fé River.

Rex Krane was the first to speak.

"So that's what we've come out for to see, is it?" he mused, aloud. "That's the precious old town that we've dodged Indians, and shot rattlesnakes, and sunburnt our noses, and rain-soaked our dress suits for! That's why we've pillowed our heads on the cushiony cactus and tramped through purling sands, and blistered our hands pullin' at eider-down ropes, and strained our leg-muscles goin' down, and busted our lungs comin' up, and clawed along the top edge of the world with nothin' but healthy climate between us and the bottom of the bottomless pit. Humph! That's what you call Santa Fé! 'The city of the Holy Faith!' Well, I need a darned lot of 'holy faith' to make me see any city there. It's just a bunch of old yellow brick-kilns to me, and I 'most wish now I'd stayed back at Independence and hunted dog-tooth violets along the Big Blue."

"It's not Boston, if that's what you were looking for; at least there's no Bunker Hill Monument nor Back Bay anywhere in sight. But I reckon it's the best they've got. I'm tired enough to take what's offered and keep still," Bill Banney declared.

I, too, wanted to keep still. I had only a faint memory of a real city. It must have been St. Louis, for there was a wharf, and a steamboat and a busy street, and soft voices--speaking a foreign tongue. But the pictures I had seen, and the talk I had heard, coupled with a little boy's keen imagination, had built up a very different Santa Fé in my mind. At that moment I was homesick for Fort Leavenworth, through and through homesick, for the first time since that April day when I had sat on the bluff above the Missouri River while the vision of the plains descended upon me. Everything seemed so different to-night, as if a gulf had widened between us and all the nights behind us.

We went into camp on the ridge, with the journey's goal in plain view. And as we sat down together about the fire after supper we forgot the hardships of the way over which we had come. The pine logs blazed cheerily, and as the air grew chill we drew nearer together about them as about a home fireside.

The long June twilight fell upon the landscape. The piñon and scrubby cedars turned to dark blotches on the slopes. The valley swam in a purple mist. The silence of evening was broken only by a faint bird-note in the bushes, and the fainter call of some wild thing stealing forth at nightfall from its daytime retreat. Behind us the mesas and headlands loomed up black and sullen, but far before us the Sangre-de-Christo Mountains lifted their glorified crests, with the sun's last radiance bathing them in crimson floods.

We sat in silence for a long time, for nobody cared to talk. Presently we heard Aunty Boone's low, penetrating voice inside the wagon corral:

"You pore gob of ugliness! Yo' done yo' best, and it's green corn and plenty of watah and all this grizzly-gray grass you can stuff in now. It's good for a mule to start right, same as a man. Whoo-ee!"

The low voice trailed off into weird little whoops of approval. Then the woman wandered away to the edge of the bluff and sat until late that night, looking out at the strange, entrancing New Mexican landscape.

"To-morrow we put on our best clothes and enter the city," my uncle broke the silence. "We have managed to pull through so far, and we intend to keep on pulling till we unload back at Independence again. But these are unsafe times and we are in an unsafe country. We are going to do business and get out of it again as soon as possible. I shall ask you all to be ready to leave at a minute's notice, if you are coming back with me!"

"Now you see why I didn't join the army, don't you, Krane?" Bill Banney said, aside. "I wanted to work under a real general."

Then turning to my uncle, he added:

"I'm already contracted for the round trip, Clarenden."

"You are going to start back just as if there were no dangers to be met?" Rex Krane inquired.

"As if there were dangers to be *met*, not run from," Esmond Clarenden replied.

"Clarenden," the young Bostonian began, "you got away from that drunken mob at Independence with your children, your mules, and your big Daniel Boone. You started out when war was ragin' on the Mexican frontier, and never stopped a minute because you had to come it alone from Council Grove. You shook yourself and family right through the teeth of that Mexican gang layin' for you back there. You took Little Trailing Arbutus at Pawnee Rock out of pure sympathy when you knew it meant a fight at sun-up, six against fifty. And there would have been a bloody one, too, but for that merciful West India hurricane bustin' up the show. You pulled us up the Arkansas River, and straddled the Gloriettas, with every danger that could ever be just whistlin' about our ears. And now you sit there and murmur softly that 'we are in an unsafe country and these are unsafe times,' so we'd better be toddlin' back home right soon. I want to tell *you* something now."

He paused and looked at Mat Nivers. Always he looked at Mat Nivers, who since the first blush one noonday long ago, so it seemed, now, never appeared to know or care where he looked. He must have had such a sister himself; I felt sure of that now.

"I want to tell *you*," Rex repeated, "that I'm goin' to stay with you. There's something *safe* about you. And then," he added, carelessly, as he gazed out toward the darkening plain below us, "my mother always said you could tie to a man who was good to children. And you've been good to this infant Kentuckian here."

He flung out a hand toward Bill Banney without looking away from the open West. "When you want to start back to God's country and the land of Plymouth Rocks and Pawnee Rocks, I'm ready to trot along."

"I'm glad to hear you say that, Krane," Esmond Clarenden said. "I shall need all the help I can get on the way back. Because we got through safely we cannot necessarily count on a safe return. I may need you in Santa Fé, too."

"Then command me," Rex replied.

He looked toward Mat again, but she and Little Blue Flower were coiling their long hair in fantastic fashion about their heads, and laughing like school-girls together.

Little Blue Flower was as a shy brown fawn following us. She had a way of copying Mat's manner, and she spoke less of Indian and Spanish and more of English from day to day. She had laid aside her Indian dress for one of Mat's neat gingham gowns. I think she tried hard to forget her race in everything except her prayers, for her own people had all been slain by Mexican ruffians. We could not have helped liking her if we had tried to do so. Yet that invisible race barrier that kept a fixed gulf between us and Aunty Boone separated us also from the lovable little Indian lass, albeit the gulf was far less deep and impassable.

To-night when she and Mat scampered away to the family wagon together, she seemed somehow to really belong to us.

Presently Jondo and Rex Krane and Bill and Beverly rolled their blankets about them and went to sleep, leaving Esmond Clarenden and myself alone beside the dying fire. The air was sharp and the night silence deepened as the stars came into the skies.

"Why don't you go to bed, Gail?" my uncle asked.

"I'm not sleepy. I'm homesick," I replied. "Come here, boy." He opened his arms to me, and I nestled in their embrace.

"You've grown a lot in these two months, little man," he said, softly. "You are a brave-hearted plainsman, and a good, strong little limb when it comes to endurance, but just once in a while all of us need a mothering touch. It keeps us sweet, my boy. It keeps us sweet and fit to live."

Oh, many a time in the years that followed did the loving embrace and the gentle words of this gentle, strong man come back to comfort me.

"Let me tell you something, Gail. I'm going to need a boy like you to help me a lot before we leave Santa Fé, and I shall count on you."

Just then a noise at the far side of the corral seemed to disturb the stock. A faint stir of awakening or surprise--just a hint in the air. All was still in a moment. Then it came again. We listened. Something, an indefinite something, somewhere, was astir. The surprise became unrest, anxiety, fear, among the mules.

"Wait here, Gail. I'll see what's up," Uncle Esmond said, in a low voice.

He hurried away toward the corral and I slipped back in the shadow of a rock and leaned against it to wait.

In the dim beams of a starlit New Mexican sky I could see clearly out toward the valley, but behind the camp all was darkness. As I waited, hidden by the shadows, suddenly the flap of the family-wagon cover lifted and Little Blue Flower slid out as softly as a cat walks in the dust. She was dressed in her own Indian garb now, with her bright blanket drawn picturesquely about her head and shoulders. Silently she moved about the camp, peering toward the shadows hiding me. Then with noiseless step she slipped toward where Beverly Clarenden lay, his boyish face upturned to the stars, sleeping the dreamless sleep of youth and health. I leaned forward and stared hard as the girl approached him. I saw her drop down on one knee beside him, and, bending over him, she gently kissed his forehead. She rose and gave one hurried look around the place and then, like a bird lifting its wings for flight, she threw up her arms, and in another moment she sprang to the edge of the ridge and slipped from view. I followed, only to see her gliding swiftly away, farther and farther, along the dim trail, until the shadows swallowed her from my sight.

A low whinny from the corral caught my ear, followed by a rush of horses' feet. As I slipped into my place again to wait for my uncle to return, the smoldering logs blazed out suddenly, lighting up the form of a man who appeared just beyond the fire, so that I saw the face distinctly. Then he, too, was gone, following the way the Indian girl had taken, until he lost himself in the misty dullness of the plains.

Presently Esmond Clarenden came back to the camp-fire.

"Gail, the pony we lost in that storm at Pawnee Rock has come back to us. It was standing outside the corral, waiting to get in, just as if it had lost us for a couple of hours. It is in good condition, too."

"How could it ever get here?" I exclaimed.

"Any one of a dozen ways," my uncle replied. "It may have run far that stormy morning when it broke out of the corral, and possibly some party coming over the Cimarron Trail picked it up and roved on this way. There is no telling how it got here, since it keeps still itself about the matter. Losing and finding and losing again is the law of events on the plains."

"But why should it find us right here to-night, like it had been led back?" I insisted.

"That's the miracle of it, Gail. It is always the strange thing that really happens here. In years to come, if you ever tell the truth about this trip, it will not be believed. When this isn't the frontier any longer, the story of the trail will be accounted impossible."

Everything seemed impossible to me as I sat there staring at the dying fire. Presently I remembered what I had seen while my uncle was away.

"Little Blue Flower has run away," I said, "and I saw the Mexican that came to Fort Leavenworth the day before I twisted my ankle. He slipped by here just a minute ago. I know, for I saw his face when the logs flared up."

Esmond Clarenden gave a start. "Gail, you have the most remarkable memory for faces of any child I ever knew," he said.

"Did he follow us, too, like the pony, or did he ride the pony after us?" I asked. "He's just everywhere we go, somehow. Did I ever see him before he came to the fort, or did I dream it?"

"You are a little dreamer, Gail," my uncle said, kindly. "But dreams don't hurt, if you do your part whenever you are needed."

"Bev and Bill Banney make fun of dreams," I said.

"Yes, they don't have 'em; but Bev and Bill are ready when it comes to doing things. They are a good deal alike, daring, and a bit reckless sometimes, with good hard sense enough to keep them level."

"Don't I do, too?" I inquired.

"Yes, you do and dream, both. That's all the better. But you mustn't forget, too, that sometimes the things we long for in our dreams we must fight for, and even die for, maybe, that those who come after us may be the better for our having them. What was it you said about Little Blue Flower?" Uncle Esmond had forgotten her for the moment.

"She's gone to Santa Fé, I reckon. Is she bad, Uncle Esmond? Tell me all about things," I urged.

"We are all here spying out the land, Mexican, Indian, trader, freighter, adventurer, invalid," Uncle Esmond replied. "I don't know what started the little Indian girl off, unless she just felt Indian, as Jondo would say; but I may as well tell you, Gail, that it may have been the Mexican who got our pony for us. He is a strange fellow, walks like a cat, has ears like a timber wolf, and the cunning of a fox."

"Is he our friend?" I asked, eagerly.

"Listen, boy. He came to Fort Leavenworth on purpose to bring me an important message, and he waited at Independence to see us off. Do you remember the two spies Krane talked about at Council Grove? I think he followed the Mexican spy across the river to our camp and sent him on east. Then he went back and got the crowd all mixed up by his report, while their own man scouted the trail out there for miles all night. He is the man who put you through town and decoyed the ruffians to one side. He located us after we had crossed the river, and then broke up their meeting and put the fellows off to wait till the next night. That is the way I worked out that Council Grove puzzle. He has a wide range, and there are big things ahead for him in New Mexico.

"Sooner or later however," my uncle went on, "we will have to reckon with that Kiowa tribe for stealing their captive. They meant to return her for a big ransom price.... Great Heavens, Gail! You seem like a man to me to-night instead of my little boy back at the fort. The plains bring years to us instead of months, with just one crossing. I am counting on you not to tell all you've been told and all you've seen. I can be sure of you if you can keep things to yourself. You'd better get to sleep now. There will be plenty to see over in Santa Fé. And there is always danger afoot. But remember, it is the coward who finds the most trouble in this world. Do your part with a gentleman's heart and a hero's hand, and you'll get to the end of every trail safely. Now go to bed."

Where I lay that night I could see a wide space of star-gemmed sky, the blue night-sky of the Southwest, and I wondered, as I looked up into the starry deeps, how God could keep so many bright bodies afield up there, and yet take time to guard all the wandering children of men.

With the day-dawn the strange events of the night seemed as unreal as the vanishing night-shadows. The bluest skies of a blue-sky land curved in fathomless majesty over the yellow valley of the Santa Fé. Against its borders loomed the silent mountain ranges--purple-shaddowed, silver-topped Ortiz and Jemez, Sandia and Sangre-de-Christo. Dusty and deserted lay the trail, save that here and there a group of dark-faced carriers of firewood prodded on their fagot-laden burros toward the distant town. As our wagons halted at the sandy borders of an arroyo the brown clad form of a priest rose up from the shade of a group of scrubby piñon-trees beside the trail.

Esmond Clarenden lifted his hat in greeting.

"Are you going our way? We can give you a ride," he paused to say.

The man's face was very dark, but it was a young, strong face, and his large, dark eyes were full of the fire of life. When he spoke his voice was low and musical.

"I thank you. I go toward the mountains. You stay here long?"

"Only to dispose of my goods. My business is brief," Esmond Clarenden declared.

The good man leaned forward as if to see each face there, sweeping in everything at one glance. Then he looked down at the ground.

"These are troublesome days. War is only a temporary evil, but it makes for hate, and hate kills as it dies. Love lives and gives life." A smile lighted his eyes, though his lips were firm. "I wish you well. Among friends or enemies the one haven of safety always is the holy sanctuary."

Uncle Esmond bowed his head reverently.

"You will find it beside the trail near the river. The walls are very old and strong, but not so old as hate, nor so strong as love. A little street runs from it, crooked--six houses away. Peace be to all of you." He broke off suddenly and his last sentence was spoken in a clear, strong tone unlike the gentler voice.

"I thank you, Father!" Jondo said, as the priest passed his wagon.

The holy man gave him one swift, searching glance. Then lifting his right hand as if in blessing, and slowly dropping it until the forefinger pointed toward the west, he passed on his way.

Jondo's brown cheek flushed and the lines about his mouth grew hard.

"Take my place, Bev," he said, as he left his wagon and joined Esmond Clarenden.

The two spoke earnestly together. Then Jondo mounted Beverly's pony.

"If you need me--" I heard him say, and he turned away and rode in the direction the priest had taken.

Uncle Esmond offered no explanation for this sudden action, and his sunny face was stern.

Usually wagon-trains were spied out long before they reached the city, and a rabble attended their entry. To-day we moved along quietly until the trail became a mere walled lane. On either side one-story adobe huts sat with their backs to the street. No windows opened to the front, and only a wooden door or a closed gateway stared in blank unfriendliness at the passer-by. Little straggling lanes led off aimlessly on either side, as narrow and silent as the strange terminal of the long trail itself.

I was only a boy, with the heart of a boy and the eyes of a boy. I could only feel; I could not understand the spell of that hour. But to me everything was alluring, wrapt as it was in the mystery of a civilization old here when Plymouth Rock felt the first Pilgrim's foot, or Pawnee Rock stared at the first bold plainsman of the pale face and the conquering soul.

I was riding beside Beverly's wagon as we neared the quaint, centuries-old, adobe church of San Miguel, rising tall and silent above the low huts about it, its rough walls suggesting a fortress of strength, while its triple towers might be an outlook for a guardsman.

"Look at that church. Bev, I wonder how old it is," I exclaimed.

"I should say about a thousand years and a day," Beverly declared. "See that flopsy steeple thing! It looks like building-blocks stacked up there."

"Maybe this is the sanctuary that priest was talking about," I suggested. "He said the walls were old as hate and strong as love, with a crooked street beside it somewhere."

"Oh, you sponge! Soaking up everything you see and hear. I wonder you sleep nights for fear the wind will tell the pine trees something you'll miss," Beverly declared. "I can tell a horse's age by its teeth, but churches don't have teeth. Go and ask Mat about it. She knows when the De Sotos and Cortéses and all the other Spanish grandaddees came to Mexico."

I had just turned back alongside of Mat's wagon--she was always our book of ready reference--when a little girl suddenly dashed out of a walled lane opening into the street behind us. She stopped in the middle of the road, almost under my pony's feet, then with a shout of laughter she dashed into the deep doorway of the church and stood there, peering out at me with eyes brimful of mischief.

I brought my pony back on its haunches suddenly. I had seen this girl before. The big dark eyes, the straight little nose, the curve of the pink cheek, the china-smooth chin and neck, and, crowning all, the cloud of golden hair shading her forehead and falling in tangled curls behind.

I did not notice all these features now. It was only the eyes, dark eyes, somewhere this side of misty mountain peaks, and maybe the halo of hair that had been in my vision on that day when Beverly and Mat Nivers and I sat on the parade-ground facing a sudden turn in our life trail.

I stared at the eyes now, only half conscious that the girl was laughing at me.

"You big brown bob-cat! You look like you had slept in the Hondo 'royo all your life," she cried, and turned to run away again.

As she did so a dark face peered round the corner of the church from the crooked street beside it. A sudden gleam of white teeth and glistening eyes, a sudden leap and grip, and a boy, larger than Beverly, caught the little girl by the shoulders and shook her viciously.

She screamed and struggled. Then, with a wild shriek as he clutched at her curls, she wrenched herself away and plunged inside the church. The boy dived in after her. Another scream, and I had dropped from my pony and leaped across the road. I pushed open the door against the two struggling together. With one grip at his coat-collar I broke his hold on the little girl and flung him outside.

I have a faint recollection of a priest hurrying down the aisle toward the fighting children, as the little girl, freed from her assailant, dashed out of the door.

"He jumped at her first, and shook her and pulled her hair," I cried, as the priest caught me by the shoulder. "I'm not going to see anybody pitched into, not a little girl, anyhow."

I jerked myself free from his grasp and ran out to my pony. At the corner of the church stood the girl, her cheeks flushed, her eyes blazing defiance, her rumpled curls in a tangle about her face.

"I hate Marcos, he's so cruel, and"--her voice softened and the defiant eyes grew mischievous--"you aren't a bob-cat. You're a--Look out!"

She shouted the last words and disappeared up the narrow, crooked street, just as a fragment of rock whizzed over my shoulder. I jumped on my pony to dash away, when another rock just missed my head, and I saw the boy, Marcos, beside the church, ready for a third hurl. His black eyes flashed fire, and the grin of malice on his face showed all his fine white teeth.

I was as mad as a boy can be. Instead of fleeing, I spurred my pony straight at him.

"You little beast, I dare you to throw that rock at me! I dare you!" I cried.

The boy dropped the missile and sped away after the girl. I followed in time to see them enter a doorway, six or seven houses up the way. Then I turned back, and in a minute I had overtaken our wagons trailing down to the ford of the Santa Fé River.

"I thought mebby you'd gone back after Jondo and that holy podder," Rex Krane greeted me. "Better begin to wink naturally and look a little pleasanter now. We'll be in the Plazzer in two or three minutes."

The drivers flourished their whips, the mules caught their spirit, and with bump and lurch and rattle we swung down the narrow crack between adobe walls that ended before the old Exchange Hotel at the corner of the Plaza.

This open square in the center of the city was shaded by trees and littered with refuse. The Palace of the Governors fronted it along the entire north side, a long, low, one-story structure whose massive adobe walls defy the wearing years. Compared to the kingly palaces of my imagination, this royal dwelling seemed a very commonplace thing, and the wide portal, or veranda, that ran along its front looked like one of the sheds about the barracks at the fort rather than an entranceway for rulers. Yet this was the house of a ruler hostile to that flag to which I had thrown a good-by kiss, up at Fort Leavenworth.

On the other three sides of the Plaza were other low adobe buildings, for the business of the city faced this central square.

A crowd was gathered there when we reached it. Somebody standing before the Palace of the Governors was haranguing in fiery Spanish, if gesture and oral vehemence are true tokens.

As our wagons rumbled up to the corner of the square the crowd broke up with a shout.

"Los Americanos! Los Carros!"

The cry went up everywhere as the rabble left the speaker to flock about us--men, women, children, Mexican, Spanish, Indian, with now and then a Saxon face among them. Our outfit was as well appointed as such a journey's end permitted. We were in our best clothes--clean-shaven gentlemen, well-dressed boys, and one girl, neat and comely in a dark-blue gown of thin stuff with white lace at throat and wrist; and last, and biggest of all, Aunty Boone, in a bright-green lawn with little white dots all over it.

As I sat on my pony beside my uncle's wagon, I caught sight of the slim figure of Little Blue Flower, well back in the shade of the Plaza. She was watching Beverly, who sat in Jondo's wagon, staring at the crowd and seeing no one in particular. A minute later a tall young Indian boy stepped in front of her, and when he moved away she was gone.

Many men came forward to greet Esmond Clarenden, and there were many inquiries regarding his goods and many exclamations of surprise that he had come alone with so valuable a cargo.

It was the first time that Beverly and I had seen him among his equals. At Fort Leavenworth, where the army overruled everything else, men stood above him in authority or below him in business affairs; and while he never cringed to the one, nor patronized the other, where there are no competitors there are no true measures. That day in the Plaza of Santa Fé the merchant was in his own kingdom, where commerce stood above everything else.

Moreover, this American merchant, following a danger-girt trail, had come in fearlessly, and those men of the Plaza knew that he was one to exact value for value in all his dealings. But I believe that his real power lay in his ready smile, his courtesy, his patience, and his up-bubbling good nature that made him a friendship-builder.

Among the men who came to make acquaintance with the American trader was a Mexican merchant. Evidently he was a man of some importance, for an interpreter hastened to introduce him, explaining that this man had been away on a journey of some weeks among the mines of New Mexico and the Southwest, and only the day before he had come in from Taos.

"You will find him a prince of merchants, a sound, unprejudiced business man. His name is Felix Narveo," the American interpreter added.

The two men shook hands, greeting each other in the Spanish tongue. This Felix Narveo was well dressed and well groomed, but I recognized him at once as the Mexican of Fort Leavenworth and Independence and Council

Grove.

There was one man in that company, however, who did not come forward at all. When I first caught sight of him he was looking at me. I stared back at him with a boy's curiosity, but he did not take his eyes from me until I had dropped my own. After that I watched him keenly. He seemed almost too fair for a Mexican--a tall, spare-built man with black hair, and eyes so steely blue that they were almost black. Everywhere I saw him--at the corners of the little crowd and in the thick of it. He was an easy mark, for he towered above the rest, and, being slender, he seemed to worm his way quickly from place to place. At sight of him, Aunty Boone, who had been peering out with shining eyes, drew her head in as quick as a snake, under the shadow of the wagon cover, and her eyes grew dull. He had not seen her, but I could see that he was watching the remainder of us, and especially my uncle; and I began to feel afraid of him and to wish that he would leave the Plaza. It was years ago that all this happened, and yet to-day my fear of that man still sticks in my memory.

When he turned away, suddenly I caught sight of the boy, whom I had flung out of the church, standing behind him, the boy whom the little girl had called Marcos. Although his face was dark and the man's was fair, there was a strong likeness between the two.

This Marcos stared insolently at all of us. Then with a laugh and a grimace at me, he ran after the man and they disappeared together around the corner of the Palace of the Governors. And in the rush of strange sights I forgot them both for a time.

VII

"SANCTUARY"

Our dwelling-place in all generations.--Psalms xc, 1.

They are wonderful to me still--those few brief days that followed. While Esmond Clarenden was forcing his business transactions to a speedy climax, he was all the time foreseeing Santa Fé under the United States Government. He had not come here as a spy, nor a speculator, but as a commerce-builder, knowing that the same business life would go on when the war cloud lifted, and that the same men who had made the plains commerce profitable under the Mexican flag would not be exiled when the Stars and Stripes should float above the old Palace of the Governors. Belief in the ethics of his calling and trust in manhood were ever a large part of his stock in trade, making him dare to go where he chose to go, and to do what he willed to do.

But no concern for commerce nor extension of national territory disturbed our young minds in those sunlit days, as Mat and Beverly and I looked with the big, quick-seeing eyes of youth on this new strange world at the end of the trail.

We were all together in the deserted dining-room on our first evening in Santa Fé when the man whom I had seen on the Plaza strolled leisurely in. He sat down at one of the farthest tables from us, and his eyes, glistening like blue-black steel, were fixed on us.

Once at Fort Leavenworth I had watched in terror as a bird fluttered helplessly toward a still, steel-eyed snake holding it in thrall. And just at the moment when its enemy was ready to strike, Jondo had happened by and shot the snake's head off. The same terror possessed me now, and I began half-consciously to long for Jondo.

In the midst of new sights I had hardly thought of him since he had left us out beyond the big arroyo. He had come into town at dusk, but soon after supper he had disappeared. His face was very pale, and his eyes had a strange look that never left them again. Something was different in Jondo from that day, but it did not change his gentle nature toward his fellow-men. During our short stay in Santa Fé we hardly saw him at all. We children were too busy with other things to ask questions, and everybody but Rex Krane was too busy to be questioned. Having nothing else to do, Rex became our chaperon, as Uncle Esmond must have foreseen he would be when he measured the young man in Independence on the day we left there.

To-night Esmond Clarenden, smiling and good-natured, paid no heed to the sharp eyes of this stranger fixed on him.

"What's the matter now, little weather-vane? You are always first to sense a coming change," he declared.

"Uncle Esmond, I saw that man watching us like he knew us, out there on the Plaza to-day. Who is he?" I asked, in a low tone.

"His name is Ferdinand Ramero. You will find him watching everywhere. Let that man alone as you would a snake," my uncle warned us.

"Is that his boy?" I asked.

"What boy?" Uncle Esmond inquired.

"Marcos, the boy I pitched endways out of the church. He's bigger than Bev, too," I declared, proudly.

"Gail Clarenden, are you crazy?" Uncle Esmond exclaimed.

"No, I'm not," I insisted, and then I told what had happened at the church, adding, "I saw Marcos with that man in the Plaza, and they went away together."

Esmond Clarenden's face grew grave.

"What kind of a looking child was she, Gail?" he asked, after a pause.

"Oh, she had yellow hair and big sort of dark eyes! She could squeal like anything. She wasn't a baby girl at all, but a regular little fighter kind of a girl."

I grew bashful all at once and hesitated, but my uncle did not seem to hear me, for he turned to Rex Krane and said, in low, earnest tones:

"Krane, if you can locate that child for me you will do me an invaluable service. It was largely on her account that I came here now, and it's a godsend to have a fellow like you to save time for me. Every man has his uses. Your service will be a big one to me."

The young man's face flushed and his eyes shone with a new light.

"If any of you happen to see that girl let me know at once," my uncle said, turning to us, "but, remember, don't act as if you were hunting for her."

"I know now right where she lives. It's up a crooked street by that church. I saw her run in there," I insisted.

"Every hut looks like every other hut, and every little Mex looks like every other little Mex," Beverly declared.

Uncle Esmond smiled, but the stern lines in his face hardly broke as he said, earnestly, "Keep your eyes open and, whatever you do, stay close to Krane while Bill helps me here, and don't forget to watch for that little girl when you are sight-seeing."

"There's not much to see, as Bev says, but the outside of 'dobe walls five feet thick," Rex Krane observed. "But if you know which wall to look through, the lookin' may be easy enough. Seein' things is my specialty, and we'll get this princess if we have to slay a giant and an ogre and take a few dozen Mexican scalps first. The plot just thickens. It's a great game." The tall New-Englander would not take life seriously anywhere, and, with our trust in his guardianship, we could want no better chaperon.

That night Beverly Clarenden and I were in fairyland.

"It's the princess, Bev, the princess we were looking for," I joyously asserted. "And, oh, Bev, she is beautiful, but snappy-like, too. She called me a 'big brown bob-cat', and then she apologized, just as nice as could be."

"And this little Marcos cuss, he'll be the ogre," Beverly declared. "But who'll we have for the giant? That priest, footing it out by that dry creek-thing they call a 'royo?'"

"Oh no, no! He and Jondo made up together, and Jondo's nobody's bad man even in a story. It will be that Ferdinand Ramero," I insisted. "But, say, Bev, Jondo wrote a new name on the register this evening, or somebody wrote it for him, maybe. It wasn't his own writing. 'Jean Deau.' I saw it in big, round, back-slanting letters. Why did he do that?"

"Well, I reckon that's his real name in big, round, back-slanting letters down here," Beverly replied. "It's French, and we have just been spelling it like it sounds, that's all."

"Well, maybe so," I commented, and when I fell asleep it was to dream of a princess and Jondo by a strange name, but the same Jondo.

The air of New Mexico puts iron into the blood. The trail life had hardened us all, but the finishing touch for Rex Krane came in the invigorating breath of that mountain-cooled, sun-cleansed atmosphere of Santa Fé. Shrewd, philosophic, brave-hearted like his historic ancestry, he laid his plans carefully now, sure of doing what he was set to do. And the wholesome sense of really serving the man who had measured his worth at a glance gave him a pleasure he had not known before. Of course, he moved slowly and indifferently. One could never imagine Rex Krane hurrying about anything.

"We'll just 'prospect,' as Daniel Boone says," he declared, as he marshaled us for the day. "We are strangers, sight-seein', got no other business on earth, least of all any to take us up to this old San Miguel Church for unholy purposes. 'Course if we see a pretty little dark-eyed, golden-haired lassie anywhere, we'll just make a diagram of the spot she's stand'n' on, for future reference. We're in this game to win, but we don't do no foolish hurryin' about it."

So we wandered away, a happy quartet, and the city offered us strange sights on every hand. It was all so old, so different, so silent, so baffling-- the narrow, crooked street; the solid house-walls that hemmed them in; the strange tongue, strange dress, strange customs; the absence of smiling faces or friendly greetings; the sudden mystery of seeking for one whom we must not seem to seek, and the consciousness of an enemy, Ferdinand Ramero, whom we must avoid--that it is small wonder that we lived in fairyland.

We saw the boy, Marcos, here and there, sometimes staring defiantly at us from some projected angle; sometimes slipping out of sight as we approached; sometimes quarreling with other children at their play. But nowhere, since the moment when I had seen the door close on her up that crooked street beside the old church, could we find any trace of the little girl.

In the dim morning light of our fifth day in Santa Fé, a man on horseback, carrying a big, bulky bundle in his arms, slipped out of the crooked, shadow-filled street beside the old church of San Miguel. He halted a moment before the structure and looked up at the ancient crude spire outlined against the sky, then sped down the narrow way by the hotel at the end of the trail. He crossed the Plaza swiftly and dashed out beyond the Palace of the Governors and turned toward the west.

Aunty Boone, who slept in the family wagon--or under it--in the inclosure at the rear of the hotel, had risen in time to peer out of the wooden gate just as the rider was passing. It was still too dark to see the man's face distinctly, but his form, and the burden he carried, and the trappings of the horse she noted carefully, as was her habit.

"Up to cussedness, that man is. Mighty long an' slim. Lemme see! Humph! I know *him*. I'll go wake up somebody."

As the woman leaned far out of the gate she caught sight of a little Indian girl crouching outside of the wall.

"You got no business here, you, Little Blue Flower! Where do you live when you *do* live?"

Little Blue Flower pointed toward the west.

"Why you come hangin' 'round here?" the African woman demanded.

"Father Josef send me to help the people who help me," she said, in her soft, low voice.

"Go back to your own folks, then, and tell your Daddy Joseph a man just stole a big bunch of something and rode south with it. He can look after that man. We can get along somehow. Now go."

The voice was like a growl, and the little Indian maiden shrank back in the shadow of the wall. The next minute Aunty Boone was rapping softly on the door of the room whose guest had registered as Jean Deau. Ten minutes later another horseman left the street beside the hotel and crossed the Plaza, riding erect and open-faced as only Jondo could ride. Then the African woman sought out Rex Krane, and in a few brief sentences told him what had been taking place. All of which Rex was far too wise to repeat to Beverly and me.

That afternoon it happened that we left Mat Nivers at the hotel, while Rex Krane and Beverly and I strolled out of town on a well-beaten trail leading toward the west.

"It looks interestin'. Let's go on a ways," Rex commented, lazily.

Nobody would have guessed from his manner but that he was indulgently helping us to have a good time with certain restriction as to where we should go, and what we might say, nor that, of the three, he was the most alert and full of definite purpose.

We sat down beside the way as a line of burros loaded with firewood from the mountains trailed slowly by, with their stolid-looking drivers staring at us in silent unfriendliness.

The last driver was the tall young Indian boy whom I had seen standing in front of Little Blue Flower in the crowd of the Plaza. He paid no heed to our presence, and his face was expressionless as he passed us.

"Stupid as his own burro, and not nearly so handsome," Beverly commented.

The boy turned quietly and stared at my cousin, who had not meant to be overheard. Nobody could read the meaning of that look, for his face was as impenetrable as the adobe walls of the Palace of the Governors.

"Bev, you are laying up trouble. An Indian never forgets, and you'll be finding that fellow under your pillow every night till he gets your scalp," Rex Krane declared, as we went on our way.

Beverly laughed and stiffened his sturdy young arms.

"He's welcome to it if he can get it," he said, carelessly. "How many million miles do we go to-day, Mr. Krane?"

"Yonder is your terminal," Rex replied, pointing to a little settlement of mud huts huddling together along the trail. "They call that little metropolis Agua Fria--'pure water'--because there ain't no water there. It's the last place to look for anybody. That's why we look there. You will go in like gentlemen, though--and don't be surprised nor make any great noise over anything you see there. If a riot starts I'll do the startin'."

Carelessly as this was said, we understood the command behind it.

Near the village, I happened to glance back over the way we had come, and there, striding in, soft-footed as a cat behind us, was that young Indian. I turned again just as we reached the first straggling houses at the outskirts of the settlement, but he had disappeared.

It was a strange little village, this Agua Fria. Its squat dwellings, with impenetrable adobe walls, had sat out there on the sandy edge of the dry Santa Fé River through many and many a lagging decade; a single trail hardly more than a cart-width across ran through it. A church, mud-walled and ancient, rose above the low houses, but of order or uniformity of outline there was none. Hands long gone to dust had shaped those crude dwellings on this sunny plain where only man decays, though what he builds endures.

Nobody was in sight and there was something awesome in the very silence everywhere. Rex lounged carelessly along, as one who had no particular aim in view and was likely to turn back at any moment. But Beverly and I stared hard in every direction.

At the end of the village two tiny mud huts, separated from each other by a mere crack of space, encroached on this narrow way even a trifle more than the neighboring huts. As we were passing these a soft Hopi voice called:

"Beverly! Beverly!" And Little Blue Flower, peeping shyly out from the narrow opening, lifted a warning hand.

"The church! The church!" she repeated, softly, then darted out of sight, as if the brown wall were but thick brown vapor into which she melted.

"Why, it's our own little girl!" Beverly exclaimed, with a smile, just as Little Blue Flower turned away, but I am sure she caught his words and saw his smile.

We would have called to her, but Rex Krane evidently did not hear her, for he neither halted nor turned his head. So, remembering our command to be quiet, we passed on.

"I guess we are about to the end of this 'pure water' resort. It's gettin' late. Let's go back home now," our leader said, dispiritedly. So we turned back toward Santa Fé.

At the narrow opening where we had seen Little Blue Flower the young Indian boy stood upright and motionless, and again he gave no sign of seeing us.

"Let's just run over to that church a minute while we are here. Looks interestin' over there," Rex suggested.

I wondered if he could have heard Little Blue Flower, and thought her suggestion was a good one, or if this was a mere whim of his.

The church, a crude mission structure, stood some distance from the trail. As we entered a priest came forward to meet us.

"Can I serve you?" he asked.

The voice was clear and sweet--the same voice that we had heard out beyond the arroyo southeast of town, the same face, too, that we had seen, with the big dark eyes full of fire. Involuntarily I recalled how his hand had pointed to the west when he had pronounced a blessing that day.

"Thank you, Father--" Rex began.

"Josef," the holy man said.

"Yes, thank you, Father Josef. We are just looking at things. No wish to be rude, you know."

Rex lifted his cap and stood bareheaded in the priestly presence.

Father Josef smiled.

"Look here, then."

He led us up the aisle to where, cuddled down on a crude seat, a little girl lay asleep. Her golden hair fell like a cloud about her face, flowing over the edge of the seat almost to the floor. Her cheeks were pink and warm, and her dimpled white hands were clasped together. I had caught Mat Nivers napping many a time, but never in my life had I seen anything half so sweet as this sleeping girl in the beauty of her innocence. And I knew at a glance that this was the same girl whom I had seen before at the door of the old Church of San Miguel.

"Same as grown-ups when the sermon is dull. Thank you, Father Josef. It's a pretty picture. We must be goin' now." Rex Krane dropped some silver in the priest's hand and we left the church.

At the door we passed the Indian boy again, and a third time he gave no sign of seeing us. I was the only one who was troubled, however, for Rex and Beverly did not seem to notice him. As we left the village I caught sight of him again following behind us.

"Look there, Bev," I said, in a low voice. Beverly glanced back, then turned and stared defiantly at the boy.

"Maybe Rex knows about Indians," he said, lightly. "That's three times I found him fooling around in less than an hour, but my scalp is still hanging over one ear."

He pushed back his cap and pulled at his bright brown locks. Happy Bev! How headstrong, brave, and care-free he walked the plains that day.

The evening shadows were lengthening and the peaks of the Sangre-de-Christo range were taking on the scarlet stains of sunset when we raced into town at last. Rex Krane went at once to find Uncle Esmond, and Beverly and I hurried to the hotel to tell Mat of all that we had seen.

Her gray eyes were glowing when she met us at the door and led us into a corner where we could talk by ourselves.

"Uncle Esmond has sold everything to that Mexican merchant, Felix Narveo, and we are going to start home just as soon as he can find that little girl."

"Oh, we've found her! We've found her!" Beverly burst out. But Mat hushed him at once.

"Don't yell it to the sides, Beverly Clarenden. Now listen!" Mat dropped her voice almost to a whisper. "He's going to take that little girl back with us as far as Fort Leavenworth, and then send her on to St. Louis where she has some folks, I guess."

"Isn't he a clipper, though," Beverly exclaimed.

"But what if the Indians should get us?" I asked, anxiously. "I heard the colonel at Fort Leavenworth just give it to Uncle Esmond one night for bringing us."

"You are safe or you are not safe everywhere. And if we got in here I reckon we can get out," Mat reasoned, philosophically. "And Uncle Esmond isn't afraid and he's set on doing it. We aren't going to take any goods back, so we can travel lots faster, and everything will be put in the wagons so we can grab out what's worth most in a hurry if we have to."

So we talked matters over now as we had done on that April day out on the parade-ground at Fort Leavenworth. But now we knew something of what might be before us on that homeward journey. Thrilling hours those were. It is no wonder that, schooled by their events, young as we were, we put away childish things.

That night while we slept things happened of which we knew nothing for many years. There was no moon and the glaring yellow daytime plain was full of gray-edged shadows, under the far stars of a midnight blue sky, as Esmond Clarenden took the same trail that we had followed in the afternoon. On to the village of Agua Fria, black and silent, he rode until he came to the church door. Here he dismounted, and, quickly securing his horse, he entered the building. The chill midnight wind swept in through the open door behind him, threatening to blot out the flickering candles about the altar. Father Josef came slowly down the aisle to meet him, while a tall man, crouching like a beast about to spring, rather than a penitent at prayer, shrank down in the shadowy corner inside the doorway.

The merchant, solid and square-built and fearless, stood before the young priest baring his head as he spoke.

"I come on a grave errand, good Father. This afternoon my two nephews and a young man from New England came in here and saw a child asleep under protection of this holy sanctuary. That child's name is Eloise St. Vrain. I had hoped to find her mother able to care for her. She--cannot do it, as you know. I must do it for her now. I come here to claim what it is my duty to protect."

At these words the crouching figure sprang up and Ferdinand Ramero, his steel-blue eyes blazing, came forward with cat-like softness. But the sturdy little man before the priest stood, hat in hand, undisturbed by any presence there.

"Father Josef," the tall man began, in a voice of menace, "you will not protect this American here. I have confessed to you and you know that this man is my enemy. He comes, a traitor to his own country and a spy to ours. He has risked the lives of three children by bringing them across the plains. He comes alone where large wagon-trains dare not venture. He could not go back to the States now. And lastly, good Father, he has no right to the child that he claims is here."

"To the child that is here, asleep beside our sacred altar," Father Josef said, sternly.

Ferdinand Ramero turned upon the priest fiercely.

"Even the Church might go too far," he muttered, threateningly.

"It might, but it never has," the holy man agreed. Then turning to Esmond Clarenden, he continued: "You must see that these charges do not stand against you. Our Holy Church offers no protection, outside of these four walls, to a traitor or a spy or even an unpatriotic speculator seeking to profit by the needs of war. Nor could it sanction giving the guardianship of a child to one who daringly imperils his own life or the lives of children, nor can it sanction any rights of guardianship unless due cause be given for granting them."

Ferdinand Ramero smiled as the priest concluded. He was a handsome man, with the sort of compelling magnetism that gives controlling power to its possessor. But because I knew my uncle so well in after years, I can picture Esmond Clarenden as he stood that night before the young priest in the little mud-walled church of Agua Fria. And I can picture the tall, threatening man in the shadows beside him. But never have I held an image of him showing a sign of fear.

"Father Josef, I am willing to make any explanation to you. As for this man whom you call Ramero here--up in the States he bears another name and I finished with him there six years ago--I have no time nor breath to waste on him. Are these your demands?" my uncle asked.

"They are," Father Josef replied.

"Do I take away the little girl, Eloise, unmolested, if you are satisfied?" Esmond Clarenden demanded, first making sure of his bargain, like the merchant he was.

Ferdinand Ramero stiffened insolently at these words, and looked threateningly at Father Josef.

"You do," the holy man replied, something of the flashing light in his eyes alone revealing what sort of a soldier the State had lost when this man took on churchly orders.

"I am no traitor to my flag, since my full commerical purpose was known and sanctioned by the military authority at Fort Leavenworth before I left there. I brought no aid to my country's enemy because my full cargo was bargained for by your merchant, Felix Narveo, before the declaration of war was made. I merely acted as his agent bringing his own to him. I have come here as a spy only in this--that I shall profit in strictly legitimate business by the knowledge I hold of commercial conditions and my acquaintance with your citizens when this war for territory ends, no matter how its results may run. I deal in wholesome trade, not in human hate. I offer value for value, not blood for blood."

Up to this time a smile had lighted the merchant's eyes. But now his voice lowered, and the lines about his mouth hardened.

"As to the guardianship of children, Father Josef, I am a bachelor who for nearly nine years have given a home, education, support, and affection to three orphan children, until, though young in years, they are wise and capable. So zealous was I for their welfare, that when word came to me--no matter how--that a company of Mexicans were on their way to Independence, Missouri, ostensibly to seek the protection of the United States Government and to settle on the frontier there, but really to seize these children in my absence, and carry them into the heart of old Mexico, I decided at once that they would be safer with me in New Mexico than without me in Missouri.

"In the night I passed this Mexican gang at Council Grove, waiting to seize me in the morning. At Pawnee Rock a storm scattered a band of Kiowa Indians to whom these same Mexicans had given a little Indian slave girl as a reward for attacking our train if the Mexicans should fail to get us themselves. Through every peril that threatens that long trail we came safely because the hand of the Lord preserved us."

Esmond Clarenden paused, and the priest bowed a moment in prayer.

"If I have dared fate in this journey," the merchant went on, "it was not to be foolhardy, nor for mere money gains, but to keep my own with me, and to rescue the daughter of Mary St. Vrain, of Santa Fé, and take her to a place of safety. It was her mother's last pleading call, as you, Father Josef, very well know, since you yourself heard her last words and closed her dead eyes. Under the New Mexican law, the guardianship of her property rests with others. Mine is the right to protect her and, by the God of heaven, I mean to do it!"

Esmond Clarenden's voice was deep and powerful now, filling the old church with its vehemence.

Up by the altar, the little girl sat up suddenly and looked about her, terrified by the dim light and the strange faces there.

"Don't be afraid, Eloise."

How strangely changed was this gentle tone from the vehement voice of a moment ago.

The little girl sprang up and stared hard at the speaker. But no child ever resisted that smile by which Esmond Clarenden held Beverly and me in loving obedience all the days of our lives with him.

Shaking with fear as she caught sight of Ferdinand Ramero, the girl reached out her hands toward the merchant, who put his arm protectingly about her. The big, dark eyes were filled with tears; the head with its sunny ripples of tangled hair leaned against him for a moment. Then the fighting spirit came back to her, so early in her young life had the need for defending herself been forced upon her.

"Where have I been? Where am I going?" she demanded.

"You are going with me now," Uncle Esmond said, softly.

"And never have to fight Marcos any more? Oh, good, good, good! Let's go now!"

She frowned darkly at Ferdinand Ramero, and, clutching tightly at Esmond Clarenden's hands, she began pulling him toward the open door.

"Eloise," Father Josef said, "you are about to go away with this good man who will be a father to you. Be a good child as your mother would want you to be." His musical voice was full of pathos.

Eloise dropped her new friend's hand and sprang down the aisle.

"I will be good, Father Josef," she said, squeezing his dark hand between her fair little palms. Then, tossing back the curls from her face, she reached up a caressing hand to his cheek.

Father Josef stooped and kissed her white forehead, and turned hastily toward the altar.

"Esmond Clarenden!" It was Ferdinand Ramero who spoke, his sharp, bitter voice filling the church.

"By order of this priest Eloise St. Vrain is yours to protect so long as you stay within these walls. The minute you leave them you reckon with me."

Father Josef whirled about quickly, but the man made a scoffing gesture.

"I brought this child here for protection this morning. But for that sickly Yankee and two inquisitive imps of boys she would have been safe here. I acknowledge sanctuary privilege. Use it as long as you choose in the church of Agua Fria. Set but a foot outside these walls and I say again you reckon with me."

His tall form thrust itself menacingly before the little man and his charge clinging to his arm.

"Set but a foot outside these walls and *you* will reckon with *me*."

It was Jondo's clear voice, and the big plainsman, towering up suddenly behind Ferdinand Ramero, filled the doorway.

"You meant to hide in the old Church of San Miguel because it is so near to the home where you have kept this little girl. But Gail Clarenden blocked your game and found your house and this child in the church door before our wagon-train had reached the end of the trail. You found this church your nearest refuge, meaning to leave it again early in the morning. I have waited here for you all day, protected by the same means that brought word to Santa Fé this morning. Come out now if you wish. You dare not follow me to the States, but I dare to come to your land. Can you meet me here?" Jondo was handsome in his sunny moods. In his anger he was splendid.

Ferdinand Ramero dropped to a seat beside Father Josef.

"I have told you I cannot face that man. I will stay here now," he said, in a low voice to the priest. "But I do not stay here always, and I can send where I do not follow," he added, defiantly.

Esmond Clarenden was already on his horse with his little charge, snugly wrapped, in his arms.

Father Josef at the portal lifted his hand in sign of blessing.

"Peace be with you. Do not tarry long," he said. Then, turning to Jondo, he gazed into the strong, handsome face. "Go in peace. He will not follow. But forget not to love even your enemies."

In the midnight dimness Jondo's bright smile glowed with all its courageous sweetness.

"I finished that fight long ago," he said. "I come only to help others."

Long these two, priest and plainsman, stood there with clasped hands, the gray night mists of the Santa Fé Valley round about them and all the far stars of the midnight sky gleaming above them. Then Jondo mounted his horse and rode away up the trail toward Santa Fé.

VIII

THE WILDERNESS CROSSROADS

I will even make a way in the wilderness. --ISAIAH.

Bent's fort stood alone in the wide wastes of the upper Arkansas valley. From the Atlantic to the Pacific shores there was in America no more isolated spot holding a man's home. Out on the north bank of the Arkansas, in a grassy river bottom, with rolling treeless plains rippling away on every hand, it reared its high yellow walls in solitary defiance, mute token of the white man's conquering hand in a savage wilderness. It was a great rectangle built of adobe brick with walls six feet through at the base, sloping to only a third of that width at the top, eighteen feet from the ground. Round bastions, thirty feet high, at two diagonal corners, gave outlook and defense. Immense wooden doors guarded a wide gateway looking eastward down the Arkansas River. The interior arrangement was after the Mexican custom of building, with rooms along the outer walls all opening into a big *patio*, or open court. A cross-wall separated this court from the large corral inside the outer walls at the rear. A portal, or porch, roofed with thatch on cedar poles, ran around the entire inner rectangle, sheltering the rooms somewhat from the glare of the white-washed court. A little world in itself was this Bent's Fort, a self-dependent community in the solitary places. The presiding genius of this community was William Bent, whose name is graven hard and deep in the annals of the eastern slopes of the Rocky Mountain country in the earlier decades of the nineteenth century.

Hither in the middle '40's the wild trails of the West converged: northward, from the trading-posts of Bent and St. Vrain on the Platte; south, over the Raton Pass from Taos and Santa Fé; westward, from the fur-bearing plateaus of the Rockies, where trappers and traders brought their precious piles of pelts down the Arkansas; and eastward, half a thousand miles from the Missouri River frontier--the pathways of a restless, roving people crossed each other here. And it was toward this wilderness crossroads that Esmond Clarenden directed his course in that summertime of my boyhood years.

The heat of a July sun beat pitilessly down on the scorching plains. The weary trail stretched endlessly on toward a somewhere in the yellow distance that meant shelter and safety. Spiral gusts of air gathering out of the low hills to the southeast picked up great cones of dust and whirled them zigzagging across the brown barren face of the land. Every draw was bone dry; even the greener growths along their sheltered sides, where the last moisture hides itself, wore a sickly sallow hue.

Under the burden of this sun-glare, and through these stifling dust-cones, our little company struggled sturdily forward.

We had left Santa Fé as suddenly and daringly as we had entered it, the very impossibility of risking such a journey again being our, greatest safeguard. Esmond Clarenden was doing the thing that couldn't be done, and doing it quickly.

In the gray dawn after that midnight ride to Agua Fria a little Indian girl had slipped like a brown shadow across the Plaza. Stopping at the door of the Exchange Hotel, she leaned against the low slab of petrified wood that for many a year served as a loafer's roost before the hotel doorway. Inside the building Jondo caught the clear twitter of a bird's song at daybreak, twice repeated. A pause, and then it came again, fainter this time, as if the bird were fluttering away through the Plaza treetops.

In that pause, the gate in the wall had opened softly, and Aunty Boone's sharp eyes peered through the crack. The girl caught one glimpse of the black face, then, dropping a tiny leather bag beside the stone, she sped away.

A tall young Indian boy, prone on the ground behind a pile of refuse in the shadowy Plaza, lifted his head in time to see the girl glide along the portal of the Palace of the Governors and disappear at the corner of the structure. Then he rose and followed her with silent moccasined feet.

And Jondo, who had hurried to the hotel door, saw only the lithe form of an Indian boy across the Plaza. Then his eye fell on the slender bag beside the stone slab. It held a tiny scrap of paper, bearing a message:

Take long trail QUICK. Mexicans follow far. Trust bearer anywhere. JOSEF.

An hour later we were on our way toward the open prairies and the Stars and Stripes afloat above Fort Leavenworth.

In the wagon beside Mat Nivers was the little girl whose face had been clear in the mystic vision of my day-dreams on the April morning when I had gone out to watch for the big fish on the sand-bars; the morning when I had felt the first heart-throb of desire for the trail and the open plains whereon my life-story would later be written.

We carried no merchandise now. Everything bent toward speed and safety. Our ponies and mules were all fresh ones--secured for this journey two hours after we had come into Santa Fé--save for the big sturdy dun creature that Uncle Esmond, out of pure sentiment, allowed to trail along behind the wagons toward his native heath in the Missouri bottoms.

We had crossed the Gloriettas and climbed over the Raton Pass rapidly, and now we were nearing the upper Arkansas, where the old trail turns east for its long stretch across the prairies.

As far as the eye could see there was no living thing save our own company in all the desolate plain aquiver with heat and ashy dry. The line of low yellow bluffs to the southeast hardly cast a shadow save for a darker dun tint here and there.

At midday we drooped to a brief rest beside the sun-baked trail.

"You all jus' one color," Aunty Boone declared. "You all like the dus' you made of 'cep' Little Lees an' me. She's white and I'm black. Nothin' else makes a pin streak on the face of the earth."

Aunty Boone flourished on deserts and her black face glistened in the sunlight. Deep in the shadow of the wagon cover the face of Eloise St. Vrain--"Little Lees," Aunty Boone had named her--bloomed pink as a wild rose in its frame of soft hair. She had become Aunty Boone's meat and drink from the moment the strange African woman first saw her. This regard, never expressed in caress nor word of tenderness, showed itself in warding from the little girl every wind of heaven that might visit her too roughly. Not that Eloise gave up easily. Her fighting spirit made her rebel against weariness and the hardships of trail life new to her. She fitted into our ways marvelously well, demanding equal rights, but no favors. By some gentle appeal, hardly put into words, we knew that Uncle Esmond did not want us to talk to her about herself. And Beverly and Mat and I, however much we might speculate among ourselves, never thought of resisting his wishes.

Eloise was gracious with Mat, but evidently the boy Marcos had made her wary of all boys. She paid no attention to Beverly and me at first. All her pretty smiles and laughing words were for Uncle Esmond and Jondo. And she was lovely. Never in all these long and varied years have I seen another child with such a richness of coloring, nor such a mass of golden hair rippling around her forehead and falling in big, soft curls about her neck. Her dark eyes with their long black lashes gave to her face its picturesque beauty, and her plump, dimpled arms and sturdy little form bespoke the wholesome promise of future years.

But the life of the trail was not meant for such as she, and I know now that the assurance of having saved her from some greater misfortune alone comforted Uncle Esmond and Jondo in this journey. For Aunty Boone was right when she declared, "They tote together always."

As we grouped together under that shelterless glare, getting what comfort we could out of the brief rest, Jondo sprang up suddenly, his eyes aglow with excitement.

"What's the matter? Because if it isn't, this is one hot day to pretend like it is," Rex Krane asserted.

He was lying on the hot earth beside the trail, his hat pulled over his face. Beverly and Bill Banney were staring dejectedly across the landscape, seeing nothing. I sat looking off toward the east, wondering what lay behind those dun bluffs in the distance.

"Something is wrong back yonder," Jondo declared, making a half-circle with his hand toward the trail behind us.

My heart seemed to stop mid-beat with a kind of fear I had never known before. Aunty Boone had always been her own defender. Mat Nivers had cared for me so much that I never doubted her bigger power. It was for Eloise, Aunty Boone's "Little Lees," that my fear leaped up.

I can close my eyes to-day and see again the desolate land banded by the broad white trail. I can see the dusty wagons and our tired mules with drooping heads. I can see the earnest, anxious faces of Esmond Clarenden and Jondo; Beverly and Bill Banney hardly grasping Jondo's meaning; Rex Krane, half asleep on the edge of the trail. I can see Mat Nivers, brown and strong, and Aunty Boone oozing sweat at every pore. But these are only the setting for that little girl on the wagon-seat with white face and big dark eyes, under the curl-shadowed forehead.

Jondo stared hard toward the hills in the southeast. Then he turned to my uncle with grim face and burning eyes; His was a wonderful voice, clear, strong and penetrating. But in danger he always spoke in a low tone.

The child stood looking at her with shining black eyes full of a wicked mischief, but he said not a word.

Just then a dull grunt caught my ear, and I half-turned to see a cot beyond mine. An Indian boy lay on it, looking straight at me. I stared back at him and neither of us spoke. His head was bandaged and his cheek was swollen, but with my memory for faces, even Indian faces, I knew him at once for the boy who had followed us into Agua Fria and out of it again.

Just then the frolickers came to the door and peered in at me.

"Are you awake?" Eloise asked.

Then seeing my face, she came romping in, followed by Mat and Beverly and little Charlie Bent, all wet and hilarious. They gave no heed to the Indian boy, who pretended to be asleep. Once, however, I caught him watching Beverly, and his eyes were like dagger points.

"We are having the best times. You must get well right away, because we are going to stay." They all began to clatter, noisily.

Rex Krane appeared at the door just then and they stopped suddenly.

"Clear out of here, you magpies," he commanded, and they scuttled away into the warm rain and the puddles again.

"Do you want anything, Gail?" Rex asked, bending over me.

I drew his head down with my right arm.

"I want that Indian out of here," I whispered.

"Out he goes," Rex returned, promptly, and almost before I knew it the boy was taken away. When we were alone the tall young man sat down beside me.

"You want to ask me a million questions. I'll answer 'em to save you the trouble," he began, in his comfortable way.

"You are wounded in your shoulder. Slight, bullet, that's Mexican; deep, arrow, that's Indian. But you are here and pretty much alive and you will be well soon."

"And Uncle Esmond? Jondo? Bill?" I began, lifting myself up on my well arm.

"Keep quiet. I'll answer faster. Everybody all right. Clarenden and Jondo leave for Independence the minute you are better, and a military escort permits."

I dropped down again.

"The U.S. Army, en route for perdition, via Santa Fé, is camping in the big timbers down-stream now. Jondo and Esmond Clarenden will leave you boys and girls here till it's safe to take you out again. And I and Daniel Boone, vestal god and goddess of these hearth-fires, will keep you from harm till that time. Bill's joining the army for sure now, and our happy family life is ended as far as the Santa Fé Trail is concerned. I'm a well man now, but not quite army-well yet, they tell me."

"Tell me about this." I pointed to my shoulder.

"All in good time. It was a nasty mess of fish. A dozen Mexicans and as many Indians had followed us all the way from the sunny side of the Gloriettas. You and Bev and Mat had got by the Mexics. Daniel Boone and 'Little Lees' were climbing the North Pole by that time. The rest of us were giving battle straight from the shoulder; and someway, I don't know how, just as we had the gang beat back behind us--you had a sniff of a bullet just then--an Indian slipped ahead in the dust. I was tendin' to mite of an arrow wound in my right calf, and I just caught him in time, aimin' at Bev; but he missed him for you. I got him, though, and clubbed his scalp a bit loose."

Rex paused and stared at his right leg.

"How did that boy get here, Rex? Is he a friendly Indian?" I asked.

"Oh, Jondo brought him in out of the wet. Says the child was made to come along, and as soon as he could get away from the gang he had to run with up here; he came right into camp to help us against them. Fine young fellow! Jondo has it from them in authority that we can trust him lyin' or tellin' the truth. *He's all right.*"

"How did he get hurt?" I inquired, still remembering in my own mind the day at Agua Fria.

"He'd got into our camp and was fightin' on our side when it happened,"

Rex replied.

"Some of them shot at him, then?" I insisted. "No, I beat him up with the butt of my gun for shootin' you," Rex said, lazily.

"At me! Why don't you tell Jondo?"

"I tried to," Rex answered, "but I can't make him see it that way. He's got faith in that redskin and he's going to see that he gets back to New Mexico safely--after while."

"Rex, that's the same boy that was down in Agua Fria, the one Bev laughed at. He's no good Indian," I declared.

"You are too wise, Gail Clarenden," Rex drawled, carelessly. "A boy of your brains had ought to be born in Boston. Jondo and I can't agree about him. His name, he says, is Santan. There's one 'n' too many. If you knock off the last one it makes him Santa--'holy'; but if you knock out the middle it's Satan. We don't knock out the same 'n', Jondo and me."

Just then the little child came tumbling noisily into the room.

"Look here, youngun. You can't be makin' a racket here," Rex said.

The boy stared at him, impudently.

"I will, too," he declared, sullenly, kicking at my cot with all his might.

Rex made no reply but, seizing the child around the waist, he carried him kicking and screaming outside.

"You stay out or I'll spank you!" Rex said, dropping him to the ground

The boy looked up with blazing eyes, but said nothing.

"That's little Charlie Bent. His daddy runs this splendid fort. His mother is a Cheyenne squaw, and he's a grim clinger of a half-breed. Some day he'll be a terror on these plains. It's in him, I know. But that won't interfere with us any. And you children are a lot safer here than out on the trail. Great God! I wonder we ever got you here!" Rex's face was very grave. "Now go to sleep and wake up well. No more thinkin' like a man. You can be a child again for a while."

Those were happy days that followed. Safe behind the strong walls of old Fort Bent, we children had not a care; and with the stress and strain of the trail life lifted from our young minds, we rebounded into happy childhood living. Every day offered a new drama to our wonder-loving eyes. We watched the big hide-press for making buffalo robes and furs into snug bales. We climbed to the cupola of the headquarters department and saw the soldiers marching by on their way to New Mexico. We saw the Ute and the Red River Comanche come filing in on their summer expeditions from the mountains. We saw the trade lines from the far north bearing down to this wilderness crossroads with their early fall stock for barter.

Our playground was the court off which all the rooms opened. And however wild and boisterous the scenes inside those walls in that summer of 1846, in four young lives no touch of evil took root. Stronger than the six-feet width of wall, higher than the eighteen feet of adobe brick guarding us round about, was the stern strength of the young Boston man interned in the fort to protect us from within, as the strength of that structure defended us from without.

And yet he might have failed sometimes, had it not been for Aunty Boone. Nobody trifled with her.

"You let them children be. An give 'em the run of this shack," she commanded of the lesser powers whose business was to domineer over the daily life there. "The man that makes trouble wide as a needle is across is goin' to meet me an' the Judgment Day the same minute."

"When Daniel gets on her crack-o'-doom voice, the mountains goin' to skip like rams and the little hills like lambs, an' the Army of the West won't be necessary to protect the frontier," Rex declared. But he knew her worth to his cause, and he welcomed it.

And so with her brute force and his moral strength we were unconsciously intrenched in a safety zone in this far-isolated place.

With neither Uncle Esmond nor Jondo near us for the first time in our remembrance, we gained a strength in self-dependence that we needed. For with the best of guardianship, there are many ways in which a child's day may be harried unless the child asserts himself. We had the years of children but the sturdy defiance of youth. So we were happy within our own little group, and we paid little heed to the things that nobody else could forestall for us.

Outside of our family, little Charlie Bent, the half-breed child of the proprietor of the fort, was a daily plague. He entered into all of our sports with a quickness and perseverance and wilfulness that was thoroughly American. He took defeat of his wishes, and the equal measure of justice and punishment, with the silent doggedness of an Indian; and on the edge of babyhood he showed a spirit of revenge and malice that we, in our rollicking, affectionate lives, with all our teasing and sense of humor, could not understand; so we laughed at his anger and ignored his imperious demands.

Behind him always was his Cheyenne mother, jealously defending him in everything, and in manifold ways making life a burden--if we would submit to the making, which we seldom did.

And lastly Santan, the young boy who had deserted his Mexican masters for Jondo's command, contrived, with an Indian's shrewdness, never to let us out of his sight. But he gave us no opportunity to approach him. He lived in his own world, which was a savage one, but he managed that it should overlap our world and silently grasp all that was in it. Beverly had persistently tried to be friendly for a time, for that was Beverly's way. Failing to do it, he had nick-named the boy "Satan" for all time.

"We found Little Blue Flower a sweet little muggins," Beverly told the Indian early in our stay at the fort. "We like good Indians like her. She's one clipper."

Santan had merely looked him through as though he were air, and made no reply, nor did he ever by a single word recognize Beverly from that moment.

The evening before we left Fort Bent we children sat together in a corner of the court. The day had been very hot for the season and the night was warm and balmy, with the moonlight flooding the open space, edging the shadows of the inner portal with silver. There was much noise and boisterous laughter in the billiard-room where the heads of affairs played together. Rex Krane had gone to bed early. Out by the rear gate leading to the fort corral, Aunty Boone was crooning a weird African melody. Crouching in the deep shadows beside the kitchen entrance, the Indian boy, Santan, listened to all that was said.

To-night we had talked of to-morrow's journey, and the strength of the military guard who should keep us safe along the way. Then, as children will, we began to speculate on what should follow for us.

"When I get older I'm going to be a freighter like Jondo, Bill and me. We'll kill every Indian who dares to yell along the trail. I'm going back to Santa Fé and kill that boy that stared at me like he was crazy one day at Agua Fria."

In the shadows of the porchway, I saw Santan creeping nearer to us as Beverly ran on flippantly:

"I guess I'll marry a squaw, Little Blue Flower, maybe, like the Bents do, and live happily ever after."

"I'm going to have a big fine house and live there all the time," Mat Nivers declared. Something in the earnest tone told us what this long journey had meant to the brave-hearted girl.

"I'm going to marry Gail when I grow up," Eloise said, meditatively. "He won't ever let Marcos pull my hair." She shook back the curly tresses, gold-gleaming in the moonlight, and squeezed my hand as she sat beside me.

"What will you be, Gail?" Mat asked.

"I'll go and save Bev's scalp when he's gunning too far from home," I declared.

"Oh, he'll be 'Little Lees's' husband, and pull that Marcos cuss's nose if he tries to pull anybody's curls. Whoo-ee! as Aunty Boone would say," Beverly broke in.

I kept a loving grip on the little hand that had found mine, as I would have gripped Beverly's hand sometimes in moments when we talked together as boys do, in the confidences they never give to anybody else.

A gray shadow dropped on the moon, and a chill night wind crept down inside the walls. A sudden fear fell on us. The noises inside the billiard room seemed far away, and all the doors except ours were closed. Santan had crept between us and the two open doorways leading to our rooms. What if he should slip inside. A snake would have seemed better to me.

A silence had fallen on us, and Eloise still clung to my hand. I held it tightly to assure her I wasn't afraid, but I could not speak nor move. Aunty Boone's crooning voice was still, and everything had grown weird and ghostly. The faint wailing cry of some wild thing of the night plains outside crept to our ears, making us shiver.

"When the stars go to sleep an' the moon pulls up the gray covers, it's time to shut your eyes an' forget." Aunty Boone's soft voice broke the spell comfortingly for us. "Any crawlin' thing that gits in my way now, goin' to be stepped on."

At the low hissing sound of the last sentence there was a swift scrambling along the shadows of the porch, and a door near the kitchen snapped shut. The big shining face of the African woman glistened above us and the court was flooded again with the moon's silvery radiance. As we all sprang up to rush for our rooms, "Little Lees" pulled me toward her and gently kissed my cheek.

"You never would let Marcos in if he came to Fort Leavenworth, would you?" she whispered.

"I'd break his head clear off first," I whispered back, and then we scampered away.

That night I dreamed again of the level plains and Uncle Esmond and misty mountain peaks, but the dark eyes were not there, though I watched long for them.

The next day we left Fort Bent, and when I passed that way again it was a great mass of yellow mounds, with a piece of broken wall standing desolately here and there, a wreck of the past in a solitary land.

———————————

II

BUILDING THE TRAIL

IX

IN THE MOON OF THE PEACH BLOSSOM

Love took me softly by the hand,
Love led me all the country o'er,
And showed me beauty in the land,
That I had never seen before.
--ANONYMOUS.

You might not be able to find the house to-day, nor the high bluff whereon it stood. So many changes have been wrought in half a century that what was green headland and wooded valley in the far '50's may be but a deep cut or a big fill for a new roadway or factory site to-day. So diligently has Kansas City fulfilled the scriptural prophecy that "every valley shall be exalted, and every mountain and hill shall be made low."

Where the great stream bends to the east, the rugged heights about its elbow, Aunty Boone, in those days, was wont to declare, did not offer enough level ground to set a hen on. Small reason was there then to hope that a city, great and gracious, would one day cover those rough ravines and grace those slopes and hilltops in the angle between the Missouri and the Kaw.

Aunty Boone had resented leaving Fort Leavenworth when the Clarenden business made the young city at the Kaw's mouth more desirable for a home. But Esmond Clarenden foresaw that a military post, when the protection it offers is no longer needed, will not, in itself, be a city-builder. The war had brought New Mexico into United States territory; railroads were slowly creeping westward toward the Mississippi River; steamboats and big covered wagons were bringing settlers into Kansas, where little cabins were beginning to mark the landscape with new hearth-stones. Congress was wrangling over the great slavery question. The Eastern lawmakers were stupidly opposing the efforts of Missouri statesmen to extend mail routes westward, or to spend any energy toward developing that so-called worthless region which they named "the great American desert." And the old Santa Fé Trail was now more than ever the highway for the commerical treasures of the Rocky Mountains and the great Southwest.

It was the time of budding things. In the valley of the Missouri the black elm boughs, the silvery sycamores and cottonwoods, and the vines on the gray rock-faced cliffs were veiled in shimmering draperies of green, with here and there a little group of orchard trees faintly pink against the landscape's dainty verdure.

Beverly Clarenden and I stood on the deck of a river steamer as it made the wharf at old Westport Landing, where Esmond Clarenden waited for us. And long before the steamer's final bump against the pier we had noted the tall, slender girl standing beside him. We had been away three years, the only schooling outside of Uncle Esmond's teaching we were ever to have. We were big boys now, greatly conscious of hands and feet in our way, "razor broke," Aunty Boone declared, brimful of hilarity and love of adventure, and eager for the plains life, and the dangers of the old trail by which we were to conquer or be conquered. In the society of women we were timid and ill at ease. Aside from this we were self-conceited, for we knew more of the world and felt ourselves more important on that spring morning than we ever presumed to know or dared to feel in all the years that followed.

"Who is she, Gail, that tall one by little fat Uncle Esmond?" Beverly questioned, as we neared the wharf. "You don't reckon he's married, Bev? He's all of twenty-four or five years older than we are, and we aren't calves any more." I replied, scanning the group on the wharf.

But we forgot the girl in our eagerness to bound down the gang-plank and hug the man who meant all that home and love could mean to us. In our three growing years we had almost eliminated Mat Nivers, save as a happy memory, for mails were slow in those days and we were poor letter-writers; and we had wondered how to meet her properly now. But when the tall, slender girl on the wharf came forward and we looked into the wide gray eyes of our old-time playmate whom, as little boys, we had both vowed to marry, we forgot everything in our overwhelming love for our comrade-in-arms, our jolliest friend and counselor.

"Oh, Mat, you miserable thing!" Beverly bubbled, hugging her in his arms.

"You are just bigger and sweeter than ever. I mistook you for Aunty Boone at first," I chimed in, kissing her on each cheek. And we all bundled away in an old-fashioned, low-swung carriage, happy as children again, with no barrier between us and the dear playmate of the past.

The new home, on the high crest overlooking the Missouri valley, nestled deep in the shade of maple and elm trees, a mansion, compared to that log house of blessed memory at Fort Leavenworth. A winding road led up the steep slope from a wooded ravine where a trail ran out from the little city by the river's edge. Vistas of sheer cliff and stretches of the muddy on-sweeping Missouri and the full-bosomed Kaw, with scrubby timbered ravines and growing groves of forest trees, offered themselves at every turn. And from the top of the bluff the world unrolled in a panorama of nature's own shaping and coloring.

The house was built of stone, with vines climbing about its thick walls, and broad veranda. And everywhere Mat's hands had put homey touches of comfort and beauty. An hundredfold did she return to Esmond Clarenden all the care and protection he had given to her in her orphaned childhood. And, after all, it was not military outposts, nor railroads, nor mail-lines alone that pushed back the wilderness frontier. It was the hand of woman that also builded empire westward.

"Mat's got her wish at last," I said, as we sat with Uncle Esmond after dinner under a big maple tree and looked out at the far yellow Missouri, churning its spring floods to foam against the snags along its high-water bound.

"What's Mat's wish?" Uncle Esmond asked.

"To have a good home and *stay there*. She wished that one night, years ago back in old Fort Bent. Don't you remember, Bev, when we were out in the court, and how scared blue we all were when the moon went under a cloud, and that Indian boy, Santan, was creeping between us and the home base?"

"No, I don't remember anything except that we were in Fort Bent. Got in by the width of a hair ahead of some Mexicans and Indians, and got out again after a jolly six weeks. What's the real job for us now, Uncle Esmond?"

Uncle Esmond was staring out toward the Kaw valley, rimmed by high bluffs in the distance.

"I don't know about Mat having her wish," he said, thoughtfully, "but never mind. Trade is booming and I'm needing help on the trail this spring. Jondo starts west in two weeks."

Beverly and I sprang up. Six feet of height, muscular, adventure-loving, fearless, we had been made to order for the Santa Fé Trail. And if I was still a dreamer and caught sometimes the finer side of ideals, where Beverly Clarenden saw only the matter-of-fact, visible things, no shrewder, braver, truer plainsman ever walked the long distances of the old Santa Fé Trail than this boy with his bright face and happy-go-lucky spirit unpained by dreams, untrammeled by fancies.

"Two weeks! We are ready to start right after supper," we declared.

"Oh, I have other matters first," Uncle Esmond said. "Beverly, you must go up to Fort Leavenworth and arrange a lot of things with Banney for this trip. He's to go, too, because military escort is short this season."

"Suits me!" Beverly declared. "Old Bill Banney and I always could get along together. And this infant here?"

"I'm going to send Gail down to the Catholic Mission, in Kansas. You remember little Eloise St. Vrain, of course?" Uncle Esmond asked.

"We do!" Beverly assured him. "Pretty as a doll, gritty as a sand-bar, snappy as a lobster's claw--she dwells within my memory yet."

All girls were little children to us, for the scheme of things had not included them in our affairs.

I threw a handful of grass in the boy's face, and Uncle Esmond went on.

"She's been at St. Ann's School at the Osage Mission down on the Neosho River for two or three years, and now she is going to St. Louis. In these troublesome times on the border, if I have a personal interest, I feel safer if some big six-footer whom I can trust comes along as an escort from the Neosho to the Missouri," Uncle Esmond explained.

And then we spoke of other things: the stream of emigration flowing into the country, the possibilities of the prairies, the future of the city that should hold the key to the whole Southwest, and especially of the chance and value of the trail trade.

"It's the big artery that carries the nation's life-blood here," Esmond Clarenden declared. "Some day when the West is full of people, and dowered with prosperity, it may remember the men who built the highway for the feet of trade to run in. And the West may yet measure its greatness somewhat by the honesty and faithfulness of the merchant of the frontier, and more by the courage and persistence of the boys who drove the ox-teams across the plains. Don't forget that you yourselves are State-builders now."

He spoke earnestly, but his words meant little to me. I was looking out toward the wide-sweeping Kaw and thinking of the journey I must make, and wondering if I should ever feel at ease in the society of women. Wondering, too, what I should say, and how I should really take care of "Little Lees," who had crossed the plains with us almost a decade ago; the girl who had held my hand tightly one night at old Fort Bent when the shadow had slipped across the moon and filled the silvery court with a gray, ghostly light.

That night the old heart-hunger of childhood came back to me, the visions of the day-dreaming little boy that were almost forgotten in the years that had brought me to young manhood. And clearly again, as when I heard Uncle Esmond's voice that night on the tableland above the valley of the Santa Fé, I heard his gentle words:

"Sometimes the things we long for in our dreams we must fight for, and even die for, that those who come after us may be the better for our having them."

But these thoughts passed with the night, and in my youth and inexperience I took on a spirit of fatherly importance as I went down to St. Ann's to safeguard a little girl on her way through the Kansas territory to the Missouri River.

It had been a beautiful day, and there was a freshness in the soft evening breeze, and an up-springing sweetness from the prairies. A shower had passed that way an hour before, and the spirit of growing things seemed to fill the air with a voiceless music.

Just at sunset the stage from the north put me down in front of St. Ann's Academy in the little Osage Mission village on the Neosho.

A tall nun, with commanding figure and dignified bearing, left the church steps across the road and came slowly toward me.

"I am looking for Mother Bridget, the head of this school," I said, lifting my hat.

"I am Mother Bridget." The voice was low and firm. One could not imagine disobedience under her rule.

"I come from Mr. Esmond Clarenden, to act as escort for a little girl, Eloise

St. Vrain, who is to leave here on the stage for Kansas City to-morrow," I hesitatingly offered my letter of introduction, which told all that I had tried to say, and more.

The woman's calm face was gentle, with the protective gentleness of the stone that will not fail you when you lean on it. One felt sure of Mother Bridget, as one feels sure of the solid rock to build upon. She looked at me with keen, half-quizzical eyes. Then she said, quietly:

"You will find the little girl down by Flat Rock Creek. The Indian girl, Po-a-be, is with her. There may be several Indian girls down there, but Po-a-be is alone with little Eloise."

I bowed and turned away, conscious that, with this good nun's sincerity, she was smiling at me back of her eyes somehow.

As I followed the way leading to the creek I passed a group or two of Indian girls--St. Ann's, under the Loretto Sisterhood, was fundamentally a mission school for these--and a trio of young ladies, pretty and coquettish, with daring, mischievous eyes, whose glances made me flush hot to the back of my neck as I stumbled by them on my way to the stream.

The last sun rays were glistening on the placid waters of the Flat Rock, and all the world was softly green, touched with a golden glamour. I paused by a group of bushes to let the spell of the hour have its way with me. I have always loved the beautiful things of earth; as much now as in my childhood days, when I felt ashamed to let my love be known; as now I dare to tell it only on paper, and not to that dear, great circle of men and women who know me best to-day.

The sound of footsteps and the murmur of soft voices fitted into the sweetness of that evening hour as two girls, one of them an Indian, came slowly down a well-worn path from the fields above the Flat Rock Valley. They did not see me as they sat down on some broad stones beside the stream.

I started forward to make myself known, but caught myself mid-step, for here was a picture to make any man pause.

The Indian girl facing me was Little Blue Flower, the Kiowas' captive, whom we had rescued at Pawnee Rock. Her heavy black hair was coiled low on her neck, a headband of fine silverwork with pink coral pendants was bound about her forehead and gleaming against her jetty hair. With her well-poised head, her pure Indian features, her lustrous dark eyes, her smooth brown skin, her cheeks like the heart of those black-red roses that grow only in richest soil--surely there was no finer type of that vanishing race in all the Indian pueblos of the Southwest. But the girl beside her! Was it really so many years ago that I stood by the bushes on the Flat Rock's edge and saw that which I see so clearly now? Then these years have been gracious indeed to me. The sun's level beams fell on the masses of golden waves that swept in soft little ripples back from the white brow to a coil of gold on the white neck, held, like the Indian girl's, with a headband of wrought silver, and goldveined turquoise; it fell on the clear, smooth skin, the pink bloom of the cheek, the red lips, the white teeth, the big dark eyes with their fringe of long lashes beneath straight-penciled dark brows; on the curves of the white throat and the round white arms. Only a master's hand could make you see these two, beautiful in their sharp contrast of deep brown and scarlet against the dainty white and gold.

"Oh, Little Blue Flower, it will not make me change."

I caught the words as I stepped toward the two, and the Indian's soft, mournful answer:

"But you are Miss St. Vrain now. You go away in the morning--and I love you always."

The heart in me stopped just when all its flood had reached my face.

"Miss St. Vrain," I repeated, aloud.

The two sprang up. That afternoon they had been dressed for a girls' frolic in some Grecian fashion. I cannot tell a Watteau pleat from window-curtain. I am only a man, and I do not name draperies well. But these two standing before me were gowned exactly alike, and yet I know that one was purely and artistically Greek, and one was purely and gracefully Indian.

"I beg your pardon. I am Mr. Clarenden," I managed to say.

At the name Little Blue Flower's eyes looked as they did on that hot May night out at Pawnee Rock when she heard Beverly Clarenden's boyish voice ring out, defiantly:

"Uncle Esmond, let's take her, and take our chances."

But the great light that had leaped into the girl's eyes died slowly out as she gazed at me.

"You are not Beverly Clarenden," she said, in a low voice.

"No, I'm Gail, the little one. Bev is up at Fort Leavenworth now," I replied.

She turned away without a word and, gathering her draperies about her, sped up the pathway toward the fields above the creek.

* * * * *

And we two were alone together--the dark-eyed girl of my boyhood vision, deep-shrined in the boy-heart's holy of holies, and I who had waited for her coming. It was the hour of golden sunset and long twilight afterglow on the glistening Flat Rock waters and the green prairies beyond the Neosho.

A sudden awakening came over me, and in one swift instant I understood my boyhood dreams and hopes and visions.

"You will pardon me for coming so abruptly, Miss St. Vrain," I said. "Mother Bridget told me I would find you here."

The girl listened to my stumbling words with eyes full of laughter.

"Don't call me Miss St. Vrain, please. Let me be Eloise, and I can call you Gail. Even with your height and your broad shoulders you haven't changed much. And in all these years I was always thinking of you growing up just as you are. Let's sit down and get acquainted again."

She offered me her hand and we sat down together. I could not speak then, for one sentence was ringing in my ears--"I was always thinking of you." In those years when Beverly and I had put away all thoughts of sweethearts-- they could not be a part of the plainsman's life before us--sweethearts such as older boys in school boasted about, "she was always thinking of me." The thought brought a keen hurt as if I had done her some great wrong, and it held me back from words.

She could not interpret my silence, and a look of timidity crept over her young face.

"I didn't mean to be so--so bold with a stranger," she began.

"You aren't bold, and we aren't strangers. I was just too stupid to think anybody else could get out of childhood except old Bev Clarenden and myself," I managed to say at last. "I even forgot Mat Nivers, who is a young lady now, and Aunty Boone, who hasn't changed a kink of her woolly hair. But we couldn't be strangers. Not after that trip across the plains and living at old Fort Bent as we did."

I paused, and the memory of that last night at the fort made me steal a glance at Eloise to see if she, too, remembered.

She was fair to see just then, with the pink clouds mirrored on the placid waters reflected in the pink of her cheeks.

"Do you remember what I called you the first time I saw you?" She looked up with shining eyes.

"You called me a big brown bob-cat, and you said I looked like I'd slept in the Hondo 'royo all my life. I know I looked it, too. I'll forgive you if you will excuse my blunder to-day. What became of that boy, Marcos? Have you ever seen him since you left Santa Fé?" I asked.

The fair face clouded, and a look of longing crept into the big, dark eyes lifted pleadingly a moment to mine. I wanted to take her in my arms right then and look about for something to kill for her sake. Yet I would not, for the gold of all the Mexicos, have touched the hem of her Grecian robe.

"Yes, I have seen Marcos many times. His father went to old Mexico after the war, but the Rameros do not stay long anywhere. Marcos made life miserable for me sometimes." She paused suddenly.

"The Rameros. Then he was the son of the man who was my uncle's enemy. Maybe you did as much for him, too, sometimes. You had the spirit to do it, anyhow," I said, lightly, to hide my real feeling.

"I was a little cat. I'm a lot better now. Let's not go too much into that time. Tell me where you have been and where you are going." Eloise changed the subject easily.

"I've been in Cincinnati, attending a boys' school for three years. I start for Santa Fé in two weeks. My uncle's store is doing a big over land business, and he keeps the ox-teams just fanning one another, coming and going across the prairies. I'm crazy to go and see the open plains again. Cincinnati is a city on stilts, and our little Independence-Westport Landing-Kansas City place, as the Cincinnati of the great American desert, is also pretty bumpy, the last place on earth to put a town--only we can see almost to Santa Fé, New Mexico, from the hilltops. Won't it be great to view that mud-walled town again? Bev is going, too--to kill a few Indians for our winter's meat, he says, in his wicked, blood-thirsty way." So I ran on, glad to be alive in the delicious beauty of that spring evening as we together went back over the days of our young years.

"Gail, may we take another passenger to-morrow?" Eloise asked, suddenly.

"Why, as many as the stage will hold! There's to be a nun and a priest and yourself. I'm chaperon. I could take the priest on my lap if he isn't too bulky," I answered.

"I want to take Po-a-be. I can't tell you why now." The lashes dropped over the brown eyes, and I wondered how she could think that I could refuse her anything.

"Oh, we'll take her on faith and the stage-coach. She can come right to Castle Clarenden and stay till she gets ready to hurdle off to her own 'wickie up'. She has grown into a beautiful Indian woman, though I couldn't call her a squaw."

"She isn't a squaw. I'm glad to hear you say that. I think it will make her very happy to stay at your home for a while. She will miss me a little when we leave here, maybe," Eloise said, looking at me with a grateful smile that sent a tingle to my fingertips.

"Won't you stay, too?" I asked, suddenly realizing that this beautiful girl might slip away as easily as she had come into my life here.

Eloise laughed at my earnestness.

"I couldn't stay long," she said, lightly.

"And why not?" I burst in, eagerly. "What have you in Santa Fé?"

"A little money and a lot of memories," she replied, seriously.

"Oh, I can bring the money up to Kansas for you in an ox-train easily enough, and you could blow up the old mud-box of a town and not hurt a hair on the head of a single memory. You know you can take them anywhere you go. I do mine."

"I'm going to St. Louis, anyhow," Eloise returned, "and you have no sacred memories--boys don't care for things like girls do."

"They don't? They don't? And I have forgotten the little girl who was afraid one moonlit night out in the court at Fort Bent and asked me that I shouldn't ever let Marcos pull her hair. Yes, boys forget."

I laid my hand on her arm and bent forward to look into her face. For just one flash those big dark eyes looked straight at me, with something in their depths that I shall never forget.

Then she moved lightly from me.

"Oh, all children remember, I suppose. I do, anyhow--a thousand things I'd like to forget. It is lovely by the river. Suppose we go down there for a little while. I must not stay out here too long."

I took her arm and we strolled down the quiet path in the twilight sweetness to where the broad Neosho, brim full from the spring rains, swept on between picturesque banks. The afterglow of sunset was flaming gorgeously above the western prairies, and the mists along the Neosho were lavender and mother-of-pearl. And before all this had deepened to purple darkness the full moon would swing up the sky, swathing the earth with a softened radiance. All the beauty of this warm spring night seemed but a setting for this girl in her graceful Greek draperies, with the waving gold of her hair and her dainty pink-and-white coloring.

A new heaven and a new earth had begun for me, and a delicious longing, clean and sweet, that swept every commoner feeling far away. What matter that the life before me be filled with danger, and all the coarse and cruel things of the hard days of the Santa Fé Trail? In that hour I knew the best of life that a young man can know. Its benediction after all these years of change is on me still. Awhile we watched the flashing ripples on the river, and the sky's darkening afterglow. Then we turned to the moonlit east.

"Do you know what the people of Hopi-land call this month?" Eloise asked.

"I don't know Hopi words for what is beautiful," I replied.

"They call it 'the Moon of the Peach Blossom', and they cherish the time in their calendar."

"Then we will be Hopi people," I declared, "for it was in their Moon of the Peach Blossom that you grew up for me from the little girl who called me a bob-cat down in the doorway of the old San Miguel Church in Santa Fé, and from Aunty Boone's 'Little Lees' at old Fort Bent, to the Eloise of St. Ann's by the Kansas Neosho."

The sound of a sweet-toned bell told us that we must not stay longer, and together we followed the path from the Flat Rock up to the academy door. And all the way was like the ways of Paradise to me, for I was in the peach-blossom moon of my own life.

X

THE HANDS THAT CLING

The hands that take
No weight from your sad cross, oh, lighter far
It were but for the burden that they bring!
God only knows what hind'ring things they are--
The hands that cling.
--ESTHER M. CLARK

The next morning three of us waited in the stage before the door of St. Ann's Academy. A thin-faced nun, who was called Sister Anita, sat beside Eloise St. Vrain, her snowy head-dress, with her black veil and somber garments, contrasting sharply with the silver-gray hat and traveling costume of her companion. Hints of pink-satin linings to coat-collar and pocket-flaps, and the pink facing of the broad hat-brim, seemed borrowed from the silver and pink of misty morning skies, with the golden hair catching the glint of all the early sunbeams. There was a tenderness in the bright face, the sadness which parting puts temporarily into young countenances. The girl looked lovingly at the church, and St. Ann's, and the green fields reaching up to the edge of the mission premises.

As we waited, Mother Bridget and Little Blue Flower came slowly out of the academy door. The good mother's arm was around the Indian girl, and her eyes filled with tears as she looked down affectionately at the dark face.

Little Blue Flower, true to her heritage, gave no sign of grief save for the burning light in her big, dry eyes. She listened silently to Mother Bridget's parting words of advice and submitted without response to the embrace and gentle good-by kiss on her brown forehead.

The good woman gazed into my face with penetrating eyes, as if to measure my trustworthiness.

"You will see that no harm comes to my little Po-a-be. The wolves of the forest are not the only danger for the unprotected lambs," she said, earnestly.

"I'll do my best, Mother Bridget," I responded, feeling a swelling pride in my double charge.

Mother Bridget patted Eloise's hand and turned away. She loved all of her girls, but her heart went out most to the Indian maidens whom she led toward her civilization and her sacred creed.

As she turned away, the priest who was to go with us came out of the church door to the stage.

Little Blue Flower sat with the other two women, facing us, her dark-green dress with her rich coloring making as strong a contrast as the nun's black robe against the pink-touched silver-gray gown. And the Indian face, strong, impenetrable, with a faintly feminine softening of the racial features, and the luminous black eyes, gave setting to the pure Saxon type of her companion.

I turned from the three to greet the priest and give him a place beside me. His face seemed familiar, but it was not until I heard his voice, in a courteous good-morning, that I knew him to be the Father Josef who had met us on the way into Santa Fé years before, and who later had shown us the little golden-haired girl asleep on the hard bench in the old mission church of Agua Fria. A page of my boyhood seemed suddenly to have opened there, and I wondered curiously at the meaning of it all. Life, that for three years had been something of a monotonous round of action for a boy of the frontier, was suddenly filling each day with events worth while. I wondered many things concerning Father Josef's presence there, but I had the grace to ask no questions as we five journeyed over the rolling green prairies of Kansas in the pleasant time of year which the Hopi calls the Moon of the Peach Blossom.

The priest appeared hardly a day older than when I had first seen him, and he chatted genially as we rode along.

"We are losing two of our stars," he said, with a gallant little bow. "Miss St. Vrain goes to St. Louis to relatives, I believe, and Little Blue Flower, eventually, to New Mexico. St. Ann's under Mother Bridget is doing a wonderful work among our people, but it is not often that a girl comes here from such a distance as New Mexico."

I tried to fancy what the Indian girl's thoughts might be as the priest said this, but her face, as usual, gave no clue to her mind's activity.

Where the Santa Fé Trail crossed the Wakarusa Father Josef left us to join a wagon-train going west. Sister Anita, who was hurrying back to Kentucky, she said, on some churchly errand, took a steamer at Westport Landing, and the three of us came to the Clarenden home on the crest of the bluff.

We had washed off our travel stains and come out on the veranda when we saw Beverly Clarenden standing in the sunlight, waiting for us. I had never seen him look so handsome as he did that day, dressed in the full regalia of the plains: a fringed and beaded buckskin coat, dark pantaloons held inside of high-topped boots, a flannel shirt, with a broad black silk tie fastened in a big bow at his throat, and his wide-brimmed felt hat set back from his forehead. Clean-shaven, his bright brown hair--a trifle long, after the custom of the frontier--flung back from his brow, his blooming face wearing the happy smile of youth, his tall form easily erect, he seemed the very embodiment of that defiant power that swept the old Santa Fé Trail clean for the feet of its commerce to run swiftly along. I am glad that I never envied him--brother of my heart, who loved me so.

He was not as surprised as I had been to find the grown-up girl instead of the little child. That wasn't Beverly's way.

"I'm mighty glad to meet you again," he said, with jaunty air, grasping Eloise by the hand. "You look just as--shall I say promising, as ever."

"I'm glad to see you, Beverly. You and Gail have been my biggest assets of memory these many years." Eloise was at ease with him in a moment. Somehow they never misunderstood each other.

"Oh, I'm always an asset, but Gail here gets to be a liability if you let him stay around too long."

"Here is somebody else. Don't you remember Little Blue Flower?" Eloise interrupted him.

"Little Blue Flower! Why, I should say I do! And are you that little blossom?"

Beverly's face beamed, and he caught the Indian girl's hand in both of his in a brotherly grasp. He wasn't to blame that nature had made him frank and unimaginative.

"I haven't forgotten the last time I saw your face in a wide crack between two adobe shacks. A 'flower in the crannied wall' in that 'pure water' sand-pile in New Mexico. I'd have plucked you out of the cranny right then, if old Rex Krane hadn't given us our 'forward march!' orders, and an Indian boy, ten feet high and sneaky as a cat, hadn't been lurking in the middle distance to pluck *me* as a brand *for* the burning. And now you are a St. Ann's girl, a good little Catholic. How did you ever get away up into Kansas Territory, anyhow?"

Beverly had unconsciously held the girl's hand as he spoke, but at the mention of the Indian boy she drew back and her bright face became expressionless.

Just then Mat Nivers joined us--Mat, whom the Lord made to smooth the way for everybody around her--and we sat down for a visit.

"We are all here, friends of my youthful days," Beverly went on, gaily. "Bill Banney and Jondo are down in the Clarenden warehouse packing merchandise for the Santa Fé trade. Even big black Aunty Boone, getting supper in there, is still a feature of this circus. If only that slim Yankee, Rex Krane, would appear here now. Uncle Esmond tells me he is to be here soon, and if all goes well he will go with us to Santa Fé again. How about it, Mat? Can't you hurry his coming a bit?"

But Mat was staring at the roadway leading to the ravine below us. Her wide gray eyes were full of eagerness and her cheeks were pink with excitement. For, sure enough, there was Rex Krane striding up the hill, with the easy swing of vigorous health. No longer the slender, slouching young idol of my boyhood days, with Eastern cut of garment and devil-may-care dejection of manner, all hiding a loving tenderness for the unprotected, and a daring spirit that scorned danger.

"It's the old settlers' picnic, eh! The gathering of the wild tribes--anything you want to call it, so we smoke the peace pipe."

Rex greeted all of us as we rushed upon him. But the first hands he reached for were the hands of our loving big sister Mat. And he held them close in his as he looked down into her beautiful eyes.

A sudden rush of memories brought back to me the long days on the trail in the middle '40's, and I knew now why he had always looked at Mat when he talked to all of us. And I used to think that he must have had a little sister like her. Now I knew in an instant why Mat could not meet his eyes to-day with that unconcern with which she met them when she was a child to me, and he, all of five years ahead of her, was very grown up. I knew more, for I had entered a new land myself since the hour by the shimmering Flat Rock in the Moon of the Peach Blossom, and I was alive to every tint and odor and musical note for every other wayfarer therein.

That was a glorious week that followed, and one to remember on the long trail days coming to us. I have no quarrel with the happy youth of to-day, but I feel no sense of loss nor spirit of envy when they tell me--all young people are my friends--when they tell me of golf-links and automobile rides, or even the daring hint of airplanes. To the heart of youth the gasolene-motor or the thrill of the air-craft to-day is no more than the Indian pony and the uncertain chance of the crude old canoe on the clear waters of the Big Blue when Kansas City was a village and the Kansas prairies were in their virgin glory.

Bill Banney had come out of the Mexican War, no longer an adventure lover, but a seasoned frontiersman. His life knew few of the gentler touches. He gave it to the plains, where so many lives went, unhonored and unsung, into the building of an enduring empire.

We would have included him in all the frolic of that wonderful week in the Moon of the Peach Blossom--but he gave us no opportunity to do so. And we were young, and the society of girls was a revelation to us. So with the carelessness of youth we forgot him. We forgot many things that week that, in Heaven's name, we had cause enough to remember in the years that followed after.

"There's a theatrical troupe come up from St. Louis to play here to-night," Rex Krane announced, after supper. "Mat, will you let me take you down to see the villain get what's due all villains? Then if we have to kill off Gail and Bev, it will not be so awkward."

"Can't we all go?" Mat suggested.

"Never mind us, Lady Nivers. Little Blue Flower, may I have the pleasure of your company? I need protection to-night," Beverly said, with much ceremony.

Little Blue Flower was sitting next to him, or it might not have begun that way.

"Oh, say yes. He's no poorer company than that company of actors down town," Rex urged.

The Indian girl assented with a smile.

She did not smile often and when she did her eyes were full of light, and her red lips and perfect white teeth were beautiful enough for a queen to envy.

"Little Lees, it seems you are doomed to depend on Gail or jump in the Kaw. I'd prefer the Kaw myself, but life is full of troubles. One more can be endured." Rex had turned to Eloise St. Vrain.

"Seems to me, having first choice, you might have been more considerate of my lot yourself," Eloise declared.

"He was. He saved you from a worse fate when he chose Mat," I broke in.

"May we have a song by the choir?" Beverly interrupted, and with his full bass voice he began to roar our some popular tune of that time.

And it went on as it began, the rambles about the rugged bluffs and picturesque ravines, where to-day the hard-surfaced Cliff Drive makes a scenic highway through the beauty spots of a populous city; the daring canoe rides on the rivers; the gatherings of the young folk in the town; and the long twilight hours on the crest of the bluff overlooking the two great waterways. And as by the first selection, Beverly and Little Blue Flower were companions. Nobody could be unhappy with Bev, least of all the shy Indian girl with a face full of sunshine, now. And I? I walked a pathway strewn with rose petals because the golden-haired Little Lees was beside me. Each day was a frolic day for us, teasing one another and making a joke of life, and for the morrow we took no thought at all.

One evening Eloise St. Vrain and I sat together on the bluff. It was the twilight hour, and all the far valley of the Kaw was full of iridescent misty lights, with gold-tipped clouds of pale lavender above, and the glistening silver of the river below. We could hear Beverly and Little Blue Flower laughing together in a big swing among the maples. Aunty Boone was crooning some African melodies in the bushes half-way down the slope. Rex and Mat had gone to the ravine below to meet Uncle Esmond.

"Little Lees, the first time I ever saw you you were away out there in such a misty light as that, and I saw only your hair and your eyes then, but as clearly as I see them now."

Eloise turned questioningly toward me, and the light in her dark eyes thrilled to the heart of me. In all her stay with us I had hardly spoken earnestly of anything before.

"When was that Gail?" she asked, the frivolous spirit gone from her, too.

"When I was a little boy, one day at Fort Leavenworth. And when I caught sight of you at the door of old San Miguel I knew you," I replied.

The girl turned her face toward the west again and was silent. I felt my cheeks flush hotly. I had made her think I was only a dream-sick fool, when I had told her of the sacredest moment of my life, and I had for the minute foolishly felt that she might understand. How could I know that it was I who could not understand?

At last she looked up with a smile as full of mischief as on that day when she had called me a big brown bob-cat.

"You must have been having a nightmare in your sleep," she declared.

"I think I was," I replied, testily. "Let me tell you something, Little Lees, something really important."

"I don't believe you know one important thing," Eloise replied, "but I'll listen, and then if it is I'll tell you something more important."

"I'm willing to hear it now. Tell me first," I replied, wondering the while how nature, that gives rough-hewn bearded faces to men, could make a face so daintily colored, in its youthful roundness, as hers.

"I'm going to start to St. Louis day after to-morrow at six o'clock in the morning. Isn't that important?"

Was there a real earnestness under the lightly spoken words, or did I imagine it so? If I had only made sure then--but I was young.

"Important! It's a tragedy! I start west in three days, at eight o'clock in the morning," I said, carelessly.

Sometimes the gray shadows fall on us when neither sunlight nor moonlight nor starlight is dimmed by any film of vapor. They fell on me then, and I shivered in my soul. How could I speak otherwise than carelessly and not show what must not be known? And how could the girl beside me know that I was speaking thus to keep down the shiver of that cold shadow? I suppose it must always be the same old story, year after year--

till the leaves of the judgment book unfold.

"What was that important something you were going to tell me? What Mat told me last night when we were watching the moon rise?" Eloise asked.

"That Rex and Mat are going to be married to-morrow evening at early candle-lighting--'early mosquito-biting,' Bev calls it. Rex has loved Mat since the day when he joined our little wagon-train out of a foolish sort of notion that he could protect us children, otherwise his life was useless to him. But something in his own boyhood made him pity all orphan children. I think it was through neglect in childhood he became an invalid at nineteen. He doesn't show the marks of it now."

I paused and looked at the young girl beside me, whose eyes were like stars in the deepening gloom of the evening. It was delicious to have her look at me and listen to me. It was delicious to live in a rose-hued twilight, and I forgot the chill of that gray shadow lurking near.

The next evening was entrancing with the soft air of spring, a night made purposely for brides. The wedding itself was simple in its appointments, as such events must needs be in the frontier years. All day we had worked to decorate the plain stone house, which the deftness of Little Blue Flower and the artistic touch of Little Lees turned into a spring bower, with trailing vines and blossoms everywhere.

Mat's wedding-gown was neither new nor elaborate, for the affair had been too hastily decided on, but Eloise had made it bride-like by draping a filmy veil over Mat's bright brown hair, and Little Blue Flower had brought her long strands of turquoise beads, "old and borrowed and blue," to fulfil the needs of every bride.

In the bridal party Beverly and I walked in front, followed by the two girls in the white Greek robes which they had worn at the school frolic at St. Ann's, and wearing their headbands, the one of silver and turquoise, the other of silver and coral. Then came Rex Krane and Bill Banney. Poor Bill! Nobody guessed that night that the bridal blossoms were flowers on the coffin of his dead hope. And last of all, Esmond Clarenden and Mat Nivers, with shining eyes, leaning on his arm. I had never seen Uncle Esmond in evening dress before, nor dreamed how splendid a figure he could make for a drawing-room in the costume in which he was so much at ease. But the handsomest man of all the large company gathered there that night was Jondo, big, broad-shouldered Jondo, his deep-blue eyes bright with joy for these two. And in the background was Aunty Boone, resplendent in a new red calico besprinkled with her favorite white dots, her head turbaned in a yellow silk bandana, and about her neck a strand of huge green glass beads. Her eyes glistened as she watched that night's events, and her comfortable ejaculations of approval were like the low purr of a satisfied cat. Then came the solemn pledges, the benediction and congratulations. There was merrymaking and singing, cake and unfermented wine of grapes for refreshing, and much good will that night.

When the guests were gone and the lights, save one kitchen candle, were all out, I had slipped from the dining-room with the last burden of dishes, when I paused a minute beside the open kitchen window to let the midnight breeze cool my face.

On the side porch, a little affair made to shelter the doorway, I saw Beverly Clarenden and Little Blue Flower. He was speaking gently, but with his blunt frankness, as he patted the two brown hands clinging to his arm. The Indian girl's white draperies were picturesque anywhere. In this dramatic setting they were startlingly beautiful, and her face, outlined in the dim light, was a thing rare to see. I could not hear her words, but her soft Hopi voice had a tender tone.

I was waiting to let them pass in when I heard Beverly's voice, and I saw him bend over the little maiden, and, putting one arm around her, he drew her close to him and kissed her forehead. I knew it was a brother's sympathetic act--and all men know how dangerous a thing that is; that there are no ties binding brother to sister except the bonds of kindred blood. The girl slipped inside the dining-room door, and a minute later a candle flickered behind her bedroom window-blind in the gable of the house. I waited for Beverly to go, determined never to mention what I had seen, when I caught the clear low voice whose tones could make my pulse thresh in its walls.

"Beverly, Beverly, it breaks my heart--" I lost the remainder of the sentence, but Beverly's words were clear and direct and full of a frank surprise.

"Eloise, do you really care?"

I turned away quickly that I might not hear any more. The rest of that night I sat wide awake and staring at the misty valley of the Kaw, where silvery ripples flashed up here and there against the shadowy sand-bars.

*****

The steamboat for St. Louis left the Westport Landing wharf at six o'clock in the morning, before the mists had lifted over the big yellow Missouri. From our bluff I saw the smoke belch from its stacks as it pulled away and started down-stream; but only Uncle Esmond and Jondo waited to wave good-by to the sweet-faced girl looking back at them from its deck. Beverly had overslept, and Little Blue Flower had left an hour earlier with a wagon-train starting west toward Council Grove. In her room lay the white Grecian robe and the headband of wrought silver with coral pendants. On the little white pin-cushion on the dressing-table the bright pin-heads spelled out one Hopi word that carries all good will and blessing

LOLOMI.

Twenty-four hours later Rex Krane left his bride, and he and Bill Banney and Beverly and I, under command of Jondo, started on our long trip overland to Santa Fé. And two of us carried some memories we hoped to lose when new scenes and certain perils should surround us.

XI

"OUR FRIENDS--THE ENEMY"

And you all know security
Is mortal's chiefest enemy.
SHAKESPEARE.

In St. Louis and Kansas City men of Esmond Clarenden's type were sending out great caravans of goods and receiving return cargoes across the plains--pioneer trade-builders, uncrowned sovereigns of national expansion--against whose enduring power wars for conquest are as flashlight to daylight. And Beverly Clarenden and I, with the whole battalion of plainsmen--"bull-whackers," in the common parlance of the Santa Fé Trail--who drove those caravans to and fro, may also have been State-builders, as Uncle Esmond had declared we would be. Yet we hardly looked like makers of empire in those summer days when we followed the great wagon-trains along the prairies and over the mountain passes.

Two of us had come home from school hilariously eager for the trail service. But the silent plains made men thoughtful and introspective. Days of endless level landscapes under wide-arching skies, and nights in the open beneath the everlasting silent stars, give a man time to get close to himself, to relive his childhood, to measure human values, to hear the voice in the storm-cloud and the song of low-purring winds, to harden against the monotonous glare of sunlight, to defy the burning heat, and to feel--aye, to feel the spell of crystal day-dawns and the sweetness of velvet-shadowed twilights. Beverly and I were typical plainsmen in that we never spoke of these things to each other--that is not the way of the plainsman.

Our company had been organized at Council Grove--three trains of twenty-six wagons each, drawn by three or four spans of mules or yoke of oxen, guarded by eightscore of "bull-whackers." And there were a dozen or more ponies trained for swift riding in cases of emergency. There were also half a dozen private outfits under protection of the large body.

The usual election before starting had made Jondo captain of the whole company. His was the controlling type of spirit that could have bent a battalion or swayed a Congress. For all the commanders and lawmakers of that day were not confined to the army and to Congress. Some of them escaped to the West and became sovereigns of service there. And Jondo had need for an intrepid spirit to rule that group of men, as that journey across the plains proved.

On the day before we left Council Grove he was sitting with the heads of the other wagon-trains under a big oak-tree, perfecting final plans for the journey.

"Gail, I want you to sign some papers here," he said. "It is the agreement for the trip among the three companies owning the trains."

I read aloud the contract setting forth how one Jean Deau, representing Esmond Clarenden, of Kansas City, with Smith and Davis, representing two other companies from St. Louis, together agreed to certain conditions regarding the journey.

Smith and Davis had already signed, and as I took the pen, a white-haired old trapper who was sitting near by burst out:

"Jean Deau! Jean Deau! Who the devil is Jean Deau?"

Jondo did not look up, but the lines hardened about his mouth.

"It's a sound. Don't get in the way, old man. Go ahead, Clarenden," Smith commanded.

Few questions were asked in those days, for most men on the plains had a history, and it was what a man could do here, not what he had done somewhere else, that counted.

So I, representing Esmond Clarenden, signed the paper and the two managers hurried away. But the old trapper sat staring at Jondo.

"Say, I'm gittin' close to the end of the trail, and the divide ain't fur off for me. D'ye mind if I say somethin'?" he asked at last.

Jondo looked up with that smile that could warm any man's heart.

"Say on," he commanded, kindly.

"You aint never signin' your own name nowhere, it sorter seems."

Jondo shook his head.

"Didn't you and this Clarenden outfit go through here 'bout ten years ago one night? Some Mexican greasers was raisin' hell and proppin' it up with a whisky-bottle that night, layin' fur you vicious."

Jondo smiled and nodded assent.

"Well, them fellers comin' in had a bargain with a passel of Kioways to git you plenty if they missed you themselves; to clinch their bargain they give 'em a pore little Hopi Injun girl they'd brung along with a lot of other Mexicans and squaws."

"I had that figured out pretty well at the time," Jondo said, with a smile.

"But, Jean Deau--" the old man began.

"No, Jondo. Go on. I'm busy," Jondo interrupted.

The old man's watery eyes gleamed.

"I just want to say friendly-like, that them Kioways never forgot the trick you worked on 'em, an' the *tornydo* that busted 'em at Pawnee Rock they laid to your bad medicine. They went clare back to Bent's Fort to fix you. Them and that rovin' bunch of Mexicans that scattered along the trail with 'em in time of the Mexican War. They'd 'a' lost you but fur a little Apache cuss they struck out there who showed 'em to you."

Jondo looked up quickly now. Santan, Beverly's "Satan," whom our captain had defended, flashed to my mind, but I knew by Jondo's face that he did not believe the old trapper's story.

"Them Kioways is still layin' fur you ever' year, I tell you, an' they're bound to git you sooner or later. I'm tellin' ye in kindness."

The old man's voice weakened a little.

"And I'm taking you in kindness," Jondo said. "You may be doing me a great service."

"I shore am. Take my word an' keep awake. Keep awake!"

In spite of his drink-bleared eyes and weakened frame, there was a hint of the commander in him, a mere shadow of the energy that had gone years ago into the wild, solitary life of the trapper who foreran the trail days here.

"One more trip to the ha'nts of the fur-bearin' and it's good-by to the mountain trails and the river courses fur me," he said, as he rose and stalked unsteadily away, and--I never saw him again.

At daybreak the next morning we were off for Santa Fé. Our wagons, loaded with their precious burdens, moved forward six abreast along the old sun-flower bordered trail. Morning, noon, and evening, pitching camp and breaking camp, yoking oxen and harnessing mules, keeping night vigil by shifts, hunting buffalo, killing rattlesnakes, watching for signs of hostile Indians, meeting incoming trains, or solitary trappers, at long intervals, breathing the sweet air of the prairies, and gathering rugged strength from sleep on the wholesome earth--these things, with the jolliest of fellowship and perfect discipline of our captain, Jondo, made this hard, free life of the plains a fascinating one. We were unshaven and brown as Indians. We lost every ounce of fat, but we were steel-sinewed, and fear, that wearing element that disintegrates the soul, dropped away from us early on the trail.

But when the full moon came sweeping up the sky, and all the prairie shadows lay flat to earth under its surge of clear light, in the stillness of the great lonely land, then the battle with home-sickness was not the least of the plains' perils.

One midnight watch of such a night, Jondo sat out my vigil with me. Our eighty or more wagons were drawn up in a rude ellipse with the stock corraled inside, for we were nearing the danger zone. And yet to-night danger seemed impossible in such a peaceful land under such clear moonlight.

"Gail, you were always a far-seeing youngster, even in your cub days," Jondo said, after we had sat silent for a long time. "We are moving into trouble from to-night, and I'll need you now."

"What makes you think so, Jondo?" I asked.

"That train we met going east at noon."

"Mexicans with silver and skins worth double our stuff, what have they to do with us?" I inquired.

"One of the best men I have ever known is a Mexican in Santa Fé. The worst man I have ever known is an American there. But I've never yet trusted a Mexican when you bunch them together. They don't fit into American harness, and it will be a hundred years before the Mexican in our country will really love the Stars and Stripes. Deep down in his heart he will hate it."

"I remember Felix Narveo and Ferdinand Ramero mighty well," I commented.

Jondo stared at me.

"Can't a boy remember things?" I inquired.

"It takes a boy to remember; and they grow up and we forget they have had eyes, ears, feelings, memories, all keener than we can ever have in later years. Gail, the Mexican train comes from Felix Narveo, and Narveo is a man of a thousand. They bring word, however, that the Kiowas are unusually friendly and that we have nothing to fear this side of the Cimarron. They don't feel sure of the Utes and Apaches."

"Good enough!" I exclaimed.

"Yes, only they lie when they say it. It's a trap to get us. No Kiowa on the plains will let a Clarenden train through peacefully, because we took their captive, Little Blue Flower. It's a hatred kept alive in the Kiowas by one man in Santa Fé through his Mexican agents with Narveo's train."

"And that man is Ramero?" I questioned.

"That man is Ramero, and his capacity for hate is appalling. Gail, there's only one thing in the world that is stronger than hate, and that is love."

Jondo looked out over the moonlit plains, his fine head erect, even in his meditative moods.

"When a Mexican says a Kiowa has turned friendly, don't believe him. And when a Kiowa says it himself--kill him. It's your only safe course," Jondo said, presently.

"Jondo, why does Ramero stir up the Indians and Mexicans against Uncle Esmond?" I asked.

"Because Clarenden drove him into exile in New Mexico before it was United States territory," Jondo replied.

"What did he do that for?" I asked.

"Because of what Ramero had done to me," Jondo replied.

"Well, New Mexico is United States territory now. What keeps this Ramero in Santa Fé, if he is there?"

"I keep him there. It's safer to know just where a man like that is. So I put a ring around the town and left him inside of it."

Jondo paused and turned toward me.

"Yonder comes Banney to go on guard now. Gail, I'll tell you all about it some day. I couldn't on a night like this."

The deep voice sent a shiver through me. There was a pathos in it, too manly for tears, too courageous for pity.

The days that followed were hard ones. Word had gotten through the camp that the Indians were very friendly, and that we need not be uneasy this side of the Cimarron country. Smith and Davis agreed with the train captain, Jondo, in taking no chances, but most of the one hundred sixty bull-whackers stampeded like cattle against precaution, and rebelled at his rigid ruling. He had begun to tighten down upon us as we went farther and farther into the heart of a savage domain. The night guard was doubled and every precaution for the stock was demanded, giving added cause for grumbling and muttered threats which no man had the courage to speak openly to Jondo's face. I knew why he had said that he would need me. Bill Banney was always reliable, but growing more silent and unapproachable every day. Rex Krane's mind was on the girl-wife he had left in the stone house on the bluff above the Missouri. Beverly was too cock-sure of himself and too light-hearted, too eager for an Indian fight. Jondo could counsel with Smith and Davis of the St. Louis trains, but only as a last resort would he dictate to them. So he turned to me.

We were nearing Pawnee Rock, but as yet no hint of an Indian trail could we find anywhere. Advance-guards and rear-guards had no news to report when night came, and the sense of security grew hourly. The day had been very warm, but our nooning was shortened and we went into camp early. Everything had gone wrong that day: harness had broken; mules had grown fractious; a wagon had upset on a rough bit of the trail; half a dozen men, including Smith and Davis of the St. Louis trains, had fallen suddenly ill;

drinking-water had been warm and muddy; and, most of all, the consciousness of wide-spread opposition to Jondo's strict ruling where there were no signs of danger made a very ugly-spirited group of men who sat down together to eat our evening meal. Bets were openly made that we wouldn't see a hostile redskin this side of Santa Fé. Covert sneers pointed many comments, and grim silence threatened more than everything else. Jondo's face was set, but there was a calmness about his words and actions, and even the most rebellious that night knew he was least afraid of any man among us.

At midnight he wakened me. "I want you to help me, Gail," he said. "The Kiowas will gather for us at Pawnee Rock. They missed us there once because they were looking for a big train, and it was there we took their captive girl. The boys are ready to mutiny to-night. I count on you to stand by me." Stand by Jondo! In my helpless babyhood, my orphaned childhood, my sturdy growing years toward young manhood, Jondo had been father, mother, brother, playmate, guardian angel. I would have walked on red-hot coals for his sake.

"I want you to slip away to-night, when Rex and Bev are on guard, and find out what's over that ridge to the north. Don't come back till you do find out. We'll get to Pawnee Rock to-morrow. I must know to-night. Can you do it? If you aren't back by sunrise, I'll follow your trail double quick."

"I'll go," I replied, proud to show both my courage and my loyalty to my captain.

The night was gray, with a dying moon in the west, and the north ridge loomed like a low black shadow against the sky. There was a weird chanting voice in the night wind, pouring endlessly across the open plains. And everywhere an eyeless, voiceless, motionless land, whereon my pony's hoof-beats were big and booming. Nature made my eyes and ears for the trail life, and matched my soul to its level spaces. To-night I was alert with that love of mastery that made me eager for this task. So I rode forward until our great camp was only a dull blot on the horizon-line, melting into mere nothingness as it grew farther away. And I was alone on the earth. God had taken out every other thing in it, save the sky over my head and the uneven short-grass sod under my feet.

On I went, veering to the northwest from instinct that I should find my journey's end soonest that way. Over the divide which hid the wide valley of the Arkansas, and into the deep draws and low bluffs of a creek with billowy hills beyond, I found myself still instinctively *smelling* my way. I grew more cautious with each step now, knowing that the chance for me to slip along unseen gave also the chance for an enemy to trail me unseen.

At last I caught that low breathing sound that goes with the sense of nearness to life. Leaving my pony by the stream, I climbed to the top of a little swell, and softly as a cat walks on a carpet, I walked straight into an Indian camp. It was well chosen for outlook near, and security from afar. There was a growing light in the sky that follows the darkness of moonset and runs before the break of dawn. Everything in the camp was dead still. I saw evidences of war-paint and a recent war-dance that forerun an Indian attack. I estimated the strength of the enemy--possibly four hundred warriors, and noted the symbols of the Kiowa tribe. Then, thrilled with pride at my skill and success, I turned to retrace my way to my pony--and looked full into the face of an Indian brave standing motionless in my path. A breath--and two more braves evolved out of gray air, and the three stood stock-still before me. Out of the tail of my eye, I caught sight of a drawn bow on either side of me. I had learned quickness with firearms years ago, but I knew that two swift arrows would cut my life-line before the sound of my ready revolver could break the stillness of the camp. Three pairs of snaky black eyes looked steadily at me, and I stared back as directly into them. Two arrow-points gently touched my ears. Behind me, a tomahawk softly marked a ring around my scalp outside of my hat. I was standing in a circle of death. At last the brave directly before me slowly drew up his bow and pointed it at me; then dropping it, he snapped the arrow shaft and threw away the pieces. Pointing to my cocked revolver, he motioned to me to drop it. At the same time the bows and tomahawks, of the other warriors were thrown down. It was a silent game, and in spite of the danger I smiled as I put down my firearms.

"Can't any of you talk?" I asked. "If you are friendly, why don't you say so?"

The men did not speak, but by a gesture toward the tallest tepee--the chief's, I supposed--I understood that he alone would talk to me.

"Well, bring him out." I surprised myself at my boldness. Yet no man knows in just what spirit he will face a peril.

One of the braves ran to the chief's tent, but the remaining five left me no chance for escape. It was slowly growing lighter. I thought of Jondo and his search at sunrise, and the moments seemed like hours. Yet with marvelous swiftness and stillness a score of Indians with their chief were mounted, and I, with my pony in the center of a solid ring, was being hurried away, alive, with friendly captors daubed with war-paint.

There was a growing light in the east, while the west was still dark. I thought of the earth as throwing back the gray shadowy covers from its morning face and piling them about its feet; I thought of some joke of Beverly's; and I wondered about one of the oxen that had seemed sick in the evening. I tried to think of nothing and a thousand things came into my mind. But of life and death and love and suffering, I thought not at all.

Meantime, Jondo waited anxiously for my coming. Rex and Beverly had gone to sleep at the end of their watch and nobody else in camp knew of my going. At dawn a breeze began to swing in from the north, and with its refreshing touch the weariness and worries of yesterday were swept away. Everybody wakened in a good humor. But Jondo had not slept, and his face was sterner than ever as the duties of the day began.

Before sunrise I began to be missed.

"Where's Gail?" Bill Banney was the first to ask.

"That's Clarenden's job, not mine," another of the bull-whackers resented a command of Jondo's.

"Gail! Gail! Anybody on earth seen Gail Clarenden this morning?" came from a far corner of the camp.

"Have you lost a man, Jondo?" Smith, still sick in his wagon, inquired.

And the sun was filling the eastern horizon with a roseate glow. It would be above the edge of the plains in a little while, and still I had not returned.

Breakfast followed, with many questions for the absent one. There was an eagerness to be off early and an uneasiness began to pervade the camp.

"Jondo, you'll have to dig up Gail now. I saw him putting out northwest about one o'clock," Rex Krane said, aside to the train captain.

"If he isn't here in ten minutes. I'll have to start out after him," Jondo replied.

Ten minutes are long to one who waits. The boys were ready for the camp order. "Catch up!" to start the harnessing of teams. But it was not given. The sun's level rays, hot and yellow, smote the camp, and a low murmur ran from wagon to wagon. Jondo waited a minute longer, then he climbed to the wagon tongue at the head of the ellipse of vehicles, his commanding form outlined against the open space, his fine face illumined by the sunlight.

"Boys, listen to me."

Men listened when Jondo spoke.

"I believe we are in danger, but you have doubted my word. I leave the days to prove who is right. At midnight I sent Gail Clarenden to find out what is beyond that ridge--a band of men running parallel with us that shadows us day by day. If he is not here in ten minutes, we must go after him."

A hush fell on the camp. The oxen switched at the first nipping insects of the morning, and the ponies and mules, with that horse-sense that all horsemen have observed in them at times, stood as if waiting for a decision to be made.

Beverly Clarenden was first to speak.

"If anybody goes after Gail, it's *me*, and I'll not stop till I get him," he cried, all the brotherly love of a lifetime in his ringing voice.

"And me!" "And me!" "And me!" came from a dozen throats. Plainsmen were always the truest of comrades in the hour of danger. Nobody questioned Jondo's wisdom now. All thought was for the missing man.

Rex Krane had leaped up on the wagon next to Jondo's and stood gazing toward the northwest. At this outburst of eagerness he turned to the crowd in the corral.

"You wait five minutes and Gail will be here. He's gettin' into sight out yonder now," he declared.

Another shout, a rush for the open, and a straining of eyes to make sure of the lone rider coming swiftly down the trail I had followed out at midnight. And amid a wild swinging of hats and whoops of joy I rode into camp, hugged by Beverly and questioned by everybody, eager for my story from the time I left the camp until I rode into it again.

"They took me to Pawnee Rock before they let me know anything, except that my scalp would hang to the old chief's war-spear if I tried one eye-wink to get away from them. But they let me keep my gun, and I took it for a sign," I told the company. "They had a lot of ceremony getting seated, and then, without any smoking-tobacco or peace-pipe, they gave their message."

"Who said the Kiowas wasn't friendly? They already sent us word enough," one man broke in.

Jondo's face, that had been bright and hopeful, now grew grave.

"They said they mean us no harm. They were grateful to Uncle Sam for the favors he had given them. That the prairies were wide, and there was room for all of us on it," I continued. "In proof, they said that we would pass that old rock to-day unharmed where once they would have counted us their enemies. And they let me go to bring you all this word. They are going northeast into the big hunting-ground, and we are safe."

No man could take defeat better than Jondo.

"I am glad if I was wrong in my opinion," he said. "Fifteen years on that trail have made me cautious. I shall still be cautious if I am your captain. They did not smoke the peace-pipe. In my judgment the Kiowas lied. Two or three days will prove it. Choose now between me and my unchanged opinion, and some new train captain."

"Oh, every man makes some bad guesses, Jondo. We'll keep you, of course, and it's a joke on you, that's all." So ran the comment, and we hurriedly broke camp and moved on.

But with all of our captain's anxiety Pawnee Rock stood like a protecting shield above us when we camped at its base, and the long bright days that followed were full of a sense of security and good cheer as we pulled away for the Cimarron crossing of the Arkansas River, miles ahead.

All day Jondo rode wide of the trail, sometimes on one side and sometimes on the other, watching for signs of an enemy. And the bluff, jovial crowd of bull-whackers laughed together at his holding on to his opinion out of sheer stubbornness.

On the second night he asked for a triple guard and nobody grumbled, for everybody really liked the big plainsman and they could afford to be good-natured with him, now that he was unquestioningly in the wrong.

The camp was in a little draw running down to the river, bordered by a mere ripple of ground on either side, growing deeper as it neared the stream and flattening out toward the level prairie in its upper portion. In spite of the triple guard, Jondo did not sleep that night; and, strangely enough, I, who had been dull to fear in the hands of the Indians two nights before, felt nervous and anxious, now when all seemed secure.

Just at daybreak a light shower with big bullet-like drops of rain pattered down noisily on our camp and a sudden flash of lightning and a thunderbolt startled the sleepy stock and brought us to our feet, dazed for an instant. Another light volley of rain, another sheet of lightning and roar of thunder, and the cloud was gone, scattering down the Arkansas Valley. But in that flash all of Jondo's cause for anxiety was justified. The widening draw was full of Kiowas, hideous in war-paint, and the ridges on either side of us were swarming with Indians beating dried skins to frighten and stampede our stock, and all yelling like fiends, while a perfect rain of arrows swept our camp. With the river below us full of holes and quicksands, our enemies had only to hold the natural defense on either side while they drove us in a harrowing wedge back to the water. If our ponies and mules should break from the corral they would rush for the river or be lost in the widening space back from the deeper draw, where a well-trained corps of thieves knew how to capture them. I had estimated the Kiowas' strength at four hundred, two nights before, which was augmented now by a roving band of Dog Indians--outcasts from all tribes, who knew no law of heaven or hell that they must obey. And so we stood, shocked wide awake, with the foe four to one, man for man against us.

Men remember details acutely in the face of danger. As I write these words I can hear the sound of Jondo's voice that morning, clear and strong above the awful din, for nature made him to command in moments of peril. In a flash we were marshalled, one force to guard the corral, one to seize and hold either bank and one to charge on the advance of the Indians down the draw. We were on the defensive, as our captain had planned we should be, and every man of us realized bitterly now how much he had done for us, in spite of our distrust of his judgment.

On came the yelling horde, with rifle-rip and singing arrow. And the sharp cry of pain and the fierce oath told where these shots had sped home. Four to one, with every advantage of well-laid plan of action against an unsuspecting sleeping force, the odds and gods were with them. Dark clouds hung overhead, but the eastern sky was aflame, casting a lurid glare across the edges of the draw as a stream of savages with painted faces and naked bedaubed bodies poured down against the corral. In an instant the chains and ropes holding the stock were severed, and our mules and oxen and ponies stampeded wildly. By some adroit movement they were herded over the low bank, and a cloud of dust hid the entire battleground as the animals, mad with fright and goaded by arrows, tossed against one another, stumbled blindly until they had cleared the ridge. A shriek of savage glee and the thunder of hoofs on the hard earth told how well the thing had been done and how furiously our animals were being whirled away.

"Go, get 'em, Gail! Stay by 'em! Run!"

Jondo's voice sounded far away, but my work was near. With a dozen bull-whackers I made a dash out of the draw and, circling wide, we rode like demons to outflank the cloud of dust that hid our precious property. On we swept, fleet and sure, in a mad burst of speed to save our own. We were gaining now, and turning the cloud toward the river. Another spurt, and we would have them checked, faced about, subdued. I saw the end, and as the boys swung forward I urged them on.

"To the river. To the river. Head 'em south!" I cried.

And Rex Krane, like a centaur, swirled by me to do the thing I ordered. Behind me rode Beverly Clarenden bareheaded, his face aglow with power. As I looked back the dust engulfed him for a moment, and then I heard an arrow sing, and a sharp cry of pain. The dust had lifted and Beverly and a huge Indian, the tallest I have ever seen, were grappling together, a scalping-knife gleaming in the morning light. I dashed forward and felled the savage with the butt of my revolver. He leaped to his feet and sprang at me just as Beverly, with unerring aim, sent a blaze of fire between us. As the savage fell again, my cousin seized his pony; and with an arrow still swinging to his arm, dashed into the chase, and left it only when the stock, with the loss of less than a fourth, was driven up the river's sandy bank and over the swell into the camp inclosure.

Meantime, Jondo at the front of his men charged into the very center of the savage battle-line as, furious for blood, they threshed across the narrow draw--the disciplined arm and courageous heart against a blood-thirsty foe. A charge, a falling back, another surge to win the lost ground, a steady holding on and sure advance, and then Jondo, with one triumphant shout of victory, struck the last fierce blow that sent the Kiowas into full flight toward the northwest, and the day was won.

Out by the river, a sudden dullness seized me. I lifted my eyes to see Beverly free and Rex directing the charge; cattle, mules, and ponies turned back toward safety, and something crawling and writhing about my feet;

Jondo's great shout of victory far away, it seemed, miles and miles to the north; a cloud of dust sweeping toward me; the crimson east aflame like the Day of judgment; the dust cloud rolling nearer; the yellow sands and slow-moving waters of the Arkansas; and six silent stalwart Kiowa braves, with snaky black eyes, looking steadily at me. Shadows, and the dust cloud upon me. Then all was night.

XII

THE BROTHERHOOD OF THE PLAINS

Deeper than speech our love, stronger than life our tether,
But we do not fall on the neck, nor kiss when we come together.
--"A SONG OF THE ENGLISH."

The whole thing was clear now, clear as the big white day that suddenly
beamed along the prairies, scattering the clouds into gray strands against the
upper heavens. The treachery of the Kiowas had been cleverly executed.
Word of their friendliness had come to us through the Mexican caravan
which could have no object in deceiving us, since it was on its way to
Kansas City to do business with the Clarenden house there. And Jondo had
sent a spy by night into the Kiowa camp as if they were not to be trusted.
Yet they had taken no offense; but, letting me keep my firearms, had led
me into their council on the top of Pawnee Rock, where they had told me
in clear English that they had nothing but love for the white brothers of the
plains. And to prove it we should pass unharmed along the trail where once
we had wronged them by stealing their captive. The prairies were wide
enough for all of us and they had forgotten--as an Indian always forgets--all
malice against us. They had sent me back to camp with greetings to my
captain, and had gone on their way to the heart of the Grand Prairie in the
northeast.

It was only Jondo, as he rode wide of the trail for two days, who could see
any mark of an Indian's track. And we had not believed Jondo. We never
made that mistake again: But trust in his shrewdness now, however, would
not bring back the oxen lost and the mules and ponies captured by the
thieving band of Dog Indians. But there was a greater loss than these. The
Kiowas had come for revenge. It was blood, not plunder, they wanted. A
dozen men with arrow wounds reported at roll call, and six men lay stark
dead under the pitiless sky. Among them Davis of the St. Louis train, who
had been too ill to take part in the struggle. One more loss was there to
report, but it was not discovered until later.

Indians seldom leave their dead on the field of battle, but the blood-stained
sod beside their fallen ponies told a story of heavy toll. Blood marked the
trail of hoofprints to the northwest in their wild rout thither. One comrade
they had missed in their flight. He lay down near the river where the
ground had been threshed over by the stampeded stock. He must have
been a giant in life, for his was the longest grave made in the prairie sod

that day. At the river's edge the sands were pricked with hoofprints, where the struggle to carry away the dead seemed to have reached clear into the thin yellow current of the Arkansas, although no trail led out on the far side of the stream.

"That's the very copper cuss with yellow trimmings who had me down when that arrow stopped me," Beverly exclaimed. "He was seven feet tall and streaked with yellow just that way. I thought ten million rattlesnakes and eight billion polecats had hit me. His club was awful. Then I caught sight of old Gail's face in the dust-storm, coming back to help me. He gave the Indian one dose and got one back, a good hard bill, and then the dust closed in and Gail was off again to the northwest out there, like a hurricane. I could hear him a mile away. Couldn't I Gail? Where is Gail?"

Where?

"Oh, back there with the stock!"

No?

"Out there looking over the draw for things that's got all scattered."

No? Not there?

"Oh, he's getting breakfast. And we are all hungry enough to eat raw Kiowas now."

No? No?

"Gail would be helping the wounded, anyhow, or straightening out dead men's limbs. Poor fellows--to lose six! It's awful!"

No? No? No?

"Bathing in the river? Where? Over there across the sand-bar?"

Nowhere! Nowhere!

"By the eternal God, they've got him!" Jondo's agonized voice rang through the camp.

"We can take care of the wounded, and those fellows lying over there don't need us. But, oh, Gail! They'll torture him to death!" Rex Krane's voice choked and he ground his teeth.

"Gail, my Gail!" Beverly sat down white and desparingly calm--Beverly, whose up-bubbling spirits nobody could repress.

The others wrung their hands and cursed and groaned aloud. Only Bill Banney, the unimaginative and stern-hearted, stood motionless with set jaws and black-frowning brows. Bill, whom the plains had made hard and unfeeling.

"We won't give up Gail, will we, Bill?" Jondo spoke sternly, but his face-- they said his face was bright with courage and that his eyes shone with the inspiration of his will. In all that crowd of eager, faithful men, he turned now to Bill Banney. Every man had his place on the plains, and Jondo out of the chrism of his own life-struggle knew that Bill was bearing a cross in silence, and that his was the martyr spirit that finds salvation only in deeds. Bill was the man for the place.

And so while straying animals were slowly recovered, while the camp was set in order, while the dead were laid with simple reverence in un-coffined graves, and the sick were crudely ministered to, while Beverly grew feverish and his arrow wound became a festering sore, and Rex Krane, master of the company, cared for every thing and everybody with that big mother-heart of his--Jondo and Bill Banney pushed alone across the desolate plains toward where the Smoky Hills wrapped in their dim gray-blue mist mark the low watershed that rims the western valley of the Kaw.

They went alone because skill, and not numbers, could save a captive from the hands of the Kiowas, and the sight of a force would mean death to the victim before he could be rescued.

A splash of water against a hot hand hanging down; a sense of light, of motion; a glimpse of coarse sands and thin straggling weeds beside the edge of the stream down which the pathway ran; a sharp aching at the base of the brain; an agony of strained muscles--thus slowly I came to my senses, to memory, to the knowledge that I was bound hand and foot to a pony's back; that the sun was hot, and the sands were hotter, and the glare on the waters blinding; that every splash of the pony's hoofs sent up glittering sparkles that stabbed my aching eyes like white-hot dagger-points; that the black and clotted dirt on the pony's shoulder was not mud, but blood; that before and behind were other splashing feet, all hiding the trail in the thin current of the wide old Arkansas; that the quick turns to follow the water and the need for speed gave no consideration to the helpless rider. The image of six pairs of snaky black eyes came to help the benumbed brain, and I knew with whom I was again captive. But there was no question about the friendly motive now, for there was no friendly motive now. And as we pushed on east, Jondo and Bill Banney were hurrying toward the northwest, and the space between us widened every minute. A wave of helplessness and despair swept over me; then a wild up-leaping prayer for deliverance to a far-away unpitying Heaven; a sudden sense of the futility of prayer in a land the Lord had forgotten; and then anger, hot and wholesome, and an unconquered, dominant will to gain freedom or to die game, swept every other feeling away, marvelously mastering the sense of pain that had ground mercilessly at every nerve. Then came that small voice which a man hears sometimes in the night stillness and sometimes in the blare of daylight wrangle. And all suddenly I knew that He who notes the sparrow's fall knew that I was alone with death, slow-lingering, inch-creeping death, out on that wide, lonely plain. The glare on the waters softened. The heat fell away. The despair and agony lifted. In all the world-- my world--there was only one, God; not a far, unpitying, book-made Lord beyond the height of the glaring blue dome above me. God beside me on, the yellow waters of the Arkansas. His hand in my hot hand! His strength about me, invisible, unbreakable, infinite. When a man enters into that shielding Presence, nothing else matters.

I do not know how many miles we went down-stream, leaving no trail in the shallow water or along its hard-baked edges. But by the time we dropped that line I had begun to think coherently and to take note of everything possible to me, bound as I was, face downward, on the pony's back. It was when we had left the river that the hard riding began, and a merciful unconsciousness, against which I fought, softened some stretches of that long day's journey. We crossed the Santa Fé Trail and were pushing eastward out of sight of it to the north. No stop, no word, nothing but ride, ride, ride. Truly, I needed the Presence that went with me on the way.

At sunset we stopped, and I was taken from my pony and thrown to the ground. I managed, in spite of my bonds, to sit up and look about me.

We were on the top of Pawnee Rock. The heat of the day was spent and all the radiant tints of evening were making the silent prairies unspeakably beautiful. I do not know why I should have noted or remembered any of this, save that the mind sometimes gathers impressions under strange stress of suffering. I had had no food all day, and when our ponies stopped to drink, the agony of thirst was maddening. My tongue was swollen and my lips were cracked and bleeding. The leather thongs that bound me cut deep now. But--only the men who lived it can know what all this meant to the pioneer of the trail.

I have sat on the same spot at sunset many a time in these my sunset years; have gazed in tranquil joy at the whole panorama of the heavens that hang over the prairies in the opalescent splendor of the after-sunset hour; have looked out over the earthly paradise of waving grain, all glowing with the golden gleam of harvest, in the heart of the rich Kansas wheat-lands--and somehow I'm glad of soul that I foreran this day and--maybe--maybe I, too, helped somewhat to build the way--the way that Esmond Clarenden had helped to clear a decade before and was building then.

The six Indians gathered near me. One of them with unmerciful mercy loosened my bonds a trifle and gave me a sup of water. They did not want me to die too soon. Then they sat down to eat and drink. I did not shut my eyes, nor turn my head. I defied their power to crush me, and the very defiance gave me strength.

The chill air of evening blew about the brow of the rock, the twilight deepened, and down in the valley the shadows were beginning to hide the landscape. But the evening hour is long on the headlands. And there was ample time for another kind of council than that to which I had listened three mornings ago, when I had been set free to bear a friendly message to my chief.

They carried me--helpless in their hands--to where, unseen myself, and secured by rock fragment and rawhide thong, I could see far up the trail to the eastward. But I could give no signal of distress, save for the feeble call of my swollen, thirst-parched throat. Then the six bronze sons of the plains sat down before me, and looked at me. Looked! I never see a pair of beady black eyes to-day--and there are many such--that I do not long to kill somebody, so vivid yet is the memory of those murdering eyes looking at me.

At last they spoke--plains English, it is true--but clear to give their meaning.

"Chief Clarenden thinks Kiowas forget. He comes with little train across the prairies; Kiowas go to meet big train east and fight fair for Mexican brothers who hate Chief Clarenden. They do not stop to look for little sneaking coyotes when they seek big game. Clarenden steals away Kiowas' captive Hopi. Cheat Kiowas of big pay that white Medicine-man Josef would give for her. Mexican brothers and Kiowa tribe hate Clarenden. They take his son, *you*, to show Clarenden they can steal, too. Hopi girl! white brave! all the same."

The speaker's words came deliberately, and he gave a contemptuous wave of the hand as he closed. And the six sat silent for a time. Then another voice broke the stillness.

"Yonder is your trail. Chief Clarenden and big white chiefs go by to Santa Fé to buy and sell and grow rich. Indian sell captives to grow rich! No! White chief not let Indians buy and sell. But we do not kill white dogs. We leave you here to watch the trail for wagon-trains. They may not come soon. They may not see you nor hear you. You can see them pass on their way to get rich. You can watch them. Hopi girl would have brought us big money. We get no richer. Watch white men go get rich. You may watch many days till sun dries your eyes. Nothing trouble you here. Watch the trail. No wild animal come here. No water drown you here. No fine meat make you ache with eating here. Watch."

The six looked long at me, and as the light faded their black eyes and dark faces seemed like the glittering eyes and hooked bills of six great dark birds of prey.

When the last sunset glow was in the west the six rose up and walked backward, still looking at me, until they passed my range of vision and I could only feel their eyes upon me. Then I heard the clatter of ponies' feet on the hard rock, the fainter stroke on the thin, sandy soil, the thud on the thickening sod. Thump, thump, thump, farther and farther and farther away. The west grew scarlet, deepened to purple and melted at last into the dull gray twilight that foreruns the darkness of night. One ray of pale gold shimmered far along toward the zenith and lost itself in the upper heavens, and the stars came forth in the blue-black eastern sky. And I was alone with the Presence whose arm is never shortened and whose ear grows never heavy.

The trail to the east was only a dull line along the darker earth. I looked up at the myriad stars coming swiftly out of space to greet me. The starlit sky above the open prairie speaks the voice of the Infinite in a grandeur never matched on land or sea.

I thought of Little Blue Flower on that dim-lighted dawning when she had showed us her bleeding hands and lashed shoulders. And again I heard Beverly's boyish voice ring out:

"Let's take her and take our chances."

And then I was beside the glistening waters of the Flat Rock, and Little Blue Flower was there in her white Grecian robe and the wrought-silver headband with coral pendants. And Eloise. The golden hair, the soft dark eyes, the dainty peach-bloom cheek. Eloise whom I had loved always and always. Eloise who loved Beverly--good, big-hearted, sunny-faced Beverly, who never had visions. Any girl would love him. Most of all, Little Blue Flower. What a loving message she had left us in the one word, *Lolomi.* God pity her.

A thousand sharp pains racked my body. I tried to move. I longed for water. Then a merciful darkness fell upon me--not sleep, but unconsciousness. And the stars watched over me through that black night, lying there half dead and utterly alone.

Out to the northwest Jondo and Bill Banney rode long on the trail of the fleeing Kiowas. A picture for an artist of the West, these two rough men in the garb and mount and trappings of the plainsman, with eyes alert and strong faces, riding only as men can ride who go to save a life more eagerly than they would save their own. Not in rash haste, but with unchecked speed, losing no mark along the trail that should guide them more quickly to their goal, so they passed side by side, and neither said a word for hours along the way. Night came, and the needs of their ponies made them pause briefly. The trail, too, was harder to follow now. They might lose it in the darkness and so lose time. And those two men were going forth to victory. Not for one single heart-beat did they doubt their power to win, and the stead-fast assurance made them calm.

Daylight again, and a fresher trail made them hurry on. They drank at every stream and ate a snatch of food as they rode. They reached the hurriedly quitted Kiowa camp, and searched for the sign of vengeance on a captive there. Jondo knew those signs, and his heart beat high with hope.

"They haven't done it yet," he said to his companion. "They want to get away first. We are safe for a day."

And they rode swiftly on again.

"There's trouble here," Bill Banney declared as he watched the ground. "Too many feet. Could it be here?"

His voice was hardly audible. The two men halted and read the ground with piercing eyes. Something had happened, for there had been a circling and chasing in and out, and the sod was cut deep with hoofprints.

"No council nor ceremony, no open space for anything." Jondo would not even speak the word he was bound not to know.

"They've divided, Jondo. Here goes the big crowd, and there a smaller one," Bill declared.

"There were a lot of Dog Indians along for thieving. They've split here. Seem to have fussed a bit over it, too. And yonder runs the Kiowa trail to the north. Here go the Dogs east." Jondo replied. "We'll follow the Kiowas a spell," he added, after a thoughtful pause.

And again they were off. It was nearing noon now, and the trail was fresher every minute. At last the plainsmen climbed a low swell, halting out of sight on the hither side. Then creeping to the crest, they looked down on the Indian camp lying in a little dry valley of a lost stream whose course ran underground beneath them.

Lying flat on the ground, each with his head behind a low bush on the top of the swell, the men read the valley with searching eyes. Then Jondo, with Bill at his heels, slid swiftly down the slope.

"Gail Clarenden isn't there. We must take the trail east, and ride hard," he said, in a hoarse voice.

And they rode hard until they were beyond the range of the Kiowa outposts.

"What's your game, Jondo?" Bill asked, at length.

"They quarreled back there. Either the Dogs have Gail, or he's lost somewhere. The Kiowas are waiting for something. I can't quite understand, but we'll go on."

It was mid-afternoon and the two riders were faint from the hardship of the chase, but nobody who knew Jondo ever expected him to give up. The sun blazed down in the heat of the late afternoon, and the baking earth lay brown and dry beneath the heat-quivering air. There was no sound nor motion on the plains as the two faithful brothers--in purpose--followed hard on the track of the Dog Indian band.

Ahead of them the trail grew clearer until they saw the object of their chase, a band nearly a hundred strong, riding slowly, far ahead. Jondo and Bill halted and dropped to the ground. No cover was in sight, but if the Indians were unsuspicious they might not be discovered. On went the outlaw band, and the two white men followed after. Suddenly the Indians halted and grouped themselves together. The plainsmen watched eagerly for the cause. Out of the south six Indians came riding swiftly into view. They, too, halted, but neither group seemed aware that the two dull, motionless spots to the west were two white men watching them. White men didn't belong there.

The six rode forward. There was much parleying and pointing eastward. Then the six rode rapidly northward and the Dog band spurted east as rapidly.

Jondo looked at Bill.

"I see it clear as day. God help us not to be too late!" he cried, triumphantly, leaping to his saddle.

"What in Heaven's name to you see?" Bill asked eagerly.

"Gail wasn't with the Kiowas back there. He wasn't with the Dogs out yonder. Don't you remember he told us about six of the devils getting him in their friendly camp that morning? Yonder go the six. They have left Gail somewhere to die and they are cutting back to join the tribe. They have sent the Dogs on east. We'll run down this trail to the south. Hurry, Bill! For God's sake, hurry! It's the Lord's mercy they didn't see us back here."

That day Pawnee Rock saw the same old beauty of sunrise; the same clear sweeping breeze; the same long shining hours on the green prairies; but it all meant nothing to me, racked with pain and choking with thirst through the awful lengths of that summer day. Fitful unconsciousness, with fever and delirium, seeing mocking faces with snaky black eyes, looking long at me; food almost touching my lips, and floods of crystal waters everywhere just out of reach. I was on the bluff above the river at Fort Leavenworth again, watching for the fish on the sand-bars. They were Indians instead of fish, and they laughed at me and called me a big brown bob-cat. Then Mother Bridget and Aunty Boone would have come to me if I could only make them hear me. But the sun beat hot upon my burning face, and my swollen lips refused to moan.

And then I looked to the eastward and hope sprang to life within me. A wagon-train was crawling slowly toward Pawnee Rock. Tears drenched my eyes until I could hardly count the wagons--twenty, thirty, forty. It must be far in the afternoon now, and they might encamp here. But they seemed to be hurrying. I could not see for pain, but I knew they were near the headland now. I could hear the rattle of the wagon-chains and the tramp of feet and shouts of the bull-whackers. I tugged masterfully at my bonds. It was a useless effort. I tried to shout, but only low moans came forth from my parched lips. I strove and raged and prayed. The wagons hurried on and on, a long time, for there were many of them. Then the rattling grew fainter, the voices were far off, the thud of hoof-beats ceased. The train had passed the Rock, never dreaming that a man lay dying in sight of the succor they would so gladly have given.

The sun began to strike in level rays across the land, and the air was cooler, but I gave no heed to things about me. Death was waiting--slow, taunting death. The stars would be kind again to-night as they had been last night, but death crouching between me and the starlight, was slowly crawling up Pawnee Rock. Oh, so slowly, yet so surely creeping on. The sun was gone and a tender pink illumined the sky. The light was soft now. If death would only steal in before the glare burst forth. I forgot that night must come first. Pity, God of heaven, pity me!

And then the Presence came, and a sweet, low voice--I hear it still sometimes, when sunsets soften to twilight, "*My presence shall go with thee, and I will give thee rest.*" I felt a thrill of triumph pulse through my being. Unconquered, strong, and glad is he who trusts.

"I shall not die. I shall live, and in God's good time I shall be saved." I tried to speak the words, but I could not hear my voice. My pains were gone and I lay staring at the evening sky all mother-of-pearl and gold above my head. And on my lips a smile.

And so they found me at twilight, as a tired child about to fall asleep. They did not cry out, nor fall on my neck, nor weep. But Bill Banney's strong arms carried me tenderly away. Water, food, unbound swollen limbs, bathed in the warm Arkansas flow, soft grass for a bed, and the eyes of the big plainsman, my childhood idol, gentle as a girl's, looking unutterable things into my eyes.

I've never known a mother's love, but for that loss the Lord gave me-- Jondo.

XIII

IN THE SHELTER OF SAN MIGUEL

Fear not, dear love, thy trial hour shall be
The dearest bond between my heart and thee.
--ALL THE YEAR ROUND.

When we reached the end of the trail and entered a second time into Santa Fé the Stars and Stripes were floating lazily above the Palace of the Governors. Out on the heights beyond the old Spanish prison stood Fort Marcy, whose battlements told of a military might, strong to control what by its strength it had secured. In its shadow was La Garita, of old the place of execution, against whose blind wall many a prisoner had started on the long trail at the word of a Spanish bullet, La Garita changed now from a thing of legalized horror to a landmark of history.

But the city itself seemed unchanged, and there was little evidence that Yankee thrift and energy had entered New Mexico with the new government. The narrow street still marked the trail's end before the Exchange Hotel. San Miguel, with its dun walls and triple-towered steeple, still good guard over the soul of Santa Fé, as it had stood for three sunny centuries. The Mexican still drove down the loaded burro-train of firewood from the mountains. The Indian basked in the sunny corners of the Plaza. The adobe dwellings clustered blindly along little lanes leading out to nowhere in particular. The orchards and cornfields, primitively cultivated, made tiny oases beside the trickling streams and sandy beds of dry arroyos. The sheep grazed on the scant grasses of the plain. The steep gray mesa slopes were splotched with clumps of evergreen shrubs and piñon trees. And over all the silent mountains kept watch.

The business house of Felix Narveo, however, did not share in this lethargy. The streets about the Plaza were full of Conestoga wagons, with tired ox-teams lying yoked or unyoked before them. Most of the traffic borne in by these came directly or indirectly to the house of Narveo. And its proprietor, the same silent, alert man, had taken advantage of a less restricted government, following the Mexican War, to increase his interests. So mine and meadow, flock and herd, trappers' snare and Indian loom and forge, all poured their treasures into his hands--a clearing-house for the products of New Mexico to swell the great overland commerce that followed the Santa Fé Trail.

For all of which the ground plan had been laid mainly by Esmond Clarenden, when with tremendous daring he came to Santa Fé and spied out the land for these years to follow.

A boy's memory is keen, and all the hours of that other journey hither, with their eager anticipation and youthful curiosity, and love of surprise and adventure, came back to Beverly Clarenden and me as we pulled along the last lap of the trail.

"Was it really so long ago, Bev, that we came in here, all eyes and ears?" I asked my cousin.

"No, it was last evening. And not an eyebrow in this Rip Van Winkle town has lifted since," Beverly replied. "Yonder stands that old church where the gallant knight on a stiff-legged pony spied Little Lees and knocked the head off of that tormenting Marcos villain, and kicked it under the door-step. Say, Gail, I'd like mighty well to see the grown-up Little Lees, wouldn't you? And I'd as soon this was Saint Louis as Santa Fé."

Since the night of Mat's wedding, I had been resolutely putting away all thought of Eloise St. Vrain. I belonged to the plains. All my training had been for this. I thought I was very old and settled now. But the mention of her pet name sent a thrill through me; and these streets of Santa Fé brought back a flood of memories and boyhood dreams and visions.

"Bev, how many auld-lang-syners do you reckon we'll meet in this land of sunshine and *chilly* beans?" I asked, carelessly.

"Well, how many of them do you remember, Mr. Cyclopedia of Prominent Men and Pretty Women?" Beverly inquired.

"Oh, there was Felix Narveo and Father Josef--and Little Blue Flower"--A shadow flitted across my cousin's face for a moment, leaving it sunny as ever again.

"And there was that black-eyed Marcos boy everywhere, and Ferdinand Ramero whom we were warned to step wide of," I went on.

"Oh, that tall thin man with blue-glass eyes that cut your fingers when he looked at you. Maybe he went out the back door of New Mexico when General Kearny peeped in at the front transom. There wasn't any fight in that man."

"Jondo says he is still in Santa Fé." Just as I spoke an Indian swept by us, riding with the ease of that born-to-the-horseback race.

"Beverly, do you remember that Indian boy that we saw out at Agua Fria?" I asked.

"The day we found Little Lees asleep in the church?" Beverly broke in, eagerly.

In our whole journey he had hardly spoken of Eloise, and, knowing Beverly as I did, I had felt sure for that reason that she had not been on his mind. Now twice in five minutes he had called her name. But why should he not remember her here, as well as I?

"Yes, I remember there was an Indian boy, sort of sneaky like, and deaf and dumb, that followed us until I turned and stared him out of it. That's the way to get rid of 'em, Gail, same as a savage dog," Beverly said, lightly.

"What if there are six of them all staring at you?" I asked.

"Oh, Gail, for the Lord's sake forget that!"

Beverly cried, affectionately. "When you've got an arrow wound rotting your arm off and six hundred and twenty degrees of fever in your blood, and the son of your old age is gone for three days and nights, and you don't dare to think where, you'll know why a fellow doesn't want to remember." There were real tears in the boy's eyes. Beverly was deeper than I had thought.

"Well, to change gradually, I wonder if that centaur who just passed us might be that same Indian of Agua Fria of long ago."

"He couldn't be," Beverly declared, confidently. "That boy got one square look at my eagle eye and he never stopped running till he jumped into the Pacific Ocean. 'I shall see him again over there.'" Half chanting the last words, Beverly, boy-hearted and daring and happy, cracked his whip, and our mule-team began to prance off in mule style the journey's latter end.

Oh, Beverly! Beverly! Why did that day on the parade-ground at Fort Leavenworth and a boy's pleading face lifted to mine, come back to me at that moment? Strange are the lines of life. I shall never clearly read them all.

Down in the Plaza a tall, slender young man was sitting in the shade, idly digging at the sod with an open pocket-knife. There was something magnetic about him, the presence that even in a crowd demands a second look.

He was dressed in spotless white linen, and with his handsome mustache, his well-groomed black hair, and sparkling black eyes, he was a true type of the leisure son of the Spanish-Mexican grandee. He stared at our travel-stained caravan as it rolled down the Plaza's edge, but his careless smile changed to an insolent grin, showing all his perfect teeth as he caught sight of Beverly and me.

We laid no claims to manly beauty, but we were stalwart young fellows, with the easy strength of good health, good habits, clear conscience, and the frank faces of boys reared on the frontier, and accustomed to its dangers by men who defied the very devil to do them harm. But even in our best clothes, saved for the display at the end of the trail, we were uncouth compared to this young gentleman, and our tanned faces and hard brown hands bespoke the rough bull-whacker of the plains.

As our train halted, the young man lighted a cigar and puffed the smoke toward us, as if to ignore our presence.

"Its mamma has dressed it up to go and play in the park, but it mustn't speak to little boys, nor soil its pinafore, nor listen to any naughty words. And it couldn't hold its own against a kitten. Nice little clothes-horse to hang white goods on!"

Beverly had turned his back to the Plaza and was speaking in a low tone, with the serious face and far-away air of one who referred to a thing of the past.

"Bev, you are a mind-reader, a character-sketcher--" I began, but stopped short to stare into the Plaza beyond him.

The young man had sprung to his feet and stood there with flashing eyes and hands clenched. Behind him was the same young Indian who had passed us on the trail. He was lithe, with every muscle trained to strength and swiftness and endurance.

He had muttered a word into the young white man's ear that made him spring up. And while the face of the Indian was expressionless, the other's face was full of surprise and anger; and I recognized both faces in an instant.

"Beverly Clarenden, there are two auld-lang-syners behind you right now. One is Marcos Ramero, and the other is Santan of Bent's Fort," I said, softly.

Beverly turned quickly, something in his fearless face making the two men drop their eyes. When we looked again they had left the Plaza by different ways.

After dinner that evening Jondo and Bill Banney hurried away for a business conference with Felix Narveo. Rex and Beverly also disappeared and I was alone.

The last clear light of a long summer day was lingering over the valley of the Rio Grande, and the cool evening breeze was rippling in from the mountains, when I started out along the narrow street that made the terminal of the old Santa Fé Trail. I was hardly conscious of any purpose of direction until I came to the half-dry Santa Fé River and saw the spire of San Miguel beyond it. In a moment the same sense of loss and longing swept over me that I had fought with on the night after Mat's wedding, when I sat on the bluff and stared at the waters of the Kaw flowing down to meet the Missouri. And then I remembered what Father Josef had said long ago out by the sandy arroyo:

"Among friends or enemies, the one haven of safety always is the holy sanctuary."

I felt the strong need for a haven from myself as I crossed the stream and followed the trail up to the doorway of San Miguel.

The shadows were growing long, few sounds broke the stillness of the hour, and the spirit of peace brooded in the soft light and sweet air. I had almost reached the church when I stopped suddenly, stunned by what I saw. Two people were strolling up the narrow, crooked street that wanders eastward beside the building--a tall, slender young man in white linen clothes and a girl in a soft creamy gown, with a crimson scarf draped about her shoulders. They were both bareheaded, and the man's heavy black hair and curling black mustache, and the girl's coronal of golden braids and the profile of her fair face left no doubt about the two. It was Marcos Ramero and Eloise St. Vrain. They were talking earnestly; and in a very lover-like manner the young man bent down to catch his companion's words.

Something seemed to snap asunder in my brain, and from that moment I knew myself; knew how futile is the belief that miles of prairie trail and strength of busy days can ever cast down and break an idol of the heart.

In a minute they had passed a turn in the street, and there was only sandy earth and dust-colored walls and a yellow glare above them, where a moment ago had been a shimmer of sunset's gold.

"The one haven of safety always is the holy sanctuary."

Father Josef's words sounded in my ears, and the face of old San Miguel seemed to wear a welcoming smile. I stepped into the deep doorway and stood there, aimless and unthinking, looking out toward where the Jemez Mountains were outlined against the southwest horizon. Presently I caught the sound of feet, and Marcos Ramero strode out of the narrow street and followed the trail into the heart of the city.

I stared after him, noting the graceful carriage, the well-fitting clothes, and the proud set of the handsome head. There was no doubt about him. Did he hold the heart of the golden-haired girl who had walked into my life to stay? As he passed out of my sight Eloise St. Vrain came swiftly around the corner of the street to the church door, and stopped before me in wide-eyed amazement. Eloise, with her clinging creamy draperies, and the vivid red of her silken scarf, and her glorious hair.

"Oh, Gail Clarenden, is it really you?" she cried, stretching out both hands toward me with a glad light in her eyes.

"Yes, Little Lees, it is I."

I took both of her hands in mine. They were soft and white, and mine were brown and horny, but their touch sent a thrill of joy through me. She clung tightly to my hands for an instant. Then a deeper pink swept her cheeks, and she dropped her eyes and stepped back.

"They told me you were--lost--on the way; that some Kiowas had killed you."

She lifted her face again, and heaven had not anything better for me than the depths of those big dark eyes looking into mine.

"Who told you, Eloise?"

The girl looked over her shoulder apprehensively, and lowered her voice as she replied:

"Marcos Ramero."

"He's a liar. I am awfully alive, and Marcos Ramero knows I am, for he saw me and recognized me down in the Plaza this afternoon," I declared.

Just then the church door opened and a girl in Mexican dress came out. I did not see her face, nor notice which way she took, for a priest following her stepped between us. It was Father Josef.

"My children, come inside. The holy sanctuary offers you a better shelter than the open street."

I shall never forget that voice, nor hear another like it. Inside, the candles were burning dimly at the altar. The last rays of daylight came through the high south windows, touching the carved old rafters and gray adobe with a red glow. Long ago human hands, for lack of trowels, had laid that adobe surface on the rough stone--hands whose imprint is graven still on those crudely dented walls.

We sat down on a low seat inside of the doorway, and Father Josef passed up the aisle to the altar, leaving us there alone.

"Eloise, Marcos Ramero is your friend, and I beg your pardon for speaking of him as I did."

I resented with all my soul the thought of this girl caring for the son of the man who in some infamous way had wronged Jondo, but I had no right to be rude about him.

"Gail, may I say something to you?" The voice was as a pleading call and the girl's farce was full of pathos.

"Say on, Little Lees," was all that I could venture to answer.

"Do you remember the day you came in here and threw Marcos Ramero out of that door?"

"I do," I replied.

"Would you do it again, if it were necessary? I mean--if--" the voice faltered.

I had heard the same pleading tone on the night of Mat's wedding when Eloise and Beverly were in the little side porch together. I looked up at the red light on the old church rafters and the rough gray walls. How like to those hand-marked walls our memories are, deep-dented by the words they hold forever! Then I looked down at the girl beside me and I forgot everything else. Her golden hair, her creamy-white dress, and that rich crimson scarf draped about her shoulders and falling across her knees would have made a Madonna's model that old Giovanni Cimabue himself would have joyed to copy.

"Is it likely to be necessary? Be fair with me, Eloise. I saw you two strolling up that little goat-run of a street out there just now. Judging from the back of his head, Marcos looked satisfied. I shouldn't want to interfere nor make you any trouble," I said, earnestly.

"It is I who should not make you any trouble, but, oh, Gail, I came here this evening because I was afraid and I didn't know where else to go, and I found you. I thought you were dead somewhere out on the Kansas prairie. Maybe it was to help me a little that you came here to-night."

Her hands were gripped tightly and her mouth was firm-set in an effort to be brave.

"Why, Eloise, I'd never let Marcos Ramero, nor anybody else, make you one little heart-throb afraid. If you will only let me help you, I wouldn't call it trouble; I'd call it by another name." The longing to say more made me pause there.

The light was fading overhead, but the church lamps gave a soft glow that seemed to shield off the shadowy gloom.

"Father Josef came all the way from New Mexico to St. Ann's to have me come back here, and Mother Bridget sent Sister Anita, you remember her, up to St. Louis to come with me by way of New Orleans. I didn't tell you that I might be here when your train came in overland because--because of some things about my own people--"

The fair head was bowed and the soft voice trembled.

"Don't be afraid to tell me anything, Little Lees," I whispered, assuringly.

"I never saw my father, but my mother was very beautiful and loving, and we were so happy together. I was still a very little girl when she fell sick and they took me away from her. I never knew when she died nor where she was buried. Ferdinand Ramero had charge of her property. He controlled everything after she went away, and I have always lived in fear of his word. I am helpless when he commands, for he has a strange power over minds; and as to Marcos--you know what a little cat I was. I had to be to live with him. It wasn't until we were all at Bent's Fort that I got over my fear of you and Beverly. The day you threw Marcos out of here was the first time I ever had a champion to defend me."

I wanted to take her in my arms and tell her what I dared not think she would let me say. So I listened in sympathetic silence.

"Then came an awful day out at Agua Fria, and Father Josef took me in his arms as he would take a baby, and sang me to sleep with the songs my mother loved to sing. I think it must have been midnight when I wakened. It was dreary and cold, and Esmond Clarenden and Ferdinand Ramero were there, and Father Josef and Jondo."

And then she told me, as she remembered them, the happenings of that night at Agua Fria, the same story that Jondo told me later. But until that evening I had known nothing of how Eloise had come to us.

"You know the rest," Eloise went on "I have had a boarding-school life, and no real friends, except the Clarenden family, outside of these schools."

"You poor little girl! One of the same Clarenden family is ready to be your friend now," I said, tenderly, remembering keenly how Uncle Esmond and Jondo had loved and protected three orphan children.

"The Rameros think nobody but a Ramero can do that now. Marcos is very much changed. He has been educated in Europe, is handsome, and courtly in his manners, and as his father's heir he will be wealthy. He came to-night to ask me, to urge and plead with me, to marry him." Eloise paused.

"Do you need the defense of a bull-whacker of the plains against these things?" I asked.

"Oh, I could depend on myself if it were only Marcos. He comes with polished ways and pleasing words," Eloise replied. "It is his father's iron fist back of him that strikes at me through his graciousness. He tells me that all the St. Vrain money, which he controls by the terms of my father's will, he can give to the Church, if he chooses, and leave me disinherited."

"We don't mind that a bit as a starter up in Kansas. Come out on our prairies and try it," I suggested.

"But, Gail, that isn't all. There is something worse, dreadfully worse, that I cannot tell you, that only the Rameros know, and hold like a sword over my head. If I marry Marcos his father will destroy all evidence of it and I shall have a handsome, talented, rich husband." Eloise bowed her head and clasped her hands, crushed by the misery of her lot.

"And if you refuse to marry this scoundrel?" I asked, bluntly.

"Then I will be a penniless outcast. The Rameros are powerful here, and the Church will be with them, for it will get my inheritance. I am helpless and alone and I don't know what to do."

I think I had never known what anger meant before. This beautiful girl, homeless, and about to be robbed of her fortune, reared in luxury, with no chance for developing self-reliance and courage, was being hemmed in and forced to a marriage by threats of poverty and a secret something against which she was powerless. All the manhood in me rallied to her cause, and she was an hundredfold dearer to me now, in her helplessness.

"Eloise, I'm a horny-handed driver of a bull-team on the Santa Fé Trail, but you will let me help you if I can. So far as your money is concerned, there's a lot of it on earth, even if the Church should grab up your little bit because Ferdinand Ramero says your father's will permits it. There are evil representatives in every Church, no matter what its name may be, Catholic, Protestant, Indian, or Jew, but Father Josef up there is bigger than his priestly coat, and you can trust that size anywhere. And as to the knowledge of this 'something' known just to Ferdinand Ramero, if he is the only one who knows it, it is too small to get far, if it were turned loose. And any man who would use such infamous means to get what he wants is too small to have much influence if he doesn't get it. This is a big, wide, good world, Little Lees, and the father of Marcos Ramero, with all his power and wealth, has a short lariat that doesn't let him graze wide. Jondo holds the other end of that lariat, and he knows."

Eloise listened eagerly, but her face was very white.

"Gail, you don't know the Ramero blood. I am helpless and terrified with them in spite of their suave manners and flattering words. Why did Father

Josef bring me back here if the Church is not with them? And then that awful shadow of some hidden thing that may darken my life. I know their cruel, pitiless hearts. They stop at nothing when they want their way. I have known them to do the most cold-blooded deeds."

Poor Eloise! The net about her had been skilfully drawn.

"I don't know Father Josef's motive, but I can trust him. And no shadow shall trouble you long, Little Lees. Jondo and Uncle Esmond `tote together,' Aunty Boone said long ago. They know something about the Ramero blood, and Jondo has promised to tell me his story some day. He must do it to-night, and to-morrow we'll see the end of this tangle. Trust me, Eloise," I said, comfortingly.

"But, Gail, I'm afraid Ferdinand will kill you if you get in his way." Eloise clung to my arm imploringly.

"Six big Kiowas got fooled at that job. Do you think this thin streak of humanity would try it?" I asked, lightly.

Eloise stood up beside me.

"I must go away now," she said.

"Then I'll go with you. Thank you, Father Josef, for your kindness," I said as the priest came toward us.

"You are welcome, my son. In the sanctuary circle no harm can come. Peace be with both of you."

There was a world of benediction in his deep tones, and his smile was genial, as he followed us to the street and stood as if watching for some one.

"I will meet you at San Miguel's to-morrow afternoon, Gail," Eloise said, as we reached a low but pretentious adobe dwelling. "This is my home now."

"Your new Mexican homes are thick-walled, and you live all on the inside," I said, as we paused at the doorway. "They make me think of the lower invertebrates, hard-shelled, soft-bodied animals. Up on the Kansas prairies and the Missouri bluffs we have a central vetebra--the family hearth-stone-- and we live all around it. That is the people who have them do. There isn't much home life for a freighter of the plains anywhere. Good by, Little

Lees." I took her offered hand. "I'm glad you have let me be your friend, a hard-shelled bull-whacker like me."

The street was full of shadows and the evening air was chill as the door closed on that sweet face and cloud of golden hair. But the pressure of warm white fingers lingered long in my sense of touch as I retraced my steps to the trail's end. At the church door I saw Father Josef still waiting, as if watching for somebody.

All that Eloise had told me ran through my mind, but I felt sure that neither financial nor churchly influence in Santa Fé could be turned to evil purposes so long as men like Felix Narveo and Father Josef were there. And then I thought of Esmond Clarenden, himself neither Mexican nor Roman Catholic, who, nevertheless, drew to himself such fair-dealing, high-minded men as these, always finding the best to aid him, and combating the worst with daring fearlessness. Surely with the priest and the merchant and Jondo as my uncle's representative, no harm could come to the girl whom I knew that I should always love.

And with my mind full of Eloise and her need I sought out Jondo and listened to his story.

XIV

OPENING THE RECORD

Fighting for leave to live and labor well,
God flung me peace and ease.
--"A SONG OF THE ENGLISH."

I found Jondo in the little piazza opening into the hotel court.

"Where did you leave Krane and Bev?" he asked, as I sat down beside him.

"I didn't leave them; they left me," I answered.

"Oh, you young bucks are all alike. You know just enough to be good to yourselves. You don't think much about anybody else," Jondo said, with a smile.

"I think of others, Jondo, and for that reason I want you to tell me that story about Ferdinand Ramero that you promised to tell me one night back on the trail."

Jondo gave a start.

"I'd like to forget that man, not talk about him," he replied.

"But it is to help somebody else, not just to be good to myself, that I want to know it," I insisted, using his own terms. And then I told him what Eloise had told me in the San Miguel church.

"Are the Ramero's so powerful here that they can control the Church in their scheme to get what they want?" I asked.

"It would be foolish to underestimate the strength of Ferdinand Ramero," Jondo replied, adding, grimly, "It has been my lot to know the best of men who could make me believe all men are good, and the worst of men who make me doubt all humanity." He clenched his fists as if to hold himself in check, and something, neither sigh nor groan nor oath nor prayer, but like them all, burst from his lips.

"If you ever have a real cross, Gail, thank the Lord for the green prairies and the open plains, and the danger-stimulus of the old Santa Fé Trail. They will seal up your wounds, and soften your hard, rebellious heart, and make you see things big, and despise the narrow little crooks in your path."

One must have known Jondo, with his bluff manner and sunny smile and daring spirit, to feel the force, of these brave sad words. I felt intuitively that I had laid bare a wound of his by my story.

"It is for Eloise, not for my curiosity, that I have come to you," I said, gently. "And you didn't come too soon, boy." Jondo was himself in a moment. "It is another cruel act in the old tragedy of Ramero against Clarenden and others."

"Will the Church be bribed by the St. Vrain estate and urge this wedding?" I asked.

"The Church considers money as so much power for the Kingdom. I have heard that the St. Vrain estate was left in Ramero's hands with the proviso that if Eloise should marry foolishly before she was twenty-five she, would lose her property. Do you see the trick in the game, and why Ramero can say that if he chooses he can take her heritage away from her? But as he keeps everything in his own hands it is hard to know the truth about anything connected with money matters."

"Would Father Josef be party to such a transaction?" I asked, angrily.

"Ramero thinks so, but he is mistaken," Jondo replied.

"What makes you think he won't be?" I insisted.

"Because I knew Father Josef before he became a priest, and why he took the vows," Jondo declared. "Unless a man brings some manhood to the altar, he will not find it in the title nor the dress there, it makes no difference whether he be Catholic, Protestant, Hebrew, or heathen. Father Josef was a gentleman before he was a priest."

"Well, if he's all right, why did he bring Eloise back here into the heart of all this trouble?" I questioned.

Jondo sat thinking for a little while, then he said, assuringly:

"I don't know his motive, unless he felt he could protect her here himself; but I tell you, my boy, he can be trusted. Let me tell you something, Gail.

When Esmond Clarenden and I were boys back in a New England college we knew two fellows from the Southwest whose fathers were in official circles at Washington. One was Felix Narveo, thoroughbred Mexican, thoroughbred gentleman, a bit lacking in initiative sometimes, for he came from the warmer, lazier lands, but as true as the compass in his character. The other fellow was Dick Verra, French father, English mother; I think he had a strain of Indian blood farther back somewhere, but he would have been a prince in any tribe or nation. A happy, wholesome, red-blooded, young fellow, with the world before him for his conquest.

"We knew another fellow, too, Fred Ramer, self-willed, imperious, extravagant in his habits, greedy and unscrupulous; but he was handsome and masterful, with a compelling magnetism that made us admire him and bound us to him. He had never known what it meant to have a single wish denied him. And with his make-up, he would stop at nothing to have his own way, until his wilful pride and stubbornness and love of luxury ruined him. But in our college days we were his satellites. He was always in debt to all of us, for money was his only god and we never dared to press him for payment. The only one of us who ever overruled him was Dick Verra. But Dick was a born master of men. There was one other chum of ours, but I'll tell you about him later. Boys together, we had many escapades and some serious problems, until by the time our college days were over we were bound together by those ties that are made in jest and broken with choking voices and eyes full of tears."

Jondo paused and I waited, silent, until he should continue.

"Things happened to that little group of college men as time went on. You know your uncle's life, leading merchant of Kansas City and the Southwest; and mine, plainsman and freighter on the Santa Fé Trail. Felix Narveo's history is easily read. Esmond Clarenden came down here at the outbreak of the Mexican War, and together he and Narveo laid the foundation for the present trail commerce that is making the country at either end of it rich and strong. Dick Verra is now Father Josef." Jondo paused as if to gather force for the rest of the story. Then he said:

"Back at college we all knew Mary Marchland, a beautiful Louisiana girl who visited in Washington and New England, and all of us were in love with her. When our life-lines crossed again Clarenden had come to St. Louis. About that time his two older brothers and their wives died suddenly of yellow fever, leaving you and Beverly alone. It was Felix Narveo who brought you up to St. Louis to your uncle."

"I remember that. The steamboat, and the Spanish language, and Felix Narveo's face. I recalled that when I saw him years ago," I exclaimed.

"You always were all eyes and ears, remembering names and faces, where Beverly would not recall anything," Jondo declared.

"And what became of your Fred Ramer?" I asked.

"He is Ferdinand Ramero here. He married Narveo's sister later. She is not the mother of Marcos, but a second wife. She owned a tract of land inherited from the Narveo estate down in the San Christobal country. There is a lonely ranch house in a picturesque cañon, and many acres of grazing-land. She keeps it still as hers, although her stepson, Marcos, claims it now. It is for her sake that Narveo doesn't dare to move openly against Ramero. And in his masterful way he has enough influence with a certain ring of Mexicans here, some of whom are Narveo's freighters, to reach pretty far into the Indian country. That's why I knew those Mexicans were lying to us about the Kiowas at Pawnee Rock. I could see Ramero's gold pieces in their hands. He joined the Catholic Church, and plays the Pharisee generally. But the traits of his young manhood, intensified, still his. He is handsome, and attractive, and rich, and influential, but he is also cold-blooded, and greedy for money until it is his ruling passion, villainously unscrupulous, and mercilessly unforgiving toward any one who opposes his will; and his capacity for undying hatred is appalling."

And this was the man who was seeking to control the life of Eloise St. Vrain. I fairly groaned in my anger.

"The failure to win Mary Marchland's love was the first time in his life that Fred Ramer's will had ever been thwarted, and he went mad with jealousy and anger. Gail, they are worse masters than whisky and opium, once they get a man down."

Jondo paused, and when he spoke again he did it hurriedly, as one who, from a sense of duty, would glance at the dead face of an enemy and turn away.

"When Fred lost his suit with Mary, he determined to wreck her life. He came between her and the man she loved with such adroit cruelty that they were separated, and although they loved each other always, they never saw each other again. Through a terrible network of misunderstandings she married Theron St. Vrain. He, by the way, was the other college chum I spoke of just now. He and his foster-brother, Bertrand, were wards of Fred

Ramer's father. But their guardian, the elder Ramer, had embezzled most of their property and there was bitter enmity between them and him. Theron and Mary were the parents of Eloise St. Vrain. It is no wonder that she is beautiful. She had Mary Marchland for a mother. Theron St. Vrain died early, and the management of his property fell into Fred Ramer's hands. At Mary's death it would descend to Eloise, with the proviso I just mentioned of an unworthy marriage. In that case, Ramer, at his own discretion, could give the estate to the Church. Nobody knows when Mary Marchland died, nor where she is buried, except Fred and his confessor, Father Josef."

"How far can a man's hate run, Jondo?" I asked.

"Oh, not so far as a man's love. Listen, Gail." Never a man had a truer eye and a sweeter smile than my big Jondo.

"Fred Ramer was desperately in need of money when he was plotting to darken the life of Mary Marchland--that was just before the birth of Eloise--and through her sorrow to break the heart of the man whom she loved--I said we college boys were all in love with her, you remember. Let me make it short now. One night Fred's father was murdered, by whom was never exactly proven. But he was last seen alive with his ward, Theron St. Wain, who, with his foster-brother, Bertrand, thoroughly despised him for his plain robbery of their heritage.

"The case was strong against Theron, for the evidence was very damaging, and it would have gone hard with him but for the foster-brother. Bertrand St. Wain took the guilt upon himself by disappearing suddenly. He was supposed to have drowned himself in the lower Mississippi, for his body, recognized only by some clothing, was recovered later in a drift and decently buried. So *he* was effaced from the records of man."

In the dim light Jondo's blue eyes were like dull steel and his face was a face of stone, but he continued:

"Just here Clarenden comes into the story. He learned it through Felix Narveo, and Felix got it from the Mexicans themselves, that Fred Ramer had plotted with them to put his father out of the way--I said he was desperately in need of money--and to lay the crime on Theron St. Vrain, by whose disgrace the life of Mary Marchland would be blighted, and Fred would have his revenge and his father's money. Narveo was afraid to act against Ramer, but nothing ever scared Esmond Clarenden away from what he wanted to do. Through his friendship for St. Vrain, to whom some suspicion still clung, and that lost foster-brother, Bertrand, he turned the screws on Fred Ramer that drove him out of the country. He landed, finally, at Santa Fé, and became Ferdinand Ramero. He managed by his charming manners to enchant the sister of Felix Narveo--and you know the rest."

Jondo paused.

"Didn't Felix Narveo go to Fort Leavenworth once, just before Uncle Esmond brought us with him to Santa Fé?" I asked.

"Yes, he went to warn Clarenden not to leave you there unprotected, for a band of Ramero's henchmen were on their way then to the Missouri River-- we passed them at Council Grove--to kidnap you three and take you to old Mexico," Jondo said. "An example of Fred's efforts to get even with Clarenden and of the loyalty of Narveo to his old college chum. The same gang of Mexicans had kidnapped Little Blue Flower and given her to the Kiowas."

"You told me that Uncle Esmond forced Ferdinand Ramero out of the country on account of a wrong done to you, Jondo," I reminded the big plainsman.

"He did," Jondo replied. "I told you that we all loved Mary Marchland. Fred Ramer broke under his loss of her, and became the devil's own tool of hate and revenge, and what generally gets tied up with these sooner or later, a passion for money and irregular means of getting it. Money is as great an asset for hate as for love, and Fred sold his soul for it long ago. Clarenden came to the frontier and lost himself in the building of the plains commerce, and his heart he gave to the three orphan children to whom he gave a home. When New Mexico came under our flag Narveo came with it, a good citizen and a loyal patriot. He married a Mexican woman of culture and lives a contented life. Dick Verra went into the Church. I came to the plains, and the stimulus of danger, and the benediction of the open sky, and the healing touch of the prairie winds, and the solemn stillness of the great distances have made me something more of a man than I should have been. Maybe I was hurt the worst. Clarenden thought I was. Sometimes I think Dick Verra got the best of all of us."

Jondo's voice trailed off into silence and I knew what his hurt was--that he was the man whom Mary Marchland had loved, from whom Fred Ramer, by his cruel machinations, had separated her--"*and although they loved each other always, they never saw each other again.*" Poor Jondo! What a man among men this unknown freighter of the plains might have been--and what a loss to the plains in the best of the trail years if Jondo had never dared its dangers for the safety of the generations to come.

But the thought of Eloise, driven out momentarily by Jondo's story, came rushing in again.

"You said you put a ring around Ramero to keep him in Santa Fé. Can't we get Eloise outside of it?" I urged, anxiously.

"Maybe I should have said that Father Josef put it around him for me," Jondo replied. "He confessed his crimes fully to the Church. He couldn't get by Father Josef. Here he is much honored and secure and we let him alone. The disgrace he holds the secret of--he alone--is that the father of Eloise killed his father, the crime for which the foster-brother fell. Ramero as guardian of Eloise and her property legally could have kept her here. Only a man like Clarenden would have dared to take her away, though he had the pleading call of her mother's last wish. Gail, I have told you the heart-history of half a dozen men. If this had stopped with us we could forgive after a while, but it runs down to you and Beverly and Eloise and Marcos, who will carry out his father's plans to the letter. So the battle is all to be fought over again. Let me leave you a minute or two. I'll not be gone long."

I sat alone, staring out at the shadowy court and, above it, the blue night-sky of New Mexico inlaid with stars, until a rush of feet in the hall and a shout of inquiry told me that Beverly Clarenden was hunting for me.

Meantime the girl in Mexican dress, who had come out of the church with Father Josef when he came to greet Eloise and me, had passed unnoticed through the Plaza and out on the way leading to the northeast. Here she came to the blind adobe wall of La Garita, whose olden purpose one still may read in the many bullet-holes in its brown sides. Here she paused, and as the evening shadows lengthened the dress and wall blended their dull tones together.

Beverly Clarenden, who had gone with Rex Krane up to Fort Marcy that evening, had left his companion to watch the sunset and dream of Mat back on the Missouri bluff, while he wandered down La Garita. He did not see the Mexican woman standing motionless, a dark splotch against a dun wall, until a soft Hopi voice called, eagerly, "Beverly, Beverly."

The black scarf fell from the bright face, and Indian garb--not Po-a-be, the student of St. Ann's and the guest of the Clarenden home, with the white

Grecian robe and silver headband set with coral pendants, as Beverly had seen her last in the side porch on the night of Mat's wedding, but Little Blue Flower, the Indian of the desert lands, stood before him.

"Where the devil--I mean the holy saints and angels, did you come from?" Beverly cried, in delight, at seeing a familiar face.

"I came here to do Father Josef some service. He has been good to me. I bring a message."

She reached out her hand with a letter. Beverly took the letter and the hand. He put the message in his pocket, but he did not release the hand.

"That's something for Jondo. I'll see that he gets it, all right. Tell me all about yourself now, Little Run-Off-and-Never-Come-Back." It was Beverly's way to make people love him, because he loved people.

It was late at last, too late for prudence, older heads would agree, when these two separated, and my cousin came to pounce upon me in the hotel court to tell me of his adventure.

"And I learned a lot of things," he added. "That Indian in the Plaza to-day is Santan, or Satan, dead sure; and you'd never guess, but he's the same redskin--Apache red--that was out at Agua Fria that time we were there long ago. The very same little sneak! He followed us clear to Bent's Fort. He put up a good story to Jondo, but I'll bet he was somebody's tool. You know what a critter he was there. But listen now! He's got his eye on Little Blue Flower. He's plain wild Injun, and she's a Saint Ann's scholar. Isn't that presumption, though! She's afraid of him, too. This country fairly teams with romance, doesn't it?"

"Bev, don't you ever take anything seriously?" I asked.

"Well, I guess I do. I found that Santan, dead loaded with jealousy, sneaking after us in the dark to-night when I took Little Blue Flower for a stroll. I took him seriously, and told him exactly where he'd find me next time he was looking for me. That I'd stand him up against La Garita and make a sieve out of him," Beverly said, carelessly.

"Beverly Clarenden, you are a fool to get that Apache's ill-will," I cried.

"I may be, but I'm no coward," Beverly retorted. "Oh, here comes Jondo. I've got a letter from Father Josef. Invitation to some churchly dinner, I expect."

Beverly threw the letter into Jondo's hands and turned to leave us.

"Wait a minute!" Jondo commanded, and my cousin halted in surprise.

"When did you get this? I should have had it two hours ago," Jondo said, sternly. "Father Josef must have waited a long time up at the church door for his messenger to come back and bring him word from me."

Beverly frankly told him the truth, as from childhood we had learned was the easiest way out of trouble.

Jondo's smile came back to his eyes, but his lips did not smile as he said: "Gail, you can explain things to Bev. This is serious business, but it had to come sooner or later. The battle is on, and we'll fight it out. Ferdinand Ramero is determined that Eloise and his son shall be married early to-morrow morning. The bribe to the Church is one-half of the St. Vrain estate. The club over Eloise is the shame of some disgrace that he holds the key to. He will stop at nothing to have his own way, and he will stoop to any brutal means to secure it. He has a host of fellows ready at his call to do any crime for his sake. That's how far money and an ungovernable passion can lead a man. If I had known this sooner, we would have acted to-night."

Beverly groaned.

"Let me go and kill that man. There ought to be a bounty on such wild beasts," he declared.

"He'd do that for you through a Mexican dagger, or an Apache arrow, if you got in his way," Jondo replied. "But what we must do is this: Twenty miles south on the San Christobal Arroyo there is a lonely ranch-house on the old Narveo estate, a forgotten place, but it is a veritable fort, built a hundred years ago, when every house here was a fort. To-morrow at daybreak you must start with Eloise and Sister Anita down there. I will see Father Josef later and tell him where I have sent you. Little Blue Flower will show you the way. It is a dangerous ride, and you must make it as quickly and as silently as possible. A bullet from some little cañon could find you easily if Ramero should know your trail. Will you go?"

There was no need for the question as Jondo well knew, but his face was bright with courage and hope, and a thankfulness he could not express shone in his eyes as he looked at us, big, stalwart, eager and unafraid.

XV

THE SANCTUARY ROCKS OF SAN CHRISTOBAL

Mark where she stands! Around her form I draw
The awful circle of our solemn church!
Set but a foot within that holy ground,
And on thy head--yea, though it wore a crown--
launch the curse of Rome.
--"RICHELIEU."

The faint rose hue of early dawn was touching the highest peaks of the
Sandia and Jemez mountain ranges, while the valley of the Rio Grande still
lay asleep under dull night shadows, when five ponies and their riders left
the door of San Miguel church and rode southward in the slowly paling
gloom. In the stillness of the hour the ponies' feet, muffled in the sand of
the way, seemed to clatter noisily, and their trappings creaked loudly in the
dead silence of the place. Little Blue Flower, no longer in her Mexican
dress, led the line. Behind her Beverly and the white-faced nun of St. Ann's
rode side by side; and behind these came Eloise St. Vrain and myself. From
the church door Jondo had watched us until we melted into the misty
shadows of the trail.

"Go carefully and fearlessly and ride hard if you must. But the struggle will
be here with me to-day, not where you are," he assured us, when we started
away.

As he turned to leave the church, an Indian rose from the shadows beyond
it and stepped before him.

"You remember me, Santan, the Apache, at Fort Bent?" he questioned.

Jondo looked keenly to be sure that his memory fitted the man before him.

"Yes, you are Santan. You brought me a message from Father Josef once."

The Indian's face did not change by the twitch of an eyelash as he replied.

"I would bring another message from him. He would see you an hour later
than you planned. The young riders, where shall I tell him they have gone?"

"To the old ranch-house on the San Christobal Arroyo," Jondo replied.

The Indian smiled, and turning quickly, he disappeared up the dark street. A sudden thrill shook Jondo.

"Father Josef said I could trust that boy entirely. Surely old Dick Verra, part Indian himself, couldn't be mistaken. But that Apache lied to me. I know it now; and I told him where our boys are taking Eloise. I never made a blunder like that before. Damned fool that I am!"

He ground his teeth in anger and disgust, as he sat down in the doorway of the church to await the coming of Ferdinand Ramero and his son, Marcos.

Out on the trail our ponies beat off the miles with steady gait. As the way narrowed, we struck into single file, moving silently forward under the guidance of Little Blue Flower, now plunging into dark cañons, where the trail was rocky and perilous, now climbing the steep sidling paths above the open plain. Morning came swiftly over the Gloriettas. Darkness turned to gray; shapeless masses took on distinctness; the night chill softened to the crisp breeze of dawn. Then came the rare June day in whose bright opening hour the crystal skies of New Mexico hung above us, and about us lay a landscape with radiant lights on the rich green of the mesa slopes, and gray levels atint with mother-of-pearl and gold.

The Indian pueblos were astir. Mexican faces showed now and then at the doorways of far-scattered groups of adobe huts. Outside of these all was silence--a motionless land full of wild, rugged beauty, and thrilling with the spell of mystery and glamour of romance. And overbrooding all, the spirit of the past, that made each winding trail a footpath of the centuries; each sheer cliff a watch-tower of the ages; each wide sandy plain, a rallying-ground for the tribes long ago gone to dust; each narrow valley a battle field for the death struggle between the dusky sovereigns of a wilderness kingdom and the pale-faced conquerors of the coat of mail and the dominant soul. The sense of danger lessened with distance and no knight of old Spain ever rode more proudly in the days of chivalry than Beverly Clarenden and I rode that morning, fearing nothing, sure of our power to protect the golden-haired girl, thrilled by this strange flight through a land of strange scenes fraught with the charm of daring and danger. Beverly rode forward now with Little Blue Flower. I did not wonder at her spell over him, for she was in her own land now, and she matched its picturesque phases with her own picturesque racial charm.

I rode beside Eloise, forgetting, in the sweet air and glorious June sunlight, that we were following an uncertain trail away from certain trouble.

The white-faced nun in her somber dress, rode between, with serious countenance and downcast eyes.

"What happened to you, Little Lees, after I left you?" I asked, as we trotted forward toward the San Christobal valley.

"Everything, Gail," she replied, looking up at me with shy, sad eyes. "First Ferdinand Ramero came to me with the command that I should consent to be married this morning. By this time I would have been Marcos' wife." She shivered as she spoke. "I can't tell you the way of it, it was so final, so cruel, so impossible to oppose. Ferdinand's eyes cut like steel when they look at you, and you know he will do more than he threatens. He said the Church demanded one-half of my little fortune and that he could give it the other half if he chose. He is as imperious as a tyrant in his pleasanter moods; in his anger he is a maniac. I believe he would murder Marcos if the boy got in his way, and his threats of disgracing me were terrible."

"But what else happened?" I wanted to turn her away from her wretched memory.

"I have not seen anybody else except Little Blue Flower. She has an Indian admirer who is Ferdinand's tool and spy. He let her come in to see me late last night or I should not have been here now. I had almost given up when she brought me word that you and Beverly would meet me at the church at daylight. I have not slept since. What will be the end of this day's work? Isn't there safety for me somewhere?" The sight of the fair, sad face with the hunted look in the dark eyes cut me to the soul.

"Jondo said last night that the battle was on and he would fight it out in Santa Fé to-day. It is our work to go where the Hopi blossom leads us, and Bev Clarenden and I will not let anything happen to you."

I meant what I said, and my heart is always young when I recall that morning ride toward the San Christobal Arroyo and my abounding vigor and confidence in my courage and my powers.

Our trail ran into a narrow plain now where a yellow band marked the way of the San Christobal River toward the Rio Grande. On either hand tall cliffs, huge weather-worn points of rock, and steep slopes, spotted with evergreen shrubs, bordered the river's course. The silent bigness of every feature of the landscape and the beauty of the June day in the June time of our lives, and our sense of security in having escaped the shadows and strife in Santa Fé, all combined to make us free-spirited. Only Sister Anita rode, alert and sorrowful-faced, between Beverly and the gaily-robed Indian girl, and myself with Eloise, the beautiful.

As we rounded a bend in the narrow valley, Little Blue Flower halted us, and pointing to an old half-ruined rock structure beside the stream, she said:

"See, yonder is the chapel where Father Josef comes sometimes to pray for the souls of the Hopi people. The house we go to find is farther up a cañon over there."

"I remember the place," Eloise declared. "Father Josef brought me here once and left me awhile. I wasn't afraid, although I was alone, for he told me I was always safe in a church. But I was never allowed to come back again."

Sister Anita crossed herself and, glancing over her shoulder, gave a sharp cry of alarm. We turned about to see a group, of horsemen dashing madly up the trail behind us. The wind in their faces blew back the great cloud of dust made by their horses hoofs, hiding their number and the way behind them. Their steeds were wet with foam, but their riders spurred them on with merciless fury. In the forefront Ferdinand Ramero's tall form, towering above the small statured evil-faced Mexican band he was leading, was outlined against the dust-cloud following them, and I caught the glint of light on his drawn revolver. "Ride! Ride like the devil!" Beverly shouted.

At the same time he and the Hopi girl whirled out and, letting us pass, fell in as a rear guard between us and our pursuers. And the race was on.

Jondo had said the lonely ranch-house whither we were tending was as strong as a fort. Surely it could not be far away, and our ponies were not spent with hard riding. Before us the valley narrowed slightly, and on its rim jagged rock cliffs rose through three hundred feet of earthquake-burst, volcanic-tossed confusion to the high tableland beyond.

As we strained forward, half a dozen Mexican horsemen suddenly appeared on the trail before us to cut off our advance. Down between us and the new enemy stood the old stone chapel, like the shadow of a great rock in a weary land, where for two hundred long years it had set up an altar to the Most High on this lonely savage plain.

"The chapel! The chapel! We must run to that now," cried Sister Anita.

Her long veil was streaming back in the wind, and her rosary and crucifix beating about her shoulders with the hard riding, but her white face was brave with a divine trust. Yet even as she urged us I saw how imposible was her plea, for the men in front were already nearer to the place than we were. At the same time a pony dashed up beside me, and Little Blue Flower's voice rang in my ears.

"The rocks! Climb up and hide in the rocks!" She dropped back on one side of Beverly, with Sister Anita on the other, guarding our rear. As I turned our flight toward the cliff, I caught sight of an Indian in a wedge of rock just across the river, and I heard the singing flight of an arrow behind me, followed almost instantly by another arrow. I looked back to see Sister Anita's pony staggering and rearing in agony, with Little Blue Flower trying vainly to catch its bridle-rein, and Sister Anita, clutching wildly at her rosary, a great stream of blood flowing from an arrow wound in her neck.

Men think swiftly in moments like these. The impulse to halt, and the duty to press on for the protection of the girl beside me, holding me in doubt. Instantly I saw the dark crew, with Ferdinand Ramero leading fiercely forward, almost upon us, and I heard Beverly Clarenden's voice filling the valley--"Run, Gail, run! You can beat 'em up there."

It was a cry of insistences and assurances and power, and withal there was that minor tone of sympathy which had sounded in the boy's defiant voice long ago in the gray-black shadows below Pawnee Rock, when his chivalric soul had been stirred by the cruel wrongs of Little Blue Flower and he had cried:

"Uncle Esmond, let's take her, and take our chances."

I knew in a flash that the three behind us were cut off, and Eloise St. Vrain and I pressed on alone. We crossed the narrow strip of rising ground to where the first rocks lay as they had fallen from the cliff above, split off by some titanic agony of nature. Up and up we went, our ponies stumbling now and then, but almost as surefooted as men, as they climbed the narrow way. Now the rocks hid us from the plain as we crept sturdily through narrow crevices, and now we clambered up an open path where nothing concealed our way. But higher still and higher, foot, by foot we pressed, while with oath and growl behind us came our pursuers.

At last we could ride no farther, and the miracle was that our ponies could have climbed so far. Above us huge slabs of stone, by some internal cataclysm hurled into fragments of unguessed tons of weight, seemed poised in air, about to topple down upon the plain below. Between these wild, irregular masses a narrow footing zigzagged upward to still other wild, irregular masses, a footing of long leaps in cramped spaces between sharp edges of upright clefts, all gigantic, unbending, now shielding by their immense angles, now standing sheer and stark before us, casting no shadows to cover us from the great white glare of the New-Mexican day.

I have said no man knows where his mind will run in moments of peril. As we left our ponies and clambered up and up in hope of safety somewhere, the face of the rocks cut and carved by the rude stone tools of a race long perished, seemed to hold groups of living things staring at us and pointing the way. And there was no end to these crude pictographs. Over and over and over--the human hand, the track of the little road-runner bird, the plumed serpent coiled or in waving line, the human form with the square body and round head, with staring circles for eyes and mouth, and straight-line limbs.

We were fleeing for safety through the sacred aisles of a people God had made; and when they served His purpose no longer, they had perished. I did not think of them so that morning. I thought only of some hiding-place, some inaccessible point where nothing could reach the girl I must protect. But these crawling serpents, cut in the rock surfaces, crawled on and on. These human hands, poor detached hands, were lifted up in mute token of what had gone before. These two-eyed, one-mouthed circles on heads fast to body-boxes, from which waved tentacle limbs, jigged by us, to give place to other coiled or crawling serpents and their companion carvings, with the track of the swift road-runner skipping by us everywhere.

At last, with bleeding hands and torn clothing, we stood on a level rock like a tiny mesa set out from the high summit of the cliff.

Eloise sat down at my feet as I looked back eagerly over the precipitous way we had come, and watched the band of Mexicans less rapidly swarming up the same steep, devious trail.

Three hundred feet below us lay the plain with the thin current of the San Christobal River sparkling here and there in the sunlight. The black spot on the trail that scarcely moved must be Beverly and Little Blue Flower with Sister Anita. No, there was only the Indian girl there, and something moving in and out of the shadow near them. I could not see for the intervening rocks.

"Gail! Gail! You will not let them take you. You will not leave me," Eloise moaned.

And I was one against a dozen. I stooped to where she sat and gently lifted her limp white hand, saying:

"Eloise, I was on a rock like this a night and a day alone on the prairie. I could not move nor cry out. But something inside told me to 'hold fast'-- the old law of the trail. You must do that with me now."

A shout broke over the valley and the rocks about us seemed suddenly to grow men, as if every pictograph of the old stone age had become a sentient thing, a being with a Mexican dress, and the soul of a devil. Just across a narrow chasm, a little below us, Ferdinand Ramero stood in all the insolence of a conqueror, with a smile that showed his white teeth, and in his steely eyes was the glitter of a snake about to spring.

"You have given us a hard race. By Jove, you rode magnificently and climbed heroically. I admire you for it. It is fine to bring down game like you, Clarenden. You have your uncle's spirit, and a six-foot body that dwarfs his short stature. And we come as gentlemen only, if we can deal with a gentleman. It wasn't our men who struck your nun down there. But if you, young man, dare to show one ounce of fighting spirit now, behind you on the rocks--don't look--as I lift my hand are my good friends who will put a bullet into the brain beneath that golden hair, and you will follow. Being a game-cock cannot help you now. It will only hasten things. Deliver that girl to me at once, or my men will close in upon you and no power on earth can save you."

Eloise had sprung to her feet and stood beside me, and both of us knew the helplessness of our plight. A startling picture it must have been, and one the cliffs above the San Christobal will hardly see again: the blue June sky arched overhead, unscarred by a single cloud-fleck, the yellow plain winding between the high picturesque cliffs, where silence broods all through the long hours of the sunny day; the pictured rocks with their furnace-blackened faces white--outlined with the story of the dim beginnings of human strivings. And standing alone and defenseless on the little table of stone, as if for sacrifice, the tall, stalwart young plainsman and the beautiful girl with her golden hair in waving masses about her uncovered head, her sweet face white as the face of the dying nun beside the sandy arroyo below us, her big dark eyes full of a strange fire.

"I order you to close in and take these two at once." The imperious command rang out, and the rocks across the valley must have echoed its haughty tone.

"And I order you to halt."

The voice of Father Josef, clear and rich and powerful, burst upon the silence like cathedral music on the still midnight air. The priest's tall form rose up on a great mass of rock across the cleft before us--Father Josef with bared head and flashing eyes and a physique of power.

Ferdinand Ramero turned like a lion at bay. "You are one man. My force number a full dozen. Move on," he ordered.

Again the voice of Father Josef ruled the listening ears.

"Since the days of old the Church has had the power to guard all that come within the shelter of the holy sanctuary. And to the Church of God was given also long ago the might to protect, by sanctuary privilege, the needy and the defenseless. Ferdinand Ramero, note that little table of rock where those two stand helpless in your grasp. Around them now I throw, as I have power to throw, the sacred circle of our Holy Church in sanctuary shelter. Who dares to step inside it will be accursed in the sight of God."

Never, never will I live through another moment like to that, nor see the power of the Unseen rule things that are seen with such unbreakable strength.

The Mexicans dropped to their knees in humble prayer, and Ferdinand Ramero seemed turned to a man of stone. A hand was gently laid upon my arm and Jondo and Rex Krane stood beside us. A voice far off was sounding in my ears.

"Go back to your homes and meet me at the church to-morrow night. You, Ferdinand Ramero, go now to the chapel yonder and wait until I come."

What happened next is lost in misty waves of forgetfulness.

XVI

FINISHING TOUCHES

"Yet there be certain times in a young man's life when through great sorrow or sin all the boy in him is burnt and seared away so that he passes at one step to the more sorrowful state of manhood."
--KIPLING.

The heat of midday was tempered by a light breeze up the San Christobal Valley, and there was not a single cloud in the June skies to throw a softening shadow on the yellow plain. A little group of Mexicans, riding northward with sullen faces, urged on their jaded ponies viciously as they thought of the gold that was to have been paid them for this morning's work, and of the gold that to-morrow night must go to pay the priest who should shrive them; and they had nothing gained wherewith to pay. Their leader, whom they had served, had been trapped in his own game, and they felt themselves abused and deceived.

Down by the brown sands of the river Father Josef waited at the door of the half-ruined little stone chapel for the strange group coming slowly toward him: Ferdinand Ramero, riding like a captured but unconquered king, his head erect, his flashing eyes seeing nobody; Jondo who could make the shabbiest piece of horseflesh take on grace when he mounted it, his tanned cheek flushed, and the spirit of supreme sacrifice looking out through his dark-blue eyes; Eloise, drooping like a white flower, but brave of spirit now, sure that her grief and anxiety would be lifted somehow. I rode beside her, glad to catch the faint smile in her eyes when she looked at me. And last of all, Rex Krane, with the same old Yankee spirit, quick to help a fellow-man and oblivious to personal danger. So we all came to the chapel, but at the door Rex wheeled and rode away, muttering, as he passed me:

"I've got business to look after, and not a darned thing to confess."

And Beverly! He was not with us.

When Rex Krane told his bride good-by up in the Clarenden home on the

Missouri bluff, Mat had whispered one last request:

"Look after Bev. He never sees danger for himself, nor takes anything seriously, least of all an enemy, whom he will befriend, and make a joke of it."

And so it happened that Rex had stayed behind to care for Beverly's arrow wound when Bill Banney had gone out with Jondo on the Kiowa trail to search for me this side of Pawnee Rock.

So also it happened that Rex had strolled down from Fort Marcy the night before, in time to see Beverly and the girl in the Mexican dress loitering along the brown front of La Garita. And his keen eyes had caught sight of Santan crouching in an angle of the wall, watching them.

"Indians and Mexes don't mix a lot. And Bev oughtn't mix with either one," Rex commented. "I'll line the boy up for review to-morrow, so Mat won't say I've neglected him."

But the Yankee took the precaution to follow the trail to the Indian's possible abiding-place on the outskirts of Santa Fé. And it was Rex who most aided Jondo in finding that the Indian had gone with Ramero's men northward.

"That fellow is Santan, of Fort Bent, Rex," Jondo said.

"Yes, you thought he was *Santa* and I took him for *Satan* then. We missed out on which to knock out of him. Bev won't care nothin' about his name. He will knock hell out of him if he gets in that Clarenden boy's way," Rex had replied.

At the chapel door now the Yankee turned away and rode down the trail toward the little angle where an Indian arrow had whizzed at our party an hour before.

In the shadow of a fallen mass of rock below the cliff Little Blue Flower had spread her blanket, with Beverly's coat tucked under it in a roll for a pillow, and now she sat beside the dying nun, holding the crucifix to Sister Anita's lips. The Indian girl's hands were blood-stained and the nun's black veil and gown were disheveled, and her white head-dress and coif were soaked with gore. But her white face was full of peace as the light faded from her eyes.

And Beverly! The boy forgot the rest of the world when one of the Apache's arrows struck down the pony and the other pierced Sister Anita's neck. Tenderly as a mother would lift a babe he quickly carried the stricken woman to the shelter of the rock, and with one glance at her he turned away.

"You can do all that she needs done for her. Give her her cross to hold," he said, gently, to Little Blue Flower.

Then he sprang up and dashed across the river, splashing the bright waters as he leaped to the farther side where Santan stood concealed, waiting for the return of Ramero's Mexicans.

At the sound of Beverly's feet he leaped to the open just in time to meet Beverly's fist square between the eyes.

"Take that, you dirty dog, to shoot down an innocent nun. And that!" Beverly followed his first blow with another.

The Apache, who had reeled back with the weight of the boy's iron fist, was too quick for the second thrust, struggling to get hold of his arrows and his scalping-knife. But the space was too narrow and Beverly was upon him with a shout.

"I told you I'd make a sieve or you the next time you tried to see me, and I'm going to do it."

He seized the Indian's knife and flung it clear into the river, where it stuck upright in the sands of the bed, parting the little stream of water gurgling against it; and with a powerful grip on the Apache's shoulders he wrenched the arrows from their place and tramped on them with his heavy boot.

The Indian's surprise and submission were gone in a flash, and the two clinched in combat.

On the one hand, jealousy, the inherited hatred of a mistreated race, the savage instinct, a gloating joy in brute strife, blood-lust, and a dogged will to trample in the dirt the man who made the sun shine black for the Apache. On the other hand, a mad rage, a sense of insult, a righteous greed for vengeance for a cruel deed against an innocent woman, and all the superiority of a dominant people. The one would conquer a powerful enemy, the other would exterminate a despicable and dangerous pest.

Back and forth across the narrow space hidden from the trail by fallen rock they threshed like beasts of prey. The Apache had the swiftness of the snake, his muscles were like steel springs, and there was no rule of honorable warfare in his code. He bit and clawed and pinched and scratched and choked and wrenched, with the grim face and burning eyes of a murderer. But the Saxon youth, slower of motion, heavier of bone and muscle, with a grip like iron and a stony endurance, with pride in a conquest by sheer clean skill, and with a purpose, not to take life, but to humble and avenge, hammered back blow for blow; and there was nothing for many minutes to show which was offensive and which defensive.

As the struggle raged on, the one grew more furious and the other more self-confident.

"Oh, I'll make you eat dust yet!" Beverly cried, as Santan in triumph flung him backward and sprang upon his prostrate form.

They clinched again, and with a mighty surge of strength my cousin lifted himself, and the Indian with him, and in the next fall Beverly had his antagonist gripped and helpless.

"I can choke you out now as easy as you shot that arrow. Say your prayers." He fairly growled out the words.

"I didn't aim at her," the Apache half whined, half boasted. "I wanted you."

At that moment Beverly, spent, bruised, and bleeding with fighting and surcharged with the lust of combat, felt all the instinct of murder urging him on to utterly destroy a poison-fanged foe to humanity. At Santan's words he paused and, flinging back the hair from his forehead, he caught his breath and his better self in the same heart-beat. And the instinct of the gentleman--he was Esmond Clarenden's brother's son--held the destroying hand.

"You aimed at me! Well, learn your lesson on that right now. Promise never to play the fool that way again. Promise the everlasting God's truth, or here you go."

The boy's clutch tightened on Santan's throat. "By all that's holy, you'll go to your happy hunting-ground *right now, unless you do*!" He growled out the words, and his blazing eyes glared threateningly at his fallen enemy.

"I promise!" Santan muttered, gasping for breath.

"You didn't mean to kill the nun? Then you'll go with me and ask her to forgive you before she dies. You will. You needn't try to get away from me. I let you thrash your strength out before we came to this settlement. Be still!" Beverly commanded, as Santan made a mad effort to release himself.

"Hurry up, and remember she is dying. Go softly and speak gently, or by the God of heaven, you'll go with her to the Judgment Seat to answer for that deed right now!"

Slowly the two rose. Their clothes were torn, their hair disheveled, the ground at their feet was red with their blood. They were as bitter, as distrustful now as when their struggle began. For brute force never conquers anything. It can only hold in check by fear of its power to destroy the body. Above the iron fist of the fighter, and the sword and cannon of the soldier, stands the risen Christ who carried his own cross up Mount Calvary--and "there they crucified him."

The two young men, spent with their struggle, their faces stained with dirt and bloody sweat, crossed the river and sought the shadowy place where Little Blue Flower sat beside Sister Anita. Twice Santan tried to escape, and twice Beverly brought him quickly to his place. It must have been here that I caught sight of them from the rock above.

"One more move like that and the ghost of Sister Anita will walk behind you on every trail you follow as long as your flat feet hit the earth," Beverly declared.

"All Indians are afraid of ghosts and I was just too tired to fight any more," he said to me afterward when he told me the story of that hour by the San Christobal River.

Sister Anita lay with wide-open eyes, her hands moving feebly as she clutched at her crucifix. Her hour was almost spent.

Santan stood motionless before her, as Beverly with a grip on his arm said, firmly:

"Tell her you did not aim at her, and ask her to forgive you. It will help to save your own soul sometime, maybe."

Santan looked at Little Blue Flower. But she gave no heed to him as she put the dropped crucifix into the weakening fingers. Murder, as such, is as horrifying to the gentle Hopi tribe as it is sport for the cruel Apache.

Beverly loosed his hold now.

"I did not want to hurt you. Forgive me!" Santan said, slowly, as though each word were plucked from him by red-hot pincers.

Sister Anita heard and turned her eyes.

"Kneel down and tell her again," Beverly said, more gently.

The Apache dropped on his knees beside the dying woman and repeated his words. Sister Anita smiled sweetly.

"Heaven will forgive you even as I do," she murmured, and closed her eyes.

"Go softly. This is sacred ground," my cousin said.

The Indian rose and passed silently down the trail, leaving Little Blue Flower and Beverly Clarenden together with the dead. At the stream he paused and pulled his knife from the sands beneath the trickling waters, and then went on his way.

But an Indian never forgets.

Rex Krane, who had hurried hither from the chapel, closed the eyes and folded the thin hands of the martyred woman, and sent Beverly forward for help to dispose of the garment of clay that had been Sister Anita. From that day something manly and serious came into Beverly Clarenden's face to stay, but his sense of humor and his fearlessness were unchanged.

That was a solemn hour in the shadow of the rock down in that yellow valley, but beautiful in its forgiving triumph. We who had gathered in the dimly lighted chapel had an hour more solemn for that it was made up of such dramatic minutes as change the trend of life-trails for all the years to come.

The chapel was very old. They tell me that only a broken portion of the circular wall about the altar stands there to-day, a lonely monument to some holy padre's faith and courage and sacrifice in the forgotten years when, in far Hesperia, men dreamed of a Quivera and found only a Calvary.

It may be that I, Gail Clarenden, was also changed as I listened to the deliberations of that day; that something of youth gave place for the stronger manhood that should stay me through the years that came after.

Eloise sat where I could see her face. The pink bloom had come back to it, and the golden hair, disordered by our wild ride and rough climb among the pictured rocks of the cliff, curled carelessly on her white brow and rippled about her shapely head. I used to wonder what setting fitted her beauty best--why wonder that about any beautiful woman?--but the gracious loveliness of this woman was never more appealing to me than in the soft light and sacred atmosphere of the church.

Father Josef's first thought was for her, but he brought water and coarse linen towels, so that, refreshed and clean-faced, we came in to his presence.

"Eloise," his voice was deep and sweet, "so long as you were a child I tried to protect and direct you. Now that you are a woman, you must still be protected, but you must live your own life and choose for yourself. You must meet sorrow and not be crushed by it. You must take up your cross and bear it. It is for this that I have called you back to New Mexico at this time. But remember, my daughter, that life is not given to us for defeat, but for victory; not for tears, but for smiles; not for idle cringing safety, but for brave and joyous struggle."

I thought of Dick Verra, the college man, whose own young years were full of hope and ambition, whose love for a woman had brought him to the priesthood, but as I caught the rich tones of Father Josef's voice, somehow, to me, he stood for success, not failure.

Eloise bowed her head and listened.

"You must no longer be threatened with the loss of your own heritage, nor coerced into a marriage for which the Church has been offered a bribe to help to accomplish. Blood money purifies no altars nor extends the limits of the Kingdom of the Christ. Your property is your own to use for the holy purposes of a goodly life wherever your days may lead you; and whatever the civil law may grant of power to control it for you, you shall no longer be harassed or annoyed. The Church demands that it shall henceforth be yours."

Father Josef's dark eyes were full of fire as he turned to Ferdinand Ramero.

"You will now relinquish all claim upon the control of this estate, whose revenue made your father and yourself to be accounted rich, and upon which your son has been allowed to build up a life expectation; and though on account of it, you go forth a poor man in wordly goods, you may go out rich in the blessing of restoration and repentance."

Ferdinand Ramero's steel eyes were fixed like the eyes of a snake on the holy man's face. Restoration and repentance do not belong behind eyes like that.

"I can fight you in the courts. You and your Church may go to the devil;" he seemed to hiss rather than to speak these words.

"We do go to him every day to bring back souls like yours," Father Josef's voice was calm. "I have waited a long time for you to repent. You can go to the courts, but you will not do it. For the sake of your wife, Gloria Ramero, and Felix Narveo, her brother, we do not move against you, and you dare not move for yourself, because your own record will not bear the light of legal investigation."

Ferdinand Ramero sprang up, the blaze of passion, uncontrolled through all his years, bursting forth in the tragedy of the hour. Eloise was right. In his anger he was a maniac.

"You dare to threaten me! You pen me in a corner to stab me to death! You hold disgrace and miserable poverty over my head, and cant of restoration and repentance! Not until here you name each thing that you count against me, and I have met them point by point, will I restore. I never will repent!"

In the vehemence of anger, Ramero was the embodiment of the dramatic force of unrestraint, and withal he was handsome, with a controlling magnetism even in his hour of downfall.

Jondo had said that Father Josef had somewhere back a strain of Indian blood in his veins. It must have been this that gave the fiber of self control to his countenance as he looked with pitying eyes at Jondo and Eloise St. Vrain.

"The hour is struck," he said, sadly. "And you shall hear your record, point by point, because you ask it now. First: you have retained, controlled, misused, and at last embezzled the fortune of Theron St. Vrain, as it was retained, controlled, misused, and embezzled by your father, Henry Ramer, in his lifetime. Any case in civil courts must show how the heritage of Eloise St. Vrain, heir to Theron St. Vrain at the death of her mother--"

"Not until the death of her mother--" Ferdinand Ramero broke in, hoarsely.

For the first time to-day the priest's cheek paled, but his voice was unbroken as he continued:

"I would have been kinder for your own sake. You desire otherwise. Yes, only after the death of Mary Marchland St. Vrain could you dictate concerning her daughter's affairs, with most questionable legality even then. Mary Marchland St. Vrain is not dead."

The chapel was as silent as the grave. My heart stood still. Before me was Jondo, big, strong, self-controlled, inured to the tragic deeds of the epic years of the West. No pen of mine will ever make the picture of Jondo's face at these words of Father Josef.

Eloise turned deathly pale, and her dark eyes opened wide, seeing nothing. It was not I who comforted her, but Jondo, who put his strong arm about her, and she leaned against his shoulder. Father and daughter in spirit, stricken to the heart.

"For many years she has lived in that lonely ranch-house on the Narveo grant in the little cañon up the San Christobal Arroyo. When the fever left her with memory darkened forever, you recorded her as dead. But your wife, Gloria Ramero, spared no pains to make her comfortable. She has never known a want, nor lived through one unhappy hour, because she has forgotten."

"A priest, confessor for men's inmost souls, who babbles all he knows! I wonder that this roof does not fall on you and strike you dead before this altar." Ferdinand Ramero's voice rose to a shout.

"It was too strongly built by one who knew men's inmost souls, and what they needed most," Father Josef replied. "You drove me to this by your insistence. I would have shielded you--and these."

He turned to Eloise and Jondo as he spoke.

"One more point, since you hold it ready to spring when I am through. You stand accused of plotting for your father's murder. The evidence still holds, and some men who rode with you to-day to seize this gentle girl and drag her back to a marriage with your son--and save your ill-gotten gold thereby--some of these men who will confess to me and do penance to-morrow night, are the same men who long ago confessed to other crimes--you can guess what they were.

"It pays well to repent before such a holy tattler as yourself." Ramero's blue eyes burned deep as their fire was centered on the priest.

"These are the counts against you," Father Josef said in review, ignoring the last outburst of wrath. "A life of ease and inheritance through money not your own, nor even rightly yours to control. A stricken woman listed with the dead, whose memory might have come again--God knows--if but the loving touch of childish hands had long ago been on her hands. It is years too late for all that now. A brave young ward rescued from your direct control by Esmond Clarenden's force of will and daring to do the right. You know that last pleading cry of Mary Marchland's, for Jondo to protect her child, and how Clarenden, for love of this brave man, came to New Mexico on perilous trails to take the little Eloise from you. And lastly in this matter, the threats to force a marriage unholy in God's sight, because no love could go with it. Your mad chase and villainous intention to use brute force to secure your will out yonder on the rocks above the cliff. You have debauched an Apache boy, making him your tool and spy. You sanctioned the seizing of a Hopi girl whose parents you permitted to be murdered, and their child sold into slavery among foreign tribes. You have stirred up and kept alive a feud of hatred and revenge among the Kiowa people against the life and property of Esmond Clarenden and all who belong to him. And, added to all these, you stand to-day a patricide in spirit, accused of plotting for the murder of your own father. Do not these things call for restoration and repentance?"

Ferdinand Ramero rose to his feet and stood in the aisle near the door. His face hardened, and all the suave polish and cool concentration and dominant magnetism fell away. What remained was the man as shaped by the ruling passions of years, from whose control only divine power could bring deliverance. And when he spoke there was a remorseless cruelty and selfishness in his low, even tones.

"You have called me a plotter for my father's life--based on some lying Mexican's love of blackmail. You do not even try to prove your charge. The man who would have killed him was Theron St. Vrain, and his brother, Bertrand. That Theron was disgraced by the fact you know very well, and the blackness of it drove him to an early grave. So this young lady here, whom I would have shielded from this stain upon her name in the marriage to my son, may know the truth about her father. He was what you, Father

Josef, try to prove me to be."

He paused as if to gather venom for his last shaft.

"These two, Theron and Bertrand, were equally guilty, but through tricks of their own, Theron escaped and Bertrand took the whole crime on himself. He disappeared and paid the penalty by his death. His body was recovered from the river and placed in an unmarked grave. Why go back to that now? Because Bertrand St. Vrain's clothes alone on some poor drowned unknown man were buried. Bertrand himself sits here beside his niece, Eloise St. Vrain. John Doe to the world, the man who lives without a name, and dares not sign a business document, a walking dead man. I could even pity him if he were real. But who can pity nothing?"

A look of defiance came into the man's glittering eyes as he took one step nearer to the door and continued:

"Esmond Clarenden drove me out of the United States with threats of implicating me in the death of my father, and I knew his power and brutal daring to do anything he chose to do. It was but his wish to have revenge for this nameless thing--"

The scorn of Ramero's eyes and voice as he looked at Jondo were withering.

"And this thing keeps me here by threats of attacks, even when he knows that by such attacks he will reveal himself. It has been a grim game." Something of a grin showed all of the man's fine teeth. "A grim game, and never played to a finish till now. I leave it to you, Father Josef, to judge who has been the stronger and who comes out of it victor. I make restoration--of what? I leave the St. Vrain money that I have guarded for Eloise, the daughter of the man who killed, or helped to kill, my father. You can control it now, among you: Clarenden, already rich; your Church, notorious in its robbery of the poor by enriching its coffers; or this uncle here, who is dead and buried in an unknown grave. That is all the restoration I can make. Repentance, I do not know what that word means. Keep it for the poor devils you will gather in to-morrow night to be shriven. They need it. I do not."

He turned and strode out of the church and, mounting his horse, rode like a madman up the yellow valley of the San Christobal. In after years I could find no term to so well describe that last act as the words of Beverly Clarenden, who came to the chapel just in time to hear Ferdinand Ramero's closing declaration, and to see his black scowl and scornful air, as, in a royal madness, he defied the power of man and denounced the all-pitying love that is big enough for the most sinful.

"It was Paradise lost," Beverly declared, "and Satan falling clear to hell before the Archangel's flaming sword. Only he went east and the real Satan dropped down to his place. But they will meet up somewhere, Ramero and the real one, and not be able to tell each other apart."

And Jondo. My boyhood idol, brave, gentle, unselfish, able everywhere! Jondo, who had kept my toddling feet from stumbling, who had taught me to ride and swim and shoot, who had made me wise in plains lore, and manly and clean among the rough and vulgar things of the Missouri frontier. Jondo, whose big, cool hand had touched my feverish face, whose deep blue eyes had looked love into my eyes when I lay dying on Pawnee Rock! A man without a name! A murderer who had by a trick escaped the law, and must walk evermore unknown among his fellow-men! Something went out of my life as I looked at him. The boy in me was burned and seared away, and only the man-to-be, was left.

He offered no word of defense from the accusation against him, nor made a plea of innocence, but sat looking straight at Father Josef, who looked at him as if expecting nothing. And as they gazed into each other's eyes, a something strong and beautiful swept the face of each. I could not understand it, and I was young. My lifetime hero had turned to nothingness before my eyes. The world was full of evil. I hated it and all that in it was, my trusting, foolish, short-sighted self most of all.

But Eloise--the heart of woman is past understanding--Eloise turned to the man beside her and, putting both arms around his neck, she pressed one fair cheek against his brown bearded one, and kissed him gently on the forehead. Then turning to Father Josef, no longer the dependent, clinging maiden, but the loving woman, strong and sure of will, she said:

"I must go to my mother. So long as she lives I will never leave her again."

She did not even look at me, nor speak a word of farewell, as if I were the murderer instead of that man, Jondo, whom she had kissed.

I saw her ride away, with Little Blue Flower beside her. I saw the green mesa, the red cliffs above the growing things, the glitter of the San Christobal water on yellow sands, the level plain where the narrow white trail crept far away toward Gloria Narveo's lonely ranch-house, strong as a fort built a hundred years ago, in a little cañon of the valley. I saw a young, graceful figure on horseback, and the glint of sunlight on golden hair. But the rider did not turn her head and I could not get one glance of those beautiful dark eyes. A great mass of rock hid the line of the trail, and the two, Eloise and Little Blue Flower, rounded the angle and rode on out of my sight.

I helped to dig open the curly mesquite and to shovel out the sand. I heard the burial service, and saw a rudely coffined form lowered into an open grave. I saw Rex Krane at the head, and Jondo at the foot, and Beverly's bleeding hands as he scraped the loose earth back and heaped it over that which had been called Sister Anita; I heard Father Josef's voice of music repeating the "Ashes to ashes, and dust to dust." And then we turned away and left the spot, as men turn every day to the common affairs of life.

Four days later Little Blue Flower came to me as I, still numb and cold and blankly unthinking, sat beside Fort Marcy and looked out with unseeing eyes at the glory of a New-Mexican sunset.

"I come from Eloise." The sadness of her face and voice even the Indian's self-control could not conceal.

"She is sad, but brave, and her mother loves her and calls her 'Little One.' She will never grow up to her mother. But"--Little Blue Flower's voice faltered and she gazed out at the far Sandia peaks wrapped in the rich purple folds of twilight, with the scarlet of the afterglow beyond them-- "Eloise loves Beverly. She will always love him. Heaven meant him for her." There were some other broken sentences, but I did not grasp them clearly then.

The world was full of gray shadows. The finishing touches had been put on life for me. I looked out at the dying glow in the west, and wondered vaguely if the sun would ever cross the Gloriettas again, or ever the Sangre-de-Christo grow radiant with the scarlet stain of that ineffable beauty that uplifts and purifies the soul of him who looks on it.

XVII

SWEET AND BITTER WATERS

Trust me, it is something to be cast
Face to face with one's self at last,
To be taken out of the fuss and strife,
The endless clatter of plate and knife,
The bore of books, and the bores of the street,
And to be set down on one's own two feet
So nigh to the great warm heart of God,
You almost seem to feel it beat
Down from the sunshine, and up from the sod.
JAMES RUSSELL LOWELL.

My hair is very white now, and my fingers hold a pen more easily than they could hold the ox-goad or the rifle, and mine to-day is all the backward look. Which look is evermore a satisfying thing because it takes in all of life behind in its true proportion, where the forward look of youth sees only what comes next and nothing more. And looking back to-day it seems that, of the many times I walked the long miles of that old Santa Fe Trail, no journey over it stands out quite so clear-cut in my memory as the home trip after I had watched the going away of Eloise, and witnessed the flight of Ferdinand Ramero, and listened to the story of Jondo's life.

When Little Blue Flower left me sitting beside Fort Marcy's wall my mind went back in swift review over the flight of days since Beverly Clarenden and I had come from Cincinnati. I recalled the first meeting of Eloise with my cousin. How easily they had renewed acquaintance, I had been surprised and embarrassed and awkward when I found her and Little Blue Flower down by the Flat Rock below St. Ann's, in the Moon of the Peach Blossom. I remembered how I had monopolized all of her time in the days that followed, leaving good-natured Bev to look after the little Indian girl who never really seemed like an Indian to him. And keen-piercing as an arrow came now the memory of that midnight hour when I had seen the two in the little side porch of the Clarenden home, and again I heard the sorrowful words:

"Oh, Beverly, it breaks my heart."

Eloise had just seen Beverly kiss Little Blue Flower in the shadows of the porch. And all the while, good-hearted, generous boy that he was, he had never tried to push his suit with her, had made her love him more, no doubt, by letting me have full command of all of her time, while he forgot himself in showing courtesy to the Indian girl, because Bev was first of all a gentleman. I thought of that dear hour in the church of San Miguel. Of course, Eloise was glad to find me there--poor, hunted, frightened child! She would have been as glad, no doubt, to have found big Bill Banney or Rex Krane, and I had thought her eyes held something just for me that night. She had not seen Beverly at the chapel beside the San Christobal River, and to me she had not given even a parting glance when she went away. If she had cared for me at all she would not have left me so. And I had climbed the tortuous trail with her and stood beside her in the zone of sanctuary safety that Father Josef had thrown about us two.

These things were clear enough to me, but when I tried to think again of all that Little Blue Flower had said an hour ago my mind went numb:

"Her mother knew her, but only as the little Eloise long lost and never missed till now. The mother, too, was very beautiful, and young in face, and child-like in her helplessness. The lonely ranch-house, old, and strong as a fort, girt round by tall cañon walls, nestled in a grassy open place; and not a comfort had been denied the woman there. For Gloria Ramero, Ferdinand's wife, had governed that. And Eloise had entered there to stay. This much was clear enough. But that which followed seemed to twist and writhe about in my mind with only one thing sure--Eloise loved Beverly, would always love him. And he could not love any one else. He could be kind to any girl, but he would not be happy. Some day when he was older-- a real man--then he would long for the girl of his heart and his own choice, and he would find her and love her, too, and she would love him and those who stood between them they both would hate. And Eloise loved Beverly. She could not send Gail any words herself, but he would understand."

So came the Indian girl's interpretation of the case, but the conclusion was the message meant for me. I wondered vaguely, as I sat there, if the vision had come to Beverly years ago as it had come to me: three men--the soldier on his cavalry mount, Jondo, the plainsman, on his big black horse, and between the two, Esmond Clarenden, neither mounted nor on foot, but going forward somehow, steady and sure. And beyond these three, this side of misty mountain peaks, the cloud of golden hair, the sweet face, with dark eyes looking into mine. I had not been a dreamer, I had been a fool.

Through Beverly I learned the next day that Ferdinand Ramero had come into Santa Fé late at night and had left early the next morning. Marcos

Ramero, faultlessly dressed, lounged about the gambling-halls, and strolled through the sunny Plaza, idly and insolently, as was his custom. But Gloria Ramero, to whom Marcos long ago ceased to be more than coldly courteous, had left the city at once for the San Christobal Valley, to devote herself to the care of the beautiful woman whom her brother Felix Narveo in his college days had admired so much.

As for Jondo, years ago when we had met Father Josef out by the sandy arroyo, he had left us to follow the good man somewhere, and had not come back to the Exchange Hotel until nightfall. Something had come into his face that day that never left it again. And now that something had deepened in the glance of his eye and the firm-set mouth. It was through that meeting with Father Josef that he had first heard of the supposed death of Mary Marchland St. Vrain, and it was through the priest in the chapel he had heard that she was still alive.

Neither Beverly nor Bill Banney nor Rex Krane knew what I had heard in the church concerning Jondo's early career, and I never spoke of it to them. But to all of us, outside of that intensified something indefinable in his face, he was unchanged. He met my eye with the open, frank glance with which he met the gaze of all men. His smile was no less engaging and his manner remained the same--fearless, unsuspicious, definite in serious affairs, good-natured and companionable in everything. I could not read him now, by one little line, but back of everything lay that withering, grievous thought--he was a murderer. Heaven pity the boy when his idol falls, and if he be a dreaming idealist the hurt is tenfold deeper.

And yet--the trail was waiting there to teach me many things, and Jondo's words rang through the aisles of my brain:

"If you ever have a real cross, Gail, thank the Lord for the open plains and the green prairies, and the danger stimulus of the old Santa Fé Trail. They will seal up your wounds, and soften your hard, rebellious heart, and make you see things big, and despise the little crooks in your path."

Our Conestoga wagons, with their mule-teams, and the few ponies for scout service, followed the old trail out of the valley of the Rio Grande to the tablelands eastward, up the steep sidling way into the passes of the Glorietta Mountains, down through lone, wind-swept cañons, and on between wild, scarred hills, coming, at last, beyond the picturesque ridges, snow-crowned and mesa-guarded, into the long, gray, waterless lands of the Cimmarron country. Here we journeyed along monotonous levels that rose and fell unnoted because of lack of landmarks to measure by, only the broad, beaten Santa Fé Trail stretched on unbending, unchanging, uneffaceable.

As the distance from spring to spring decreased, every drop of water grew precious, and we pushed on, eager to reach the richer prairies of the Arkansas Valley. Suddenly in the monotony of the way, and the increasing calls of thirst, there came a sense of danger, the plains-old danger of the Comanche on the Cimarron Trail. Bill Banney caught it first--just a faint sign of one hostile track. All the next day Jondo scouted far, coming into camp at nightfall with a grave report.

"The water-supply is failing," he told us, "and there is something wrong out there. The Comanches are hovering near, that's certain, and there is a single trail that doesn't look Comanche to me that I can't account for. All we can do is to 'hold fast,'" he added, with his cheery smile that never failed him.

That night I could not sleep, and the stars and I stared long at each other. They were so golden and so far away. And one, as I looked, slipped from its place and trailed wide across the sky until it vanished, leaving a stream of golden light that lingered before my eyes. I thought of the trail in the San Christobal Valley, and again I saw the sunlight on golden hair as Eloise with Little Blue Flower passed out of sight around the shoulder of a great rock beside the way. At last came sleep, and in my dreams Eloise was beside me as she had been in the church of San Miguel, her dark eyes looking up into mine. I knew, in my dream, that I was dreaming and I did not want to waken. For, "Eloise loved Beverly, would always love him." Little Blue Flower had said it. The face was far away, this side of misty mountain peaks, and farther still. I could see only the eyes looking at me. I wakened to see only the stars looking at me. I slept again deeply and dreamlessly, and wakened suddenly. We were far and away from the Apache country, but there, for just one instant, a face came close to mine--the face of Santan-- the Apache. It vanished instantly as it had come. The night guard passed by me and crossed the camp. The stars held firm above me. I had had another dream. But after that I did not sleep till dawn.

The day was very hot, with the scorching breeze of the plains that sears the very eyeballs dry. Through the dust and glare we pressed on over long, white, monotonous miles. Hovering near us somewhere were the Comanches--waiting; with us was burning thirst; ahead of us ran the taunting mirage--cool, sparkling water rippling between green banks-- receding as we approached, maddening us by the suggestion of its refreshing picture, the while we knew it was only a picture. For it is Satan's own painting on the desert to let men know that Dante's dream is mild compared to the real art of torment. Men and animals began to give way under the day's burden, and we moved slowly. In times like these Jondo stayed with the train, sending Bill Banney and Beverly scouting ahead. That was the longest day that I ever lived on the Santa Fé Trail, although I followed its miles many times in the best of its freighting years.

The weary hours dragged at last toward evening, and a dozen signs in plains lore told us that water must be near. As we topped a low swell at the bottom of whose long slide lay the little oasis we were seeking, we came upon Bill Banney's pony lying dead across the trail. And near it Bill himself, with bloated face and bleared eyes, muttering half-coherently:

"Water-hole! Poison! Don't drink!"

And then he babbled of the muddy Missouri, and the Kentucky blue grass, and cold mountain springs in the passes of the Gloriettas, warning us thickly of "death down there."

"Down there," beside the little spring shelved in by shale at the lower edge of the swell, we found a tiny cairn built of clumps of sod and bits of shale. Fastened on it was a scrap from Bill's note-book with the words

Spring poisoned. Bev gone for water not very far on.--BILL.

So Bill had drunk the poisoned water and had tried to reach us. But for fear he might not do it, he had scrawled this warning and left it here. Brave Bill! How madly he had staggered round the place and threshed the ground in agony when he tried to mount his poisoned pony, and his first thought was for us. The plains made men see big. Jondo had told me they could do it. Poor Bill, moaning for water now and tossing in agony in Jondo's wagon! The Comanches had been cunning in their malice. How we hated them as we stood looking at the waters of that poisoned spring!

Rex Krane's big, gentle hands were holding Bill's. Rex always had a mother's heart; while Jondo read the ground with searching glance.

"We will wait here a little while. Bev will report soon, I hope. Come, Gail," he said to me. "Here is something we will follow now."

A single trail led far away from the beaten road toward a stretch of coarse dry yucca and loco-weeds that hid a little steep-sided draw across the plains. At the bottom of it a man lay face downward beside a dead pony. We scrambled down, shattering the dry earth after us as we went. Jondo gently lifted the body and turned it face upward. It was Ferdinand Ramero.

The big plainsman did not cry out, nor drop his hold, but his face turned gray, and only the dying man saw the look in the blue eyes gazing into his. Ramero tried to draw away, fear, and hate, and the old dominant will that ruled his life, strong still in death. As he lay at the feet of the man whose life hopes he had blasted, he expected no mercy and asked for none.

"You have me at last. I didn't put the poison in that spring. I would not have drunk it if I had. It was the one below I fixed for you. And I'm in your power now. Be quick about it."

For one long minute Jondo looked down at his enemy. Then he lifted his eyes to mine with the victory of "him that overcometh" shining in their blue depths.

"If I could make you live, I'd do it, Fred. If you have any word to say, be quick about it now. Your time is short."

The sweetness of that gentle voice I hear sometimes to-day in the low notes of song-birds, and the gentle swish of refreshing summer showers.

Ferdinand Ramero lifted his cold blue eyes and looked at the man bending over him.

"Leave me here--forgotten--"

"Not of God. His Mercy endureth forever," Jondo replied.

But there was no repentance, no softening of the hard, imperious heart.

We left him there, pulling down the loose earth from the steep sides of the draw to cover him from all the frowning elements of the plains. And when we went back to the waiting train Jondo reported, grimly:

"*No enemy in sight.*"

We laid Bill Banney beside the poisoned spring, from whose bitter waters he had saved our lives. So martyrs filled the unknown graves that made the milestones of the way in the days of commerce-building on the old Santa Fé Trail.

The next spring was not far ahead, as Bill's note had said, but the stars were thick above us and the desolate land was full of shadows before we reached it--a thirst-mad, heart-sore crowd trailing slowly on through the gloom of the night.

Beverly was waiting for us and the refreshing moisture of the air above a spring seemed about him.

"I thought you'd never come. Where's Bill? There's water here. I made the spring myself," he shouted, as we came near.

The spring that he had digged for us was in the sandy bed of a dry stream, with low, earth-banks on either side. It was full of water, hardly clear, but plentiful, and slowly washing out a bigger pool for itself as it seeped forth.

"There is poison in the real spring down there." Beverly pointed toward the diminished fountain we had expected to find. "I've worked since noon at this."

We drank, and life came back to us. We pitched camp, and then listened to Beverly's story of the sweet and bitter waters of the trail that day. And all the while it seemed as if Bill Banney was just out of sight and might come galloping in at any moment.

"You know what happened up the trail," my cousin said, sadly. "Bill was ahead of me and he drank first, and galloped back to warn me and beg me to come on for water. I thought I could get down here and take some water back to Bill in time. It's all shale up there. No place to dig above, nor below, even if one dared to dig below that poison. But I found a dead coyote that had just left here, and all springs began to look Comanche to me. I lariated my pony and crept down under the bank there to think and rest. Everything went poison-spotted before my eyes."

"Where's your pony now, Bev?" Jondo asked.

"I don't know sure, but I expect he is about going over the Raton Pass by this time," Beverly replied. "Down there things seemed to swim around me like water everywhere and I knew I'd got to stir. Just then an Indian came slipping up from somewhere to the spring to drink. He didn't look right to me at all, but I couldn't sit still and see him kill himself. If he needed killing I could have done it for him, for he never saw me. Just as he stooped I saw his face. It was that Apache--Santan--the wander-foot, for I never heard of an Apache getting so far from the mountains. I ought to have kept still, Jondo"--Beverly's ready smile came to his face--"but I'd made that fellow swear he'd let me eternally alone when we had our little fracas up by the

San Christobal Arroyo, so something like conscience, mean as the stomach-ache, made me call out:

"'Don't drink there; it's poison.'

"He stopped and stared at me a minute, or ten minutes--I didn't count time on him--and then he said, slow-like:

"'It's the spring west that is poisoned. I put it there for you. You will not see your men again. They will drink and die. Who put this poison here?'

"'Lord knows. I didn't,' I told him. 'Two of you carrying poison are two too many for the Cimarron country.'

"And I hadn't any more conscience after that, but I was faint and slow, and my aim was bad for eels. He could have fixed me right then, but for some reason he didn't."

Beverly's face grew sad.

"He made six jumps six ways, and caught my pony's lariat. I can hear his yell still as he tore a hole in the horizon and jumped right through. Then I began on that spring. 'Dig or die. Dig or die.' I said over and over, and we are all here but Bill. I wish I'd got that Apache, though."

Jondo and I looked at each other.

"The thing is clear now," he said, aside to me. "That single trail I found back yonder day before yesterday was Santan's running on ahead of us to poison the water for us and then steal a horse and make his way back to the mountains. An Apache can live on this cactus-covered sand the same as a rattlesnake. He fixed the upper spring and came down here to drink. Only Beverly's conscience saved him here. Heaven knows how Fred Ramer got out here. He may have come with some Mexicans on ahead of us and left them here to drop his poison in this lower spring. Then he turned back toward Santa Fé and found his doom up there at Santan's spring.

"I'm like Bev. I wish he had gotten the Apache, now. I don't know yet how I was fooled in him, for he has always been Fred Ramer's tool, and Father Josef never trusted him. And to think that Bill Banney, in no way touching any of our lives, should have been martyred by the crimes of Fred and this Apache! But that's the old, old story of the trail. Poor Bill! I hope his sleep will be sweet out in this desolate land. We'll meet him later somewhere."

The winds must have carried the tale of poisoned water across the Cimarron country, for the Comanches' trail left ours from that day. Through threescore and ten miles to the Arkansas River we came, and there was not a well nor spring nor sign of water in all that distance. What water we had we carried with us from the Cimarron fountains. But the sturdy endurance of the days was not without its help to me. And the wide, wind-swept prairies of Kansas taught me many things. In the lonely, beautiful land, through long bright days and starlit nights, I began to see things bigger than my own selfish measure had reckoned. I thought of Esmond Clarenden and his large scheme of business; Felix Narveo, the true-hearted friend; and of Father Josef and his life of devotion. And I lived with Jondo every day. I could not forget the hour in the little ruined chapel in the San Christobal Valley, and how he himself had made no effort to clear his own name. But I remembered, too, that Father Josef, mercilessly just to Ferdinand Ramero, had not even asked Jondo to defend himself from the black charge against him.

The sunny Kansas prairies, the far open plains, and the wild mountain trails beyond, had brought their blessing to Jondo, whose life had known so much of tragedy. And my cross was just my love for a girl who could not love me. That was all. Jondo had never forgotten nor ceased to love the mother of Eloise St. Vrain. I should be like Jondo in this. But the world is wide. Life is full of big things. Henceforth, while I would not forget, I, too, would be big and strong, and maybe, some time, just as sunny-faced as my big Jondo.

The trail life, day by day, did bring its blessing to me. The clear, open land, the far-sweeping winds, the solitude for thought, the bravery and gentleness of the rough men who walked the miles with me, the splendor of the day-dawn, the beauty of the sunset, the peace of the still starlit night, sealed up my wounds, and I began to live for others and to forget myself; to dream less often, and to work more gladly; to measure men, not by what had been, but by how they met what was to be done.

From all the frontier life, rough-hewn and coarse, the elements came that helped to make the big brave West to-day, and I know now that not the least of source and growth of power for these came out of the strength and strife of the things known only to the men who followed the Santa Fé Trail.

III

DEFENDING THE TRAIL

XVIII

WHEN THE SUN WENT DOWN

The mind hath a thousand eyes,
And the heart but one.
--BOURDILLON.

Busy years, each one a dramatic era all its own, made up the annals of the Middle West as the nation began to feel the thrill for expansion in its pulse-beat. The territorial days of Kansas were big with the tragic events of border warfare, and her birth into statehood marked the commencement of the four years of civil strife whose record played a mighty part in shaping human destiny.

Meanwhile the sunny Kansas prairies lay waiting for the hearthstone and the plow. And young men, trained in camp and battle-field, looked westward for adventure, fortune, future homes and fame. But the tribes, whose hunting-grounds had been the green and grassy plains, yielded slowly, foot by foot, their stubborn claim, marking in human blood the price of each acre of the prairie sod. The lonely homesteads were the prey of savage bands, and the old Santa Fé Trail, always a way of danger, became doubly perilous now to the men who drove the vans of commerce along its broad, defenseless miles. The frontier forts increased: Hays and Harker, Larned and Zarah, and Lyon and Dodge became outposts of power in the wilderness, whose half-forgotten sites to-day lie buried under broad pasture-lands and fields of waving grain.

One June day, as the train rolled through the Missouri woodlands along rugged river bluffs, Beverly Clarenden and I looked eagerly out of the car window, watching for signs of home. It was two years after the close of the Civil War. We had just finished six years of Federal service and were coming back to Kansas City. We were young men still, with all the unsettled spirit that follows the laying aside of active military life for the wholesome but uneventful life of peace.

The time of our arrival had been uncertain, and the Clarenden household had been taken by surprise at our coming.

"I wonder how it will seem to settle down in a store, Bev, after toting shooting-irons for six years," I said to my cousin, as the train neared

Kansas City.

"I don't know," Beverly replied, with a yawn, "but I'm thinking that after we see all the folks, and play with Mat's little boys awhile, and eat Aunty Boone's good stuff till we begin to get flabby-cheeked and soft-muscled, and our jaws crack from smiling so much when we just naturally want to get out and cuss somebody--about that time I'll be ready to run away, if I have to turn Dog Indian to do it."

"There's a new Clarenden store at a place called Burlingame out in Kansas now, somewhere on the old trail. Maybe it will be far enough away to let you get tamed gradually to civil life there, if Uncle Esmond thinks you are worth it," I suggested.

"Rex Krane is to take charge of that as soon as we get home. Yonder are the spires and minarets and domes of Kansas City. Put on your company grin, Gail," Beverly replied, as we began to run by the huts and cabins forming the outworks of the little city at the Kaw's mouth.

Six years had made many changes in the place, but the same old welcome awaited us, and we became happy-hearted boys again as we climbed the steep road up the bluff to the Clarenden house. On the wide veranda overlooking the river everybody except one--Bill Banney, sleeping under the wind-caressed sod beside the Cimarron spring--was waiting to greet us. There were Esmond Clarenden and Jondo, in the prime of middle life, the one a little bald, and more than a little stout; the other's heavy hair was streaked with gray, but the erect form and tremendous physical strength told how well the plains life had fortified the man of fifty for the years before him. The prairies had long since become his home; but whether in scout service for the Government, or as wagon-master for a Clarenden train on the trail, he was the same big, brave, loyal Jondo.

And there was Rex Krane, tall, easy-going old Rex, with his wife beside him. Mat was a fair-faced young matron now, with something Madonna-like in her calm poise and kindly spirit. Two little boys, Esmond, and Rex, Junior, clinging to her gown, smiled a shy welcome at us.

In the background loomed the shining face and huge form of Aunty Boone. She had never seemed bigger to me, even in my little-boy days, when I considered her a giant. Her eyes grew dull as she looked at us.

"Clean faces and finger-nails now. Got to stain 'em up 'bout once more 'fore you are through. Hungry as ever, I'll bet. I'll get your supper right away. Whoo-ee!"

As she turned away, Mat said:

"There is somebody else here, boys, that you will be glad to meet. She has just come and doesn't even know that you are expected. It is 'Little Lees.'"

A rustle of silken skirts, a faint odor of blossoms, a footfall, a presence, and Eloise St. Vrain stood before us. Eloise, with her golden hair, the girlish roundness of her fair face, her big dark eyes and their heavy lashes and clear-penciled brows, her dainty coloring, and beyond all these the beauty of womanly strength written in her countenance.

Her dress was a sort of pale heliotrope, with trimmings of a deeper shade, and in her hands she carried a big bunch of June roses. She stopped short, and the pink cheeks grew pale, but in an instant the rich bloom came back to them again.

"I tried to find you, Eloise. The boys have just come in almost unannounced," Mat said.

"You didn't mean to hide from us, of course," Beverly broke in, as he took the girl's hand, his face beaming with genuine joy at meeting her again.

Eloise met him with the same frank delight with which she always greeted him. Everything seemed so simple and easy for these two when they came together. Little Blue Flower was right about them. They seemed to fit each other.

But when she turned to me her eyes were downcast, save for just one glance. I feel it yet, and the soft touch of her hand as it lay in mine a moment.

I think we chatted all together for a while. I had a wound at Malvern Hill that used to make me dizzy. That, or an older wound, made my pulse frantic now. I know that it was a rare June day, and the breeze off the river came pouring caressingly over the bluff. I remember later that Uncle Esmond and Jondo and Rex Krane went to the Clarenden store, and that Mat was helping Aunty Boone inside, while Beverly let the two little Kranes take him down the slope to see some baby squirrels or something. And Eloise and I were left alone beneath the trees, where once we had sat together long ago in the "Moon of the Peach Blossom." For me, all the strength of the years wherein I had built a wall around my longing love, all my manly loyalty to my cousin's claims, were swept away, as I have seen the big Missouri floods, joined by the lesser Kaw, sweep out bridges, snapping like sticks before their power.

"Eloise, it seems a hundred years since I saw you and Little Blue Flower ride away up the San Christobal River trail out of my sight," I said.

"It has been a long time, but we are not yet old. You seem the same. And as for me, I feel as if the clock had stopped awhile and had suddenly started to ticking anew."

It was wonderful to sit beside her and hear her voice again. I did not dare to ask about her mother, but I am sure she read my thoughts, for she went on:

"My mother is gone now. She was as happy as a child and never had a sorrow on her mind after her dreadful fever, although the doctors say she might have been restored if I had only been with her then. But it is all ended now."

Eloise paused with saddened face, and looked out toward the Missouri River, boiling with June rains and melted snows.

"It is all right now," she went on, bravely. "Sister Gloria--you know who she was--stayed with me to the last. And I have a real mound of earth in the cemetery beside my father." The last two words were spoken softly. "Sister Gloria is in the convent now. Marcos is a common gambler. His father disappeared and left him penniless. Esmond Clarenden says that his father died out on the plains somewhere."

"And Father Josef?" I inquired.

"Is still the same strong friend to everybody. He spends much time among the Hopi people. I don't know why, for they are hopelessly heathen. Their own religion has so many beautiful things to offset our faith that they are hard to convert."

"And Little Blue Flower--what became of her?" I asked. "Is she a squaw in some hogan or pueblo, after all that the Sisterhood of St. Ann's did for her?"

A shadow fell on the bright face beside me.

"Let's not talk of her to-day." There was a pleading note in Eloise's voice. "Life has its tragedies everywhere, but I sometimes think that none of them--American, English, Spanish, French, Mexican, nor any others of our pale-faced people, have quite such bitter acts as the Indian tragedy among a gentle race like the people of Hopi-land."

"I hope you will stay with us now."

I didn't know what I really did hope for. I was no longer a boy, but a young man in the very best of young manhood's years. I had seen this girl ride away from me without one good-by word or glance. I had heard her message to me through Little Blue Flower. I had suffered and outgrown all but the scar. And now one touch of her hand, one smile, one look from her beautiful eyes, and all the barrier of the years fell down. I wondered vaguely now about Beverly's wish to turn Dog Indian if things became too monotonous. I wondered about many things, but I could not think anything.

"I have no present plans. Father Josef and Esmond Clarenden thought it would be well for me to come up to Kansas and look at green prairies instead of red mesas for a while; to rest my eyes, and get my strength again--which I have never lost," Eloise said, with a smile. "And Jondo says--"

She did not tell me what Jondo had said, for Beverly and Mat and the two rollicking boys joined us just then and we talked of many things of the earlier years.

I cannot tell how that June slipped by, nor how Eloise, in the full bloom of her young womanhood, with the burdens lifted from her heart and hands, was no more the clinging, crushed Eloise who had sat beside me in the church of San Miguel, but a self-reliant and deliciously companionable girl-woman. With Beverly she was always gay, matching him, mood for mood; and if sometimes I caught the fleeting edge of a shadow in her eyes, it was gone too soon to measure. I did not seek her company alone, because I knew that I could not trust myself. Over and over, Jondo's words, when he had told me the story of Mary Marchland, came back to me:

"And although they loved each other always, they never saw each other again."

Nobody, outside of those touched by it, knew Jondo's story, except myself. He was Theron St. Vrain's brother, yet Eloise never called him uncle, and, except for the one mention of her father's grave, she did not speak of him.

He was not even a memory to her. And both men's names were forever stained with the black charge against them.

One evening in late June, Uncle Esmond called me into council.

"Gail, Rex leaves to-morrow for the new store at Burlingame, Kansas. It is two days out on the Santa Fé Trail. Bev will go with him and stay for a while. I want you to drive through with Mat and the children and Eloise a day or two later."

"Eloise?" I looked up in surprise.

"Yes; she will visit with Mat for a while. She has had some trying years that have taxed her heavily. The best medicine for such is the song of the prairie winds," Uncle Esmond replied.

"And after that?" I insisted.

"We will wait for 'after that' till it gets here," my uncle smiled as he spoke. "There are more serious things on hand than where out Little Lees will eat her meals. She seems able to take care of herself anywhere. Wonderfully beautiful and charming young woman she is, and her troubles have strengthened her character without robbing her of her youth and happy spirits."

Esmond Clarenden spoke reminiscently, and I stared at him in surprise until suddenly I remembered that Jondo had said, "We were all in love with Mary Marchland." Eloise must seem to him and Jondo like the Mary Marchland they had known in their young manhood. But my uncle's mood passed quickly, and his face was very grave as he said:

"The conditions out on the frontier are serious in every way right now. The Indians are on the war-path, leaving destruction wherever they set foot. Something must be done to protect the wagon-trains on the Santa Fé Trail. I have already lost part of two valuable loads this season, and Narveo has lost three. But the appalling loss of property is nothing compared to the terror and torture to human life. The settlers on the frontier claims are being massacred daily. The Governor of Kansas is doing all he can to get some action from the army leaders at Washington. But you haven't been in military service for six years without finding out that some army leaders are flesh and blood, and some are only wood--plain wooden wood. Meantime, the story of one butchery doesn't get to the Missouri River before the story of another catches up with it. It's bad enough when it's ruinous to just my own commercial business--but in cases like this, humanity is my business."

What a man he was--that Esmond Clarenden! They still say of him in Kansas City that no sounder financier and no bigger-hearted humanitarian ever walked the streets of that "Gateway to the Southwest" than the brave little merchant-plainsman who builded for the generations that should follow him.

"What will be the outcome, Uncle Esmond? Are we to lose all we have gained out here?" I asked.

"Not if we are real Westerners. It's got to be stopped. The question is, how soon," my uncle replied.

That night in a half-waking dream I remembered Aunty Boone's prophetic greeting a few days before, and how her eyes had narrowed and grown dull as she said, "One more stainin' of your hands 'fore you are through."

I had given six good years to army service--the years which young men give to college and to establishing themselves in their life-work. But the vision of the three men whom I had seen under the elm-tree at Fort Leavenworth came back to me, and only one--the cavalry man--moved westward now. I knew that I was dreaming, but I did not want to waken till the vision of a fair face whose eyes looked into mine should come to make my dream sweet and restful.

But in my waking hours, in spite of the gravity of conditions that troubled Esmond Clarenden, in spite of the terrible tidings of daily killings on the unprotected plains, I forgot everything except the girl beside me as I went with her and Mat and the children to the new home in the village of Burlingame beside the Santa Fé Trail.

Eloise St. Vrain had come up to Kansas to let the green prairies shut out the memory of tall red mesas. About the little town of Burlingame the prairies were waiting for her eyes to see. It nestled beside a deep creek under the shelter of forest trees, with the green prairie lapping up to its edges on every side. The trail wound round the shoulder of a low hill, and, crossing the stream, it made the main street of the town, then wandered on westward to where a rim of ground shut the view of its way from the settlement under the trees by the creek. A stanch little settlement it was, and, like many Kansas towns of the '60's, with big, but never-to-be realized, ambition to become a city. Into its life and up-building Rex Krane was to throw his good-natured Yankee shrewdness, and Mat her calm, generous spirit; vanguards they were, among the home-makers of a great State.

My stay in the place was brief, and I saw little of Eloise until the evening before I was to return to Kansas City. I had meant to go away, as she had left me in the San Christobal Valley, without one backward look, but I couldn't do it; and at the close of my last day I went to the Krane home, where I found her alone. It was the long after-sunset hour, with the refreshing evening breezes pouring in from all the green levels about us.

"Rex is at the store, and the others are all gone fishing," Eloise said, in answer to my inquiry for the family.

"Mat and Bev always did go fishing on every occasion that I can remember, and they will make fishermen of little Esmond and Rex now. Would you like to go up to the west side of town and look into New Mexico?" I asked, wondering why Beverly should go fishing with Mat when Eloise was waiting for his smile.

But I was desperately lonely to-night, and I might not see Eloise again until after she and Beverly--I could not go farther. She smiled and said, lightly:

"I'm just honin' for a walk, as Aunty Boone would say, but I'm not quite ready to see New Mexico yet."

"Oh, it's only a thing made of evening mists rising from the meadows, and bits of sunset lights left over when the day was finished," I assured her.

So we left the shadow of the tall elms and strolled up the main street toward the west.

Where the one cross-street cut the trail in the center of the village there was a public well. The ground around it was trampled into mud by many hoofs. A Mexican train had just come in and was grouped about this well, drinking eagerly.

"What news of the plains?" I asked their leader as we passed.

"I cannot tell you with the lady here," he replied, bowing courteously. "It is too awful. A spear hung with a scalp of pretty baby hair like hers. I see it yet. The plains are all *alive--alive* with hostile red men; and the worst one of all--he that had the golden scalp--is but a half-breed Cheyenne Dog. Never the Apaches were so bad as he."

The cattle horned about the well, with their drivers shouting and struggling to direct them, as we went wide to avoid the mud, then passed up to the rise beyond which lay the old trail's westward route.

The mists were rising from the lowlands; along the creek the sunset sky was all a flaming glory, under whose deep splendor the June prairies lay tenderly green and still; down in the village the sounds of the Mexicans settling into camp; the shouting of children, romping late; and out across the levels, the mooing call of milking-time from some far-away settler's barn-yard; a robin singing a twilight song in the elms; crickets chirping in the long grass; and the gentle evening breeze sweet and cool out of the west--such was the setting for us two. We paused on the crest of the ridge and sat down to watch the afterglow of a prairie twilight. We did not speak for a long time, but when our eyes met I knew the hour had been made for me. In such an hour we had sat beside the glistening Flat Rock down in the Neosho Valley. I was a whole-hearted boy when I went down there, full of eagerness for the life of adventure on the trail, and she a girl just leaving boarding-school. And now--life sweetens so with years.

"I think I can understand why your uncle thought it would be well for me to come to Kansas," Eloise said at last. "There is an inspiration and soothing restfulness in a thing like this. Our mountains are so huge and tragical; and even their silences are not always gentle. And our plains are dry and gray. And yet I love the valley of the Santa Fé, and the old Ortiz and Sandia peaks, and the red sunset's stain on the Sangre-de-Christo. Many a time I have lifted up my eyes to them for help, as the shepherd did to his Judean hills when he sang his psalms of hope and victory."

"Yes, Nature is kind to us if we will let her be. Jondo told me that long ago, and I've proved it since. But I have always loved the prairies. And this ridge here belongs to me," I replied.

Eloise looked up inquiringly.

"I'll tell you why. When I was a little boy, years ago, a day-dreaming, eager-hearted little boy, we camped here one night. That was my first trip over the trail to Santa Fé. You haven't forgotten it and what a big brown bob-cat I looked like when I got there. I grew like weeds in a Kansas corn-field on that trip."

"Oh, I remember you. Go on," Eloise said, laughingly.

"That night after supper, everybody had left camp--Mat and Bev were fishing--and I was alone and lonely, so I came up here to find what I could see of the next day's trail. It was such an hour as this. And as I watched the twilight color deepen, my own horizon widened, and I think the soul of a man began, in that hour, to look out through the little boy's eyes; and a new mile-stone was set here to make a landmark in my life-trail. The boy who went back slowly to the camp that night was not the same little boy that had run up here to spy out the way of the next day's journey."

The afterglow was deepening to purple; the pink cloud-flecks were turning gray in the east, and a kaleidoscope of softest rose and tender green and misty lavender filled the lengthening shadows of the twilight prairie.

"Eloise, I had a longing that night, still unfulfilled. I wish I dared to tell you what it was."

I turned to look at the fair girl-woman beside me. In the twilight her eyes were always like stars; and the golden hair and the pink bloom of her cheeks seemed richer in their shadowy setting. To-night her gown was white--like the Greek dress she had worn at Mat's wedding, on the night when she met Beverly in the little side porch at midnight. Why did I recall that here?

"What was your wish, Gail?" The voice was low and sweet.

I took her hand in mine and she did not draw away from me.

"That I might some day have a real home all my own down there among the trees. I was a little homesick boy that night, and I came up here to watch the sunset and see the open level lands that I have always loved. Eloise, Jondo told me once of three young college men who loved your beautiful mother, and because of that love they never married anybody, but they lived useful, happy lives. I can understand now why they should love her, and why, because they could not have her love, they would not marry anybody else. One was my uncle Esmond, and one was Father Josef."

"And the third?" The voice was very low and a tremor shook the hand I held.

"He did not tell me. And I speak of it now only to show you that in what I want to say I am not altogether selfish and unkind. I love you, Eloise. I have loved you since the day, long ago, when your face came before me on the parade-ground at Fort Leavenworth. I told you of that once down on the bluff by the Clarenden home at Kansas City. I shall love you, as the Bedouin melody runs,

Til the sun grows cold,
And the stars are old,
And the leaves of the judgment
Book unfold!

"But I know that it will end as Uncle Esmond's and Father Josef's loving did, in my living my life alone."

Eloise quickly withdrew her hand, and the pain in her white face haunts me still.

"I do not want to hurt you, oh, Eloise. I know I do wrong to speak, but to-night will be the last time. I thought that night in the church at San Miguel, and that next day when we rode for our lives together, that you cared for me who would have walked through fire for you. But in that hour in the little chapel a barrier came between us. You rode away without one word or glance. And I turned back feeling that my soul was falling into ruins like that half-ruined little pile of stone that some holy padre had built his heart into years and years ago. Then Little Blue Flower brought your message to me and I knew as I sat beside Fort Marcy's wall that night, and saw the sun go down, that the light of my life was going out with it."

"But, Gail," Eloise exclaimed, "I said I could not send you any word, but you would understand. I--I couldn't say any more than that." Her voice was full of tears and she turned away from me and looked at the last radiant tints edging the little cloud-flecks above the horizon.

"Of course I understand you, Eloise, and I do not blame you. I never could blame you for anything." I sprang to my feet. "You'll hate me if I say another word," I said, savagely.

She rose up, too, and put her hand on my arm. Oh, she was beautiful as she stood beside me. So many times I have pictured her face, I will not try to picture it as it looked now in this sweet, sacred moment of our lives.

"Gail, I could never hate you. You do not understand me. I cannot help what is past now. I hoped you might forget. And yet--" She paused.

All men are humanly alike. In spite of my strong love for Beverly and my sense of right, the presence of the woman whose image for so many years had been in the sacredest shrine of my heart, Eloise, in all her beauty and her womanly strength and purity, standing beside me, her hand still on my arm--all overpowered me.

I put my arms about her and held her close to me, kissing her forehead, her cheek, her lips. The world for one long moment was rose-hued like the sunset's afterglow; and sky and prairie, lowlands along the winding creek, and tall elm-trees above the deepening shadows, were all engulfed in a mist of golden glory, shot through with amethyst and sapphire, the dainty coraline pink of summer dawns, and the iridescent shimmer of mother-of-pearl.

Heaven opens to us here and there such moments on the way of life. And the memory of them lingers like perfume through all the days that follow.

We turned our faces toward the darkening village street and the tall elms above the gathering shadows, and neither spoke a word until we reached the door where I must say good night.

"I cannot ask you to forgive me, Little Lees, because you let me have a bit of heaven up there. I shall go away a better man. And, remember, that no blessing in your life can be greater than I would wish for you to have."

The brave white face was before my eyes and the low voice was in my ears long after I had left her door.

"Gail, I cannot help what has been, but I do not blame you. I should almost wish myself shut in again by the tall red mesas; but maybe, after all, the prairies are best for me. I am glad I have known you. Good night."

"Goodnight," I said, and turned away.

And that was all. The last light of day had gone from the sky, and the stars overhead were hidden by the thick leafage of the Burlingame elms.

XIX

A MAN'S PART

Don't you guess that the things we're seeing now will haunt us through the
years;
Heaven and hell rolled into one, glory and blood and tears;
Life's pattern picked with a scarlet thread, where once we wove with a gray,
To remind us all how we played our part in the shock of an epic day?
--ROBERT W. SERVICE.

However darkly the sun may go down on hope and love, the real sun shines
on, day after day, with its inexorable call to duty. In less than a week after I
had left Eloise and the vague hope of a home of my own under the big
elm-trees of Burlingame, Governor Crawford of Kansas sent forth a call
for a battalion of four companies of soldiers, and I heard the call and
answered it.

It was to be known as the Eighteenth Kansas Cavalry, with Col. Horace L.
Moore, a veteran soldier of tried mettle, at the head. We were to go at once
to Fort Harker, in the valley of the Smoky Hill River, to begin a campaign
against the Indians, who were laying waste the frontier settlements and
attacking wagon-trains on the Sante Fé Trail.

On the evening before I left home I sat on the veranda of the Clarenden
house, waiting for Uncle Esmond to join me, when suddenly Beverly
Clarenden strode over the edge of the hill. The sunny smile and the merry
twinkle of his eye were Bev's own, and there wasn't a line on his face to
show whether it belonged to the happy lover or the rejected suitor. I
thought I could always read his moods when he had any. He had none to-
night.

"I just got in from Burlingame. At what hour do you leave to-morrow? I'm
going along to chaperon you, as usual," he declared.

"Why, Beverly Clarenden, I thought you were fixed at Burlingame, selling
molasses and calico by the gallon," I exclaimed, but my real thought was
not given to words.

"And let the Cheyennes, and Kiowas, and Arapahoes, and other
desperadoes of the plains gnaw clear into the heart of us? Not your uncle

Esmond Clarenden's nephew. And, Gail, this won't be anything like we have had since those six Kiowas staked you out on Pawnee Rock once. The thoroughbred Indians are bad enough, but there is a half-breed leader of a band of Dog Indians that's worst of all. He's of the yellow kind, with wolf's fangs. A Mexican on the trail told me that this half-breed ties up with the worst of every tribe from the Coast Range mountains to Tecumseh, Kansas," Beverly declared.

"I remember that Mexican. I saw him at the well in Burlingame," I replied, turning to look at the Kaw winding far away, for the memory of everything in Burlingame was painful to me.

Aunty Boone's huge form appearing around the corner of the house shut off my view of the river just then. Her face was glistening, but her eyes were dull as she looked us over.

"You stainin' your hands again," she purred. "Yes, Aunty. We are going to lick the redskins into ribbons," Beverly replied.

"You never get that done. Lickin' never settles nobody. You just hold 'em down till they strong enough to boost you off their heads again, and up they come. Whoo-ee!"

The black woman gave a chuckle.

"Well, I'd rather sit on their heads than have them sitting on mine, or yours, Aunty Boone," Beverly returned, laughingly.

Aunty Boone's eyes narrowed and there was a strange light in them as she looked at us, saying:

"You get into trouble, Mr. Bev, you see me comin', hot streaks, to help you out. Whoo-ee!"

She breathed her weird, African whoop and turned away.

"I'll depend on you." Beverly's face was bright, and there was no shadow in his eyes, as he called after her retreating form.

We chatted long together, and I hoped--and feared--to have him tell me the story of his suit with Eloise, and why in such a day, of all the days of his life, he should choose to run away to the warfare of the frontier. He could not have failed, I thought. Never a disappointed lover wore a smile like this. But Beverly had no story to tell me that night.

* * * * *

The mid-July sun was shining down on a treeless landscape, across which the yellow, foam-flecked Smoky Hill River wound its sinuous way. Beside this stream was old Fort Harker, a low quadrangle of quarters, for military man and beast, grouped about a parade-ground for companionship rather than for protection. The frontier fort had little need for defensive strength. About its walls the Indian crawled submissively, fearful of munitions and authority. It was not here, but out on lonely trails, in sudden ambush, or in overwhelming numbers, or where long miles, cut off from water, or exhausting distance banished safe retreat, that the savage struck in all his fury.

Eastward from Harker the scattered frontier homesteads crouched, defenseless, in the river valleys. Far to the northwest spread the desolate lengths of a silent land where the white man's foot had hardly yet been set. Miles away to the southwest the Santa Fé Trail wound among the Arkansas sand-hills, never, in all its history, less safe for freighters than in that summer of 1867.

In this vast demesne the raiding Cheyenne, the cruel Kiowa, the blood-thirsty Arapahoe, with bands of Dog Indians and outlaws from every tribe, contested, foot by foot, for supremacy against the out-reaching civilization of the dominant Anglo-American. The lonely trails were measured off by white men's graves. The vagrant winds that bear the odor of alfalfa, and of orchard bloom to-day, were laden often with the smoke of burning homes, and often, too, they bore that sickening smell of human flesh, once caught, never to be forgotten. The story of that struggle for supremacy is a tragic drama of heroism and endurance. In it the Eighteenth Kansas Cavalry played a stirring part.

It seems but yesterday to me now, that July day so many years ago, when our four companies, numbering fewer than four hundred men, detrained from the Union Pacific train at Fort Harker on the Smoky Hill. And the faces of the men who were to lead us are clear in memory. Our commander, Colonel Moore, always brave and able; and our captains, Henry Lindsay, and Edgar Barker, and George Jenness, and David Payne, with the shrewd, courageous scout, Allison Pliley, and the undaunted, clear-thinking, young lieutenant, Frank Stahl. Ours was not to be a record of unfading glory, as national military annals show, yet it may count mightily when the Great Records are opened for final estimates. Those men who marched two thousand miles, back and forth, upon the trackless plains in that four months' campaign, have been forgotten in the debris of uneventful years. Our long-faded trails lie buried under wide alfalfa-fields and the paved streets of western Kansas towns. From the far springs that quenched our burning thirst comes water, trickling through a nickel faucet into a marble basin, now. Where the fierce sun seared our eyeballs, in a treeless, barren waste, green groves, atune with song-birds, cast long swaths of shade on verdant sod. The perils and the hardships of the Eighteenth Kansas Cavalry are now but as a tale that is told.

And yet of all the heroes whose life-trails cut my own, I account among the greatest those men under whose command, and with whose comradeship, I went out to serve the needs of my generation among the vanguards of the plains. And if in a sunset hour on the west ridge beyond the little town of Burlingame I had left a hopeless love behind me, I put a man's best energy into the thing before me.

The battle-field alone is not the soldier's greatest test. I had kept step with men who charge an enemy on an open plain or storm a high defense in the face of sure defeat. I had been ordered with my company to take redoubts against the flaming throats of bellowing cannon in the life-and-death grip before Richmond. I had felt the awful thrill of carnage as my division surged back and forth across the blood-soaked lengths of Gettysburg, and I never once fell behind my comrades. The battle-field breeds courage, and self-forgetfulness, and exaltation, from the sense of duty squarely met.

There were no battle-fields in 1867, where Greek met Greek in splendid gallantry, out on the Kansas plains. Over Fort Harker hung the pall of death, and in the July heat the great black plague of Asiatic cholera stalked abroad and scourged the land. Men were dying like rats, lacking everything that helps to drive death back. The volunteer who had offered himself to save the settlers from the scalping-knife had come here only to look into an open grave, and then, in agony, to drop into it. Such things test soldiers more than battle-fields. And our men turned back in fear, preferring the deserter's shame to quick, inglorious martyrdom by Asiatic cholera. I had a battle of my own the first night at Fort Harker. There was a growing moon and the night breeze was cool after the heat of the day. Beverly Clarenden and I went down to the river, whose tawny waters hardly hid the tawny sands beneath them. The plains were silent, but from all the hospital tents about the fort came the sharp, agonized cries of pain that forerun the last collapse of the plague-stricken sufferers. To get away from the sound of it all we wandered down the stream to where the banks of soft, caving earth on the farther side were higher than a man's head, and their shadow hid the current. We sat down and stared silently at the waters, scarcely whispering as they rolled along, and at the still shade of the farther bank upon them. The shadows thickened and moved a little, then grew still. We also grew still. Then they moved again just opposite us, and fell into three parts, as three men glided silently along under the bank's protecting gloom. We waited until they had reached the edge of the moonlight, and saw three soldiers pass swiftly out across the unprotected sands to other shadowy places further on.

"Deserters!" Beverly said, half aloud. "You can stay here if you want to, Gail. I'd rather go up and listen to those poor wretches groan than stick down here and listen to the fiend inside of me to-night."

He rose and stalked away, and I sat listening to myself. I could join those three men easily enough. The world is wide. I had no bond to hold me to one single place in it. I was young and strong, and life is sweet. Why let the black plague snuff me out of it? I had come here to serve the State. I should not serve it in a plague-marked grave. I rose to follow down the stream, to go to where the Smoky Hill joins the big Republican to make the Kaw, and on to where the Kaw reaches to the Missouri. But I would not stop there. I'd go until I reached the ocean somewhere.

Would I?

The memory of Jondo's eyes when they looked into mine on Pawnee Rock came unbidden across my mind. Jondo had lived a nameless man. How strong and helpful all his years had been! How starved had been my life without his love! I would be another Jondo, somewhere on earth.

I stared after three faintly moving shadows down the stream. 'Twas well I waited, for Esmond Clarenden came to me now, clean-cut, honest, everybody's friend. How firm his life had been; and he had built into me a hatred of deceit and lies. And Jondo was another Uncle Esmond. In spite of the black shadow on his name, he walked the prairies like a prince always. I could not be like him if I were a deserter. Up-stream death was waiting for me; down-stream, disgrace. I turned and followed up the river's course, but the strength that forced me to it was greater than that which made me brave on battle-fields. And ever since that night beside the Smoky Hill I have felt gentler toward the man who falls.

We were not idle long for Fort Harker had just been informed of an assault on a wagon-train on the Santa Fé Trail and our cavalry squadron hurried away at once to overtake and punish the assailants.

We came into camp on the bank of Walnut Creek, at the close of a long summer day of blazing light and heat over the barren trails where there was no water; a day of long hours in the saddle; a day of nerve-wearing watchfulness. But we believed that we had left the plague-cursed region behind us, so we were light-hearted and good-natured; and we ate, and drank, and took our lot cheerfully.

Among the men at mess that night I saw a new face which was nothing remarkable, except that something in it told me that I had already seen that face somewhere, some time. It is my gift never to forget a face, once seen, no matter how many years may pass before I see it twice. This soldier was a pleasant fellow, too, and, in a story he was telling, clever at imitating others.

"Who is that man, Bev? The third one over there?" I asked my cousin.

"Stranger to me. I don't believe I ever saw him before. Who is the fellow with the smile, Captain?" Beverly asked the officer beside him.

"I don't know. He's not in my company. I'm finding new faces every day," the captain replied.

As twilight fell I saw the man again at the edge of the camp. He smiled pleasantly as he passed me, turning to look at Beverly, who did not see him, and in a minute he was cantering down to the creek beside our camp. I saw him cross it and ride quickly out of sight. But that smile brought to the face the thing that had escaped me.

"I know that fellow now," I said to Beverly and the officer who came up just then. "He's Charlie Bent, the son of Colonel Bent. Don't you remember the little dinner at old Fort Bent, Bev?"

"I do, and what a vicious little reptile he was," Beverly replied. "But Uncle Esmond told me that his father took him away early and had him schooled like a gentleman in the best Saint Louis had to give. I wonder whose company he is in."

The officer stared at us.

"You mean to say you know that cavalryman to be Charlie Bent?" he fairly gasped.

"Of course it's Charlie. I never missed a face in all my life. That's his own," I replied.

"The worst Indian on the plains!" the captain declared. "He stirs up more fiendishness than a whole regiment of thoroughbred Cheyennes could ever think of. He's led in every killing here since March."

"Not Colonel Bent's son!" I exclaimed.

"Yes, he's the half-breed devil that we'll have to fight, and here he comes and eats with us and rides away."

"He must be the fellow that the Mexican told us about back at Burlingame, Gail. I remember now he did say the brute's name was Bent, but I didn't rope him up with our Fort Bent chum. Gail would have run him down in half a minute if he had heard the name. I never could remember anything," Beverly said, in disgust. But the smile was peeping back of his frown, and he forgot the boy he was soon to have cause enough to remember.

"We must run that rascal down to-night," the Captain declared, as he hurried away to consult with the other officers.

But Charlie Bent was not run down that night. Before we had time to get over our surprise a scream of pain rang through the camp. Another followed, and another, and when an hour had passed a third of our forces was writhing in the clutches of the cholera.

I shall never forget the long hours of that night beside the Walnut, nor Beverly Clarenden's face as he bent over the suffering men. For all of us who were well worked mightily to save our plague-stricken comrades, whose couches were of prairie grass and whose hospital roof was the starlit sky. However forgetful Beverly might be of names and faces, his strong hand had that soothing firmness that eased the agony of cramping limbs. Dear Bev! He comforted the sick, and caught the dying words, and straightened the relaxed bodies of the dead, and smiled next day, and forgot that he had done it.

At last the night of horror passed, and day came, wan and hot and weary out of the east. But five of our comrades would see no earthly day again; and three dozen strong men of the day before lay stretched upon the ground, pulseless and shrunken and purple, with wrinkled skin and wide, unseeing eyes.

- 221 -

Before the sun had risen our dead, coffined only by their army blankets, lay in unmarked graves. Our helpless living were placed in commissary wagons, and we took the trail slowly and painfully toward the Arkansas River.

If Charley Bent had gathered up his band to strike that night there would have been a different chapter in the annals of the plains.

I cannot follow with my pen the long marches of that campaign, and there was no honorable nor glorious warfare in it. It is a story of skirmishes, not of battles; of attack and repulse; of ambush and pursuit and retreat. It is a story of long days under burning skies, by whose fierce glare our brains seemed shriveling up and the world went black before our heat-bleared eyes. A story of hard night-rides, when weary bodies fought with watchful minds the grim struggle that drowsiness can wage, though sleep, we knew, meant death. It is a story of fevered limbs and bursting pulse in hospitals whose walls were prairie distances. A story of hunger, and exhausted rations; of choking thirst, with only alkali water mocking at us. And never could the story all be told. There is no rest for cavalrymen in the field. We did not suffer heavy loss, but here and there our comrades fell, by ones, and twos, at duty's post; and where they fell they lie, in wayside graves, waiting for glorious mention until the last reveille shall sound above the battlements of heaven.

And I was one among these vanguards of the plains, making the old Santa Fé Trail safe for the feet of trade; and the wide Kansas prairies safe for homes, and happiness, and hope, and power. I lived the life, and toughened in its grind. But in my dreams sometimes my other life returned to me, and a sweet face, with a cloud of golden hair, and dark eyes looking into mine, came like a benediction to me. Another face came sometimes now--black, big, and glistening, with eyes of strange, far vision looking at me, and I heard, over and over, the words of Esmond Clarenden's cook.

"If you get into trouble, Mr. Bev, I'll come, hot streaks, to help you."

But trouble never stuck to "Mr. Bev," because he failed to know it when it came.

Mid-August found us at Fort Hays on the Smoky Hill, beyond whose protecting guns the wilderness ruled. A wilderness checkered by faint trails of lawless feet, a wilderness set with bloody claws and poison stings and cruel fangs, and slow, agonizing death. And with all a wilderness of weird, fascinating distances and danger, charm and beauty. The thrill of the explorer of new lands possessed us as we looked far into the heart of it.

Here in these August days the Cheyenne and Arapahoe and Kiowa bands were riding trails blood-stained by victims dragged from lonely homesteads, and butchered, here and there, to make an Indian holiday. The scenes along the valleys of the Sappa and the Beaver and the Prairie Dog creeks were far too brutal and revolting to belong to modern life. Against these our Eighteenth Kansas, with a small body of United States cavalry, struck northward from Fort Hays. We rested through the long, hot days and marched by night. The moon was growing toward the full, and in its clear, white splendor the prairies lay revealed for miles about us. Our command was small and meagerly equipped, and we were moving on to meet a foe of overwhelming numbers. Men took strange odds with Fate upon the plains.

Beyond the open, level lands lay a rugged region hemming in the valley of the Prairie Dog Creek. Here picturesque cliffs and deep, earth-walled cañons split the hills, affording easy ambush for a regiment of red men. And here, in a triangle of a few miles area, a new Thermopylae, with no Leonidas but Kansas plainsmen, was staged through two long August days and nights. One hundred and fifty of us against fifteen hundred fighting braves.

In the early morning of a long, hot August day, we came to an open plain beyond the Prairie Dog Creek. Our supply-wagons and pack-mules were separated from us somewhere among the bluffs. We had had no food since the night before, and our canteens were empty--all on account of the blundering mismanagement of the United States officer who cammanded us. I was only a private, and a private's business is not to question, but to obey. And that major over us, cashiered for cowardice later, was not a Kansas man. Thank heaven for that!

A score of us, including my cousin and myself, under a sergeant, and with good Scout Pliley, were suddenly ordered back among the hills.

"Where do we go, and why?" Beverly asked me as we rode along.

"I don't know," I replied. "But Captain Jenness and a file of men were lost out here somewhere last night. And Indian tracks step over one another all around here. I guess we are out to find what's lost, maybe. It isn't a twenty minutes' job, I know that."

"And all our canteens empty, too! Why cut off all visible means of support in a time like this? Look at these bluffs and hiding-places, will you! A handful of Indians could scoop our whole body up and pitch us into the Prairie Dog Creek, and not be missed from a set in a war-dance," Beverly insisted. "Keep it strictly in the Clarenden family, Gail, but our honorable commander is a fool and a coward, if he is a United States major."

"You speak as one expecting a promotion, Bev," I suggested.

"I'd know how to use it if I got it," he smiled brightly at me as we quickened our pace not to fall behind.

Every day of that campaign Beverly grew dearer to me. I am glad our lives ran on together for so many years.

The cañons deepened and the whole region was bewildering, but still we struggled on, lost men searching for lost men. The sun blazed hotly, and the soft yellow bluffs of bone-dry earth reached down to the dry beds of one-time streams.

High noon, and still no food, no water, and no lost men discovered. We had pushed out to a little opening, ridged in on either side by high, brown bluffs, when a whoop came from the head of the line.

"Yonder they are! Yonder they are!"

Half a dozen men, led by Captain Jenness, were riding swiftly to join us and we shouted in our joy. For some among us that was the last joyous shout. At that moment a yell from savage throats filled the air, and the thunder of hoofs shook the ground. Over the west ridge, half a mile away, five hundred Indians came swooping like a hurricane down upon us. And we numbered, altogether, twenty-nine. I can see that charge to-day: the blinding, yellow sky, the ridge melting into a cloud of tawny dust, the surge of ponies with their riders bending low above them; fronting them, our little group of cavalrymen formed into a hollow square, on foot, about our mounts; the Indians riding, in a wide circle around us, with blankets flapping, and streamer-decked lances waving high. And as I see, I hear again that wild, unearthly shriek and taunting yell and fiendish laughter. From every point the rifle-balls poured in upon us, while out of buffalo wallow and from behind each prairie-dog hillock a surge of arrows from unmounted Indians swept up against us. I had been on battle-fields before, but this was a circle out of hell set 'round us there. And every man of of knew, as we sent back ball for ball, what capture here would mean for us before the merciful hand of death would seal our eyes.

Suddenly, as we moved forward, the frantic circle halted and a hundred braves came dashing in a fierce charge upon us. Their leader, mounted on a great, white horse, rode daringly ahead, calling his men to follow him, and taunting us with cowardice. He spoke good English, and his voice rang clear and strong above the din of that strange struggle. Straight on he came, without once looking back, a revolver in each hand, firing as he rode. A volley from our carbines made his fellows stagger, then waver, break, and run. Not so the rider of the splendid white horse, who dared us to strike him down as he dashed full at us.

"Come on, you coward Clarenden boys, and I'll fight you both. I've waited all these years to do it. I dare you. Oh, I dare you!"

It was Charlie Bent.

Nine balls from Clarenden carbines flew at him. Beverly and I were listed among the cleverest shots in Kansas, but not one ball brought harm to the daring outlaw. A score of bullets sung about his insolent face, but his seemed a charmed life. Right on he forged, over our men, and through the square to the Indian's circle on the other side, his mocking laughter ringing as he rode. A bloody scalp hung from his spear, and, turning 'round just out of range of our fire, shaking his trophy high, he shouted back:

"We got all of the balance of your men. We'll get you yet."

The sun glared fiercely on the bare, brown earth. A burning thirst began to parch our lips. We had had no food nor drink for more than twenty hours. Our horses, wounded with many arrows, were harder to care for than our brave, stricken men.

Night came upon the cañons of the Prairie Dog, and with the darkness the firing ceased. Somewhere, not far away, there might be a wagon-train with food for us. And somewhere near there might be a hundred men or more of our command trying to reach us. But, whether the force and supplies were safe or the wagons were captured and all our comrades killed, as Charlie Bent had said, we could not know. We only knew that we had no food; that one man, and all but four of our cavalry horses lay dead out in the valley; that two men in our midst were slowly dying, and a dozen others suffering from wounds of battle, among these our captain and Scout Pliley; that we were in a wild, strange land, with Indians perching, vulture-like, on every hill-top, waiting for dawn to come to seize their starving prey.

We heard an owl hoot here and there, and farther off an answering hoot; a coyote's bark, a late bird's note, another coyote, and a fainter hoot, all as night settled. And we knew that owl and coyote and twilight song-bird were only imitations--sentinel signals from point to point, where Indian videttes guarded every height, watching the trail with shadow-piercing eyes.

The glossy cottonwood leaves, in the faint night breeze, rippled like pattering rain-drops on dry roofs in summertime, and the thin, willow boughs swayed gently over us. The full moon swept grandly up the heavens, pouring a flood of softened light over the valley of the Prairie Dog, whose steep bluffs were guarded by a host of blood-lusting savages, and whose cañons locked in a handful of intrepid men.

If we could only slip out, undiscovered, in the dark we might find our command somewhere along the creek. It was a perilous thing to undertake, but to stay there was more perilous.

"Say, Gail," Beverly whispered, when we were in motion, "somebody said once, 'There have been no great nations without processions,' but this is the darndest procession I ever saw to help to make a nation great. Hold on, comrade. There! Rest on my arm a bit. It makes it softer."

The last words to a wounded soldier for whom Bev's grip eased the ride.

It was a strange procession, and in that tragic gloom the boy's light-hearted words were balm to me.

Silently and slowly we moved forward. The underbrush was thick on either side of the narrow, stony way that wound between sheer cliffs. We had torn up our blankets and shirts to muffle the horses' feet, that no sound of hoofs, striking upon the rocky path, might reach the ears of the Cheyenne and his allies crouching watchfully above us. At the head marched Captain Jenness and Scout Pliley, each with his carbine for a crutch and leaning on each other for support. Followed five soldiers as front guard through the defile. And then four horses, led by careful hands, bearing nine suffering, silent men upon their backs. Two of the horses carried three, and one bore two, and the last horse, one--a dying boy, whispering into my ear a message for his mother, as I held his hand. Behind us came the sergeants with the remainder, for rear-guard. And so we passed, mile after mile, winding in and out, to find some sheltering spot where, sinking in exhaustion, we might sleep.

The midnight winds grew chill, and the tense strain of that slow march was maddening, but not a groan came from the wounded men. The vanguards of the plains knew how to take perilous trails and hold their peace.

When the sun rose on the second day the hills about us swarmed with savages, whose demoniac yells rent the air. Leonidas had his back against a rock at old Thermopylae, but our Kansas plainsmen fought in a ring of fire.

At day-dawn, our brave scout, Pliley, slipped away, and, after long hours among the barren hills, he found the main command.

Men never gave up hope in the plains warfare, but each of us had saved one bullet for himself, if we must lose this game. The time for that last bullet had almost come when the sight of cavalrymen on a distant ridge told us that our scout was on its way to us again. It took a hero's heart to thread unseen the dangerous trails and find our comrades with the cavalry major and bring back aid, but Pliley did it for us--a man's part. May the sod rest lightly where he sleeps to-day. Meantime, on the day before, the main force of our cavalry, who had given us up for lost, had had their own long, fearful struggle. In the early morning, Lieutenant Stahl, scouting forward in an open plain, rushed back to give warning of Indians everywhere. And they were everywhere--a thousand strong against a feeble hundred caught in their midst. They rode like centaurs, and their aim was deadly true as they poured down, a murderous avalanche, from every hillslope. Their ponies' tails, sweeping the ground, lengthened by long horse-hair braids, with sticks thrust through at intervals by way of ornament; their waving blankets, and streamered lances held aloft; the savage roar from ten hundred throats; the mad impetus of their furious charge through clouds of dust and rifle smoke--all made the valley of the Prairie Dog seem but a seething hell bursting with fiendins shouts, shot through with quivering arrows, shattered by bullets, rocked with the thunderous beat of horses' hoofs, trampling it into one great maelstrom of blood and dirt.

All day, with neither food nor water, amid bewildering bluffs and gorges, alive with savage warriors, the cavalrymen had striven desperately. Night fell, and in the clear moonlight they forced their way across the Prairie Dog, and neither man nor horse dared to stop to drink because an instant's pause meant death.

And the evening and the morning were the first day. And the second was like unto it, albeit we were no longer a triangle, made up of wagon-train here and main command there, and our twenty-nine--less two lost ones-- under Captain Jenness, at a third point. Before noon, our force was all united and we joined hands for the finish.

Beverly and I rode side by side all day. Everywhere around us the half-breed, Charlie Bent, dashed boldly on his big, white horse calling us cowardly dogs and taunting us with lack of marksmanship.

"I'm getting tired of that fellow, Gail. I'll pick his horse out from under him pretty soon, see if I don't." My cousin called to me as Bent's insolent cry burst forth:

"Come out, and let me show you how to shoot."

Beverly leaped out toward the Indian horde surrounding Bent. He raised his carbine, and with steady aim, fired far across the field of battle, the cleanest shot I ever saw. Years ago my cousin had urged Uncle Esmond to let him practise shooting on horseback. He was a master of the art now. Charlie Bent's splendid white steed fell headlong, hurling its rider to the ground and dragging him, face downward, in the dirt.

I cannot paint that day's deeds with my pen, nor ever artist lived whose brush could reproduce it. If we should lose here, it meant the turning of the clock from morning back to midnight on the Kansas plains.

Between this and the safety of the prairies stood fewer than a hundred and fifty men, against a thousand warriors, led by cunning half-breeds skilled in the white man's language and the red man's fiendishness.

If we should lose--We did not go out there to lose. When each man does a man's part there is no failure possible at last.

As the sun sank toward late afternoon, the savage force massed for its great, crushing blow that should annihilate us. The strong center, made up of the flower of every tribe engaged, was on the crest of a long, westward-reaching slope, a splendid company of barbaric warriors--strong, eager, vengeful, doggedly determined to finish now the struggle with the power they hated

The air was very clear, and in its crystal distances we could see every movement and hear each command.

The valley rang with the taunts and jeers and threats and mocking laughter of our foes, daring us to come out and meet them face to face, like men. And we went out and met them face to face, like men.

A little force of soldiery fighting, not for ourselves, but for the hearthstones of a nobler people, our cavalry swung up that long, western slope in the face of a murderous fire, into the very heart of Cheyenne strength, enforced by all the iron of the allied tribes. I marvel at it now, when, in solid phalanx, our foes might easily have mowed us down like a thin line of standing grain; for their numbers seemed unending, while flight on flight of arrows and fierce sheets of rifle-fire swept our ranks as we rode on to death or victory. But each man's face among us there was bright with courage, and with our steady force unchecked we swept right on to the very crest of the high slope, scattering the enemy, at last, like wind-blown autumn leaves, until upon our guidons victory rested and the long day was won.

XX

GONE OUT

I wander alone at dead of night,
But ever before me I see a light,
In darkest hours more clear, more bright;
And the hope that I bear fails never.
FREDRICH RÜCKERT.

The waters of the Smoky Hill flowed yellow, flecked with foam, beside our camp, where, in a little grove of cottonwood trees, we rested from a long day's march. The heat of a late Kansas summer day was fanned away at twilight by the cool prairie breeze. There was an appealing something in the air that evening hour that made me homesick. So I went down beside the river to fight out my daily battle and let the wide spaces of the landscape soothe me, and all the opal tints of sunset skies and the soft radiance of a prairie twilight bring me their inspiration.

Each day my heart-longing for the girl I must not love grew stronger. I wondered, as I sat here to-night, what trail would open for me when Beverly and Eloise should meet again, as lovers must meet some time. We had not once spoken her name between us, Bev and I, in all the days and nights since we had been in service on the plains.

As I sat lonely, musing vaguely of a score of things that all ran back to one fair face, Beverly dropped down beside me. His face was grave and his eyes had a gentle, pleading look, something strange and different from the man whose moods I knew.

"I'm homesick, Gail." He smiled as he spoke, and all the boy of all the years was in that smile.

"So am I, Bev. It must be in the water here," I replied, lightly.

But neither one misunderstood the other.

"I'd like to see Little Lees to-night. Wouldn't you?" he asked, suddenly.

The question startled me. Maybe my cousin wanted to confide in me here. I would not be selfish with him.

"Yes, I always like to see her. Why to-night, though?" I asked, encouragingly.

Beverly looked steadily into my face.

"I want to tell you something, Gail. I haven't dared to speak before, but something tells me I should speak to-night," he said slowly.

I looked away along the winding valley of the Smoky Hill. I must hear it some time. Why be a coward now?

"Say on, I'm always ready to hear anything from you, Beverly."

I tried to speak firmly, and I hoped my voice did not seem faltering to him. He sat silent a long while. Then he rose and straightened to his full height-- a splendid form of strength and wholesomeness and grace.

"I'll tell you some time soon, but not to-night. Honor is something with me yet."

And so he left me.

I dreamed of him that night with Eloise. And all of us were glad. I wakened suddenly. Beverly was standing near me. He turned and walked away, his upright form and gait, even in the faint light, individually Bev's own. I saw him lie down and draw his blanket about him, then sit up a moment, then nestle down again. Something went wrong with sleep and me for a long time, and once I called out, softly:

"Bev, can't you sleep?"

"Oh, shut up! Not if you fidget about me," he replied, with the old happy-go-lucky toss of the head and careless tone.

It was dim dawn when I wakened. My cousin was sleeping calmly just a few feet away. An irresistible longing to speak to him overcame me and I slipped across and gently kicked the slumbering form. Two cavalry blankets rolled apart. A note pinned to the edge of one caught my eye. I stooped to read:

DEAR GAIL, Don't hate me. I'm sick of army life. They will call me a coward and if they get me they will shoot me for a deserter. I have disgraced the Clarenden name. You'll never see me again. Good-bye, old boy.

BEV.

Deserter!

The yells of all the tribes in the battle on the Prairie Dog Creek shrieked not so fiercely in my ears as that word rang now. And all the valley of the Smoky Hill echoed and re-echoed it.

Deserter!

My Beverly--who never told a lie, nor feared a danger, nor ever, except in self-defense, hurt a creature God had made. I could bury Bev, or stand beside him on his wedding-day. But Beverly disgraced! O, God of mercy toward all cowards, pity him!

I sat down beside the blankets I had kicked apart and looked back over my cousin's life. It offered me no help. I thought of Eloise--and his longing to see her on the night before; of his struggle to tell me something. I knew now what that something was. Poor boy!

He was not a boy, he was a man--strong, fearless, happy-hearted. How could the plains make cowards out of such as he? They had made a man of Jondo, who had all excuse to play the coward. The mystery of the human mind is a riddle past my reading--and I had always thought of Beverly's as an open book. The only one to whom I could turn now was not Eloise, nor my uncle, nor Mat nor Rex, but Jondo, John Doe, the nameless man, with whom Esmond Clarenden had walked all these years and for whose sake he had rescued Eloise St. Vrain. They had "toted together," as Aunty Boone had said. Oh, Aunty Boone with dull eyes of prophecy! I could hear her soft voice saying:

"If you get into trouble, Mr. Bev, I come, hot streaks, to help you."

She could not come "hot streaks" now, for Beverly had deserted. But there was Jondo.

I wrote at once to him, inclosing the crumpled note, and then, as one who walks with neither sight nor feeling any more, I rode the plains and did a man's part in that Eighteenth Cavalry campaign of '67. The days went slowly by, bringing the long, bright autumn beauty to the plains and turning all the elms to gold along the creek at Burlingame. Time took away the sharp edge from our grief and shame, and left the dull pain that wears deeper and deeper, unnoticed by us; and all of us who had loved Beverly lived on and were cheerful for one another's sake.

When Jondo--as only Jondo could--bore the news of my letter to Esmond Clarenden, he made no reply, but sat like an image of stone. Rex Krane broke down and sobbed as if his heart would break. But Mat, calm, poised, and always merciful, merely said:

"We must wait awhile."

It was many days before she broke the news to Eloise St. Vrain, who only smiled and said:

"Gail is mistaken. Beverly couldn't desert."

It was when the word came to Aunty Boone that the storm broke. They told me afterward that her face was terrible to see, and that her eyes grew dull and narrow. She went out to the bluff's edge and sat staring up the valley of the Kaw as if to see into the hidden record of the coming years.

One October day, when the Kranes and Eloise sat with my uncle and Jondo in the soft afternoon air, looking out at the beauty of the Missouri bluffs, Aunty Boone loomed up before them suddenly.

"I got somebody's fortune, just come clear before me," she declared, in her soft voice. "Lemme see you' hand, Little Lees!"

Eloise put her shapely white hand upon the big, black paw.

Aunty Boone patted it gently, the first and last caress she ever gave to any of us.

"You' goin' to get a letter from a dark man. You' goin' to take a long journey. And somebody goin' with you. An' the one tellin' this is goin' away, jus' one more voyage to desset sands again, and see Africy and her own kingdom. Whoo-ee!"

Never before, in all the years that we had known her, had she expressed a wish for her early home across he seas. Her voice trailed off weirdly, and she gazed at the Kaw Valley for a long moment. Then she said, in a low tone that thrilled her listeners with its vibrant power:

"Bev ain't no deserter. He's gone out! Jus' gone out. Whoo-ee!"

She disappeared around the corner of the house and stood long in the little side porch where Beverly had kissed Little Blue Flower one night in the "Moon of the Peach-Blossom," and Eloise had found them there, and I had unwittingly heard what was said.

"Is there no variation in palmistry?" Rex Krane asked. "I never knew a gypsy in all my life who read a different set of prophecies. It's always the dark man--I'm light (darn the luck)--and a journey and a letter. But I thought maybe an African seer, a sort of Voodo, hoodoo, bugaboo, would have it a light man and a legacy and company coming, instead of you taking a journey, Eloise."

Eloise smiled.

"You musn't envy me my good fortune, Rex," she declared. "Aunty Boone says she is going back to Africa, too. You'll need a new cook, Uncle Esmond. Let me apply for the place right now."

My uncle smiled affectionately on her.

"I could give you a trial, as I gave her. I remember I told her if she could cook good meals I'd keep her; if not, she'd leave. Do you want to take the risk?"

"That's where you'll get your journey of the prophecy, Eloise," Jondo suggested.

"Well, you leave out the best part of it all," Mat broke in. "She added that Beverly isn't a deserter, he's just 'gone out.' Why don't you believe it all, serious or frivolous?"

A shadow lifted from the faces there as a glimpse of hope came slowly in.

"And as to letters, Eloise," Uncle Esmond said, "I must beg your pardon. I have one here for you that I had forgotten. It came this morning."

"See if it isn't from a dark man, inviting you to take a journey," Rex suggested.

"It must be, it's from Santa Fé," Eloise said, opening the letter eagerly.

Aunty Boone had come back again and was standing by the corner of the veranda, half hidden by vines, watching Eloise with steady eyes. The girl's face grew pale, then deadly white, and her big, dark eyes were opened wide as she dropped the letter and looked at the faces about her.

"It is from Father Josef," she gasped. "He writes of Little Blue Flower somewhere in Hopi-land. He asks me to go to Santa Fé at once for her sake. And it says, too--" The voice faltered and Eloise turned to Esmond Clarenden. "It says that Beverly is there somewhere and he wants you. Read it, Uncle Esmond."

As Eloise rose and laid the letter in my uncle's hand, Aunty Boone, hidden by the vines, muttered in her soft, strange tone:

"He's jus' gone out. Thank Jupiter! He's jus' gone out. I'm goin', hot streaks, to help him, too. Then I go to my own desset where I'm honin' o to be, an' stay there till the judgment Day. Whoo-ee!"

In the early morning of a rare October day upon the plains I sat on my cavalry horse beside Fort Hays, waiting for one last word from my superior officer, Colonel Moore. He was my uncle's friend, and he had been kind to the Clarenden boys, as military kindness runs.

"You are honorably discharged," he said. "Take these letters to Fort Dodge. You will meet your friends there, and have some safeguard from there on, by order of General Sheridan. God bless you, Gail. You have ridden well. I wish you a safe journey, and I hope you'll find your cousin soon. He was a splendid boy until this happened. He may be cleared some day."

"He is splendid still to me in spite of everything," I replied.

"Yes, yes," my colonel responded. "Never a Clarenden disgraced the name before. That is why General Sheridan is granting you a squad to help you. It is a great thing to have a good name. Good-by."

"Good-by. I thank you a thousand times," I said, saluting him.

"And I thank you. A chain, you know, is as strong as its weakest link. A cavalry troop is as able as its soldiers make it."

He turned his horse about, and I rode off alone across the lonely plains a hundred miles away toward old Fort Dodge, beside the Arkansas River. Jondo and Rex were to meet me there for one more trip on the long Santa Fé Trail.

Late September rains had blessed the valley of the Arkansas. The level land about Fort Dodge showed vividly green against the yellow sand-hills across the river, and the brown, barren bluffs westward, where a little city would one day rise in pretty picturesqueness. The scene was like the Garden of Eden to my eyes when I broke through the rough ridges to the north on the last lap of my long ride thither and hurried down to the fort. I grant I did not appear like one who had a right to enter Eden, for I was as brown as a Malayan. Nearly four months of hard riding, sleeping on the ground, with a sky-cover, eating buffalo meat, and drinking the dregs of slow-drying pools, had made a plainsman of me, of the breed that long since disappeared. Golf-sticks and automobile steering-wheels are held by hands to-day no less courageous than those that swung the carbine into place, and flung aside the cavalry bridle-rein in a wild onslaught in our epic day. Each age grows men, flanked by the coward and the reckless daredevil.

Rex Krane was first to recognize me when I reached the fort.

"Oh, we are all here but Mat: Clarenden, Jondo, Aunty Boone, and Little Lees; and a squad of half a dozen cavalry men are ready to go with us." Rex drawled in his old Yankee fashion, hiding an aching heart underneath his jovial greeting.

"All of us!" I exclaimed.

"Yes. Here they all come!" Rex retorted.

They all came, but I saw only one, veiling the joy in my eyes as best I could. For with the face of Eloise before me, I knew the hardest battle of my life was calling me to colors. I had forgotten how womanly she was, or else her summer by the blessed prairies that lap up to the edge of the quiet town of Burlingame had brought her peace and helped her to put away sad memories of her mother.

Behind her--a black background for her fair, golden head--was Aunty Boone.

"Our girl was called to Santa Fé, and Daniel here goes with her. I couldn't stay behind, of course," my uncle said. "The Comanches are making trouble all along the Cimarron, and we will go up the Arkansas by the old trail route. It is farther, but the soldiers say much safer right now, and maybe just as quick for us. There is no load of freight to hinder us--two wagons and our mounts. Besides, the cavalrymen have some matters to look after near the mountains, or we might not have had their protection granted us."

The beauty of that early autumn on the plains and mountains lingers in my memory still, though half a century has passed since that journey on the old, long trail to Santa Fé.

At the closing of an Indian summer day we pitched our camp outside the broken walls of old Fort Bent. Every day found me near Eloise, although the same barrier was between us that had risen up the day she left me in the ruined chapel by the San Christobal River. Every day I longed to tell her what Beverly had said to me the night he--went out. It was due her that she should know how tenderly he had thought of her.

The night was irresistible, soft and balmy for the time of year, as that night had been long ago when we children were marooned inside this stronghold. A thin, growing moon hung in the crystal heavens and all the shadowy places were softened with gray tones. Jondo and Uncle Esmond and Rex Krane were talking together. Aunty Boone was clearing up after the evening meal. The soldiers were about their tasks or pastimes. Only Eloise and I were left beside the camp-fire.

"Let's go and find the place where we spent our last evening here, Little Lees," I said, determined to-night to tell her of Beverly.

"And just as many other places as we can remember," Eloise replied.

We clambered over heaps of fallen stone in the wide doorway, and stood inside the half-roofless ruin that had been a stronghold at the wilderness crossroads.

The outer walls were broken here and there. The wearing elements were slowly separating the inner walls and sagging roofs. Heaps of debris lay scattered about. Over the caving well the well-sweep stuck awry, marking a place of danger. Everywhere was desolation and slow destruction.

We sat down on some fallen timbers in the old court and looked about us.

"It was a pity that Colonel Bent should have blown up this splendid fortress, and all because the Government wouldn't pay him his price for it," I declared.

"Destroyed what he had built so carefully, and what was so useful," Eloise commented. "Sometimes we wreck our lives in the same way."

I have said the twilight seemed to fit her best, although at all times she was fair. But to-night she was a picture in her traveling dress of golden brown, with soft, white folds about her throat. I wondered if she thought of Beverly as she spoke. It hurt me so to be harsh with his memory.

"Yes, Charlie Bent blew up all that the Colonel built into him, of education and the ways of cultured folks--a leader of a Dog Indian band, he is a piece of manhood wrecked. And by the way," I went on, "Beverly shot his beautiful white horse on the Prairie Dog Creek. You should have seen that shot. It was the cleanest piece of long-range marksmanship I ever saw. He hated Bev for that."

"Maybe he gloats over our lost Beverly to-day. He is only 'gone out' to me," Eloise said softly.

"Let me tell you something, Little Lees. Beverly and I never spoke of you-- you can guess why--until that last night beside the Smoky Hill. He wanted to tell me something that night."

"And did he?" Eloise asked, eagerly.

"No. He said honor was something with him still. I thought he meant to tell me of himself and you. Forgive me. I do not want any confidences not freely given. But now I know it was the struggle in which he went down that night that he wanted to tell me about. He said first, 'I'm homesick. I'd like to see Little Lees.' And his eyes were full of sympathy as he looked at me."

"Did he say anything more?" Eloise's voice was almost a whisper.

"That was all. I thought that night I should hunt a lonely trail--when he went home to claim--happiness. But now I feel that I could live beside him always--to have him safe with us again."

As I turned to look at Eloise something was in her big, dark eyes-- something that disappeared at once. I caught only a fleeting glimpse of it, and I could not understand why a thrill of something near to happiness should sweep through me. It was but the shadow of what might have been for me and was not.

"Do you recall our prophecies here that night when we were children?" Eloise asked.

"Yes, every one. Mat wanted a home, Bev to fight the Indians, and you wanted me to keep Marcos Ramero in his place. I tried to do it," I replied.

And both of us recalled, but did not speak of, the warm, childish kiss of Little Lees upon my lips, and how we gripped hands in the shadows when the moon went cold and grey. Life was so simple then.

"It may be, if our problems and our tragedies crowd into our younger years, they clear the way for all the bright, unclouded years to follow," Eloise said, as we rose to go back to the camp-fire.

"I hope they will leave us strong to meet the bright, unclouded years," I answered her.

On the next day the cavalrymen left us for a time, and we went on alone southward toward our journey's end.

Autumn on the mountain slopes, and in the mesa-girdled valleys of New Mexico hung rainbow-tinted lights by day, with star-beam pointed paths trailing across the blue night-sky. And all the rugged beauty of a picturesque land, basking in lazy warmth, out-breathing sweet, pure air, made the old trail to Santa Fé an enchanting highway to me, despite the burden of a grief that weighed me down. For I could not shut from my mind the pitiful call of Little Blue Flower that had come to Eloise, nor all the uncertainty surrounding my cousin somewhere in the Southwest wanting us.

The little city of adobe walls seemed not to have changed a hair's turn in the six years since I had seen it last. Out beyond the sandy arroyo again Father Josef waited for us. The same strong face and dark eyes, full of fire, the same erect form and manly bearing were his. Except for a few streaks of gray in his close-cropped hair the years had wrought no change in him, save that his countenance betokened the greater benediction of a godly life upon it. As we rode slowly to the door of San Miguel I fell behind. The years since that day when the saucy little girl had called me a big, brown, bob-cat here came back upon my mind, and, though my hope had vanished, still I loved the old church.

Before we had passed the doorway Eloise left her wagon and stood beside my horse.

"Gail, let us stop here with Father Josef while the others go down to Felix Narveo's. It always seems so peaceful here."

"You are always welcome here, my children," Father Josef said, graciously, as I leaped from my horse and stuck its lariat pin down beside the doorway.

Inside there were the same soft lights from the high windows, the same rare old paintings about the altar, the same seat beside the door.

The priest spoke to us in low tones befitting sanctuary stillness. "You have come on a long journey, but it is one of mercy. I only pray you do not come too late," he said.

"Tell us about it, Father," Eloise urged. "The men will get the story from Felix Narveo, but Gail and I seem to belong up here." She smiled up at me with the words.

I could have almost hoped anew just then, but for the thought of Beverly.

"Let us pray first," the holy man replied.

Beverly and I had been confirmed in the Episcopalian faith once long ago, but the plains were hard on the religion of a high-church man. And yet, all sacred forms are beautiful to me, and I always knew what reverence means.

"You may not know," Father Josef said, "that I have Indian blood in my veins--a Hopi strain from some French ancestors. Po-a-be, our Little Blue Flower, is my heathen cousin, descended from the same chief's daughter. The Hopi's faith is a part of him, like his hand or eye, and I have never gained much with the tribe save through blood-ties. But because of that I have their confidence."

"You have all men's confidence, Father Josef," I said, warmly.

"Thank you, my son," the priest replied. "When Santan, the Apache, came back from a long raid eastward, he told Little Blue Flower that Beverly had spared his life beside a poisoned spring in the Cimarron valley, urging him to go back and marry her; life had other interests now to white men who must forget all about Indian girls, he declared, and with Apache adroitness he pressed his claims upon her. But Santan had slain Sister Anita beside the San Christobal Arroyo. A murderer is abhorrent to a Hopi, who never takes life, save in self-defense or in legitimate warfare--if warfare ever is legitimate," he added, gravely.

"My little cousin was heart-broken, for all the years since her rescue at Pawnee Rock she had cherished one face in memory; and maybe Beverly in his happy, careless way had given her cause to do so."

"We understand, I think," Eloise said, turning inquiringly to me.

I nodded, and Father Josef went on. "She knew her love was foolish, but few of us are always wise in love. So Santan's suit seemed promising for a time. But the Hopi type ran true in her, and she put off the Apache year after year. It is a strange case in Indian romance, but romance everywhere is strange enough. The Apache type also ran true to dogged purpose. Besides being an Apache, Santan has some Ramero blood in his veins, to be accounted for in the persistence of an evil will. He was as determined to win Po-a-be as she that he should fail. And he was cunning in his schemes."

Father Josef paused and looked at Eloise.

"To make the story short," he began again, "Santan could not make the Hopi woman hate Beverly, although she knew that her love was hopeless, as it should be. Pardon me, daughter," Father Josef said, gently. "She heard you two talking in a little porch one night at the Clarenden home, and she has believed ever since that you are lovers. That is why she sent for you to come to help her now."

"I saw Beverly give Little Blue Flower a brotherly kiss that night, and I told him, frankly, how it grieved me, because I had known at St. Ann's about her love for him. I had urged her to go with me to the Clarendens', hoping that when she saw Beverly again she would quit dreaming of him."

I looked away, at the paintings and the crucifix above the altar, and the long shafts of light on gray adobe walls, wondering, vaguely, what the next act of this drama might reveal.

"Beverly was always lovable," Father Josef said. "But now the message comes that he is out in the heart of Hopi-land, and because Little Blue Flower is protecting him her people may turn against her. For Beverly's sake, and for her sake, too, my daughter, we must start at once to find her and maybe save his life. She wants you. It is the call of sisterhood. Sister Gloria and I will go with you. I have much influence with my Hopi people."

"Will they put Beverly to death?" I asked.

"I cannot tell, but--see how long the arm of hate can be, my son--Santan, the Apache, has been informed of Beverly's coming by Marcos Ramero, gambler and debauchee. And Marcos got it in some way from Charlie Bent, a Cheyenne half-breed, son of old Colonel Bent, a fine old gentleman. Maybe you knew young Bent?"

"Yes, he holds a grudge against the Clarenden name because we made him play square with us at the old fort when we were children," I told the priest. "He yelled defiance at us in the battle on the Prairie Dog Creek last August. Bev shot his horse from under him just to humble the insolent dog! Beverly never was a coward," I insisted, all my affection for my cousin overwhelming me.

"This makes it clearer," Father Josef said. "Through Bent to Ramero and Ramero to Santan, the word went, somehow. The Apache has gathered up a band of the worst of his breed and they are moving against the Hopis to get Beverly. You and Jondo and Clarenden and Krane will join the little squad of cavalry you left up in the mountains, and turn the Apache back, and all of us must start at once, or we may be too late. May heaven bless our hands and make them strong."

We bowed in reverence for a moment. When we hurried from the dim church into the warm October sunlight, Aunty Boone sat on the door-step beside my horse.

"'He's jus' gone out,' I told 'em so, back there on the Missouri River. He's gone out an' I'm goin', hot streaks, to find him, Little Lees. Whoo-ee!"

XXI

IN THE SHADOW OF THE INFINITE

And though there's never a grave to tell,
Nor a cross to mark his fall,
Thank God! we know that he "batted well"
In the last great Game of all.
--SERVICE.

We left Santa Fé within an hour, and struck out toward the unknown land where Beverly Clarenden, in the midst of uncertain friends, was being hunted down by an Apache band. As our little company passed out on the trail toward Agua Fria, I recalled the day when we had gone with Rex Krane to this little village beside the Santa Fé River. Eloise and Father Josef and Santan and Little Blue Flower were all there that day; and Jondo, although we did not know it then. Rex Krane had told Beverly, going out, that an Indian never forgets. In all the years Santan had not forgotten.

To-day we covered the miles rapidly. Jondo and Father Josef rode ahead, with Esmond Clarenden and Felix Narveo following them; then came Eloise St. Vrain with Sister Gloria; behind them, Aunty Boone, with Rex and myself bringing up the rear. Three pack-mules bearing our equipment went tramping after us with bobbing ears and sturdy gait.

I looked down the line of our little company ahead. The four men in the lead were college chums once, and all of them had loved the mother of the girl behind them. I have said the girl looked best by twilight. I had not seen her in a coarse-gray riding-dress when I said that. I had seen her when she needed protection from her enemies. I had not seen her until to-day, going out to meet hardship fearlessly, for the sake of one who wanted her--only an Indian maiden, but a faithful friend. In the plainest face self-forgetfulness puts a beauty all its own. That beauty shone resplendent now in the beautiful face of Mary Marchland's daughter.

The world can change wonderfully in sixty minutes. As we rode out toward the Rio Grande, the yellow sands, the gray gramma grass, the purple sage, the tall green cliffs, and, high above, the gleaming snow-crowned peaks, took on a beauty never worn for me before. Why should a hope spring up within me that would die as other hopes had died? But back of all my thought was the longing to help Beverly, and a faith in Aunty Boone's weird, prophetic grip on things unseen. He had just "gone out" to her--why not to all of us? I could not understand Little Blue Flower's part in this tragedy, so I let it alone.

A day out from Santa Fé we were joined by the little squad of cavalrymen with whom we had parted company back at the Fort Bent camping-place. With these we had little cause to dread personal danger. The Apache band was a small, vicious gang that could do much harm to the Hopis, but it seemed nothing for us to fear.

Our care was to reach Beverly before the Hopis should rise up against Little Blue Flower, or the band led by Santan should fall upon them. Father Josef had sent a runner on to tell them of our coming and to warn them of the Apache raid. But runners sometimes come to grief.

It is easy enough now to sleep most of the hours away across the and lands that lie between the Rockies and the Coast Range mountains, where the great "through limiteds," swinging down their long trail of steel, sweep farther in one day than we crept in two long, weary weeks in that October fifty years ago. Only Father Josef's unerring Indian accuracy brought us through.

We crawled up rugged mountain trails and skirted the rims of dizzy chasms; we wound through cañons, with only narrow streams for paths, between sheer walls of rock; we pitched our camp at the bases of great, red sand stone mesas, barren of life; we followed long, yellow ways over stretches of unending plain; we wandered in the painted-desert lands, where all the colors God has made bewilder with their beauty, in the barest, dreariest, most unlovely bit of unfinished world that our great continent holds; the lands forgotten, maybe, when, in Creation's busy week, the evening and the morning were the sixth day, and the Great Builder looked on His work and called it good.

We found the Hopi trails, but not the Hopi clan that we were seeking. We found Apache trails behind them, but only dimly marked, as if they blew one moccasin track full of sand before they made another.

The October days were dreams of loveliness, and dawn and sunset on the desert were indescribably beautiful. But the nights were bitterly cold. Eloise and Sister Gloria were native to the Southwest and they knew how to dress warmly for it. Aunty Boone had never felt such chilling night breezes, but not one word of complaint came from her lips in all that journey.

One night we gathered into camp beneath the shelter of a little butte. We had overtaken Father Josef's Indian runner an hour before. He had not found the Hopis yet, and so we held a council.

"The Hopi is ahead of us northwest," the Indian declared.

"Is the Apache following?" Jondo asked.

The runner nodded. "They have been pursued, but they have slipped away; the Apache goes north, they turn north-west. They take the dry lands and the pine forests beyond; their last chance. If they hold out till the Apache leaves, they will return safely. You follow them, wait for them, or go back without them. It is your choice."

We turned toward the three women, one in the bloom of her young womanhood, one with the patient endurance of the nun, one black and strong and always unafraid.

"I do not want to leave Little Blue Flower in her hour of peril," Eloise said.

"I can go where I am needed," Sister Gloria declared.

"This is my land, I never know Africa was right out here. I thought they was oceans on both sides of it. I go where Bev's gone out an then I come here and stay. Whoo-ee!"

We smiled at her mistaken dream of her far African home, and, cheering one another on, when morning came we moved northwest.

Jondo rode beside me all that day, and we talked of many things.

"Gail," he said, "Aunty Boone is right. This is her Africa. I don't believe she will ever leave it."

"She can't stay here, Jondo," I replied.

"She will, though. You will see. Did she ever fail to have her way?"

"No. She is a type of her own, never to be reproduced, but like a great dog in her faithful loyalty," I declared.

"And shrewder than most men," Jondo went on. "She supplied the lost link with Santan for me last night. Years ago, when Little Blue Flower brought me a message from Father Josef on the morning that we took Eloise from Santa Fé, I caught a glimpse of the Apache across the plaza and read the message--'*trust the bearer anywhere*'--to mean that boy. Aunty Boone had just peered out and scared the little girl away. She told me all about it last night, when she was bewailing Beverly's hard fate. How small a thing can open the road to a big tragedy. I trusted that whelp till that day at San Christobal."

"I hope we will finish this soon," I said. "I don't understand Beverly at all and I marvel at Little Blue Flower's love for him. Don't you?"

Jondo looked up with a pathos in his dark-blue eyes.

"Don't hurry, Gail. The trails all end somewhere soon. Life is a stranger thing from day to day, but the one thing that no man will ever fully understand is a woman's love for man. There is only one thing higher, and that is mother-love."

"The kind that you and Uncle Esmond have," I said.

"Oh, I am only a man, but Clarenden has a woman's heart, as you and Beverly and my sister's child all know."

"Your sister's child?" I gasped.

"Yes. When her parents went with yellow fever, too, I could not adopt Mat--you know why. Clarenden did it for me. She has always known that I am her uncle, but Mat was always a self-contained child."

I loved Mat more than ever from that hour.

The next day our trail ran into pine forests, where tall, shapely trees point skyward. Not a dense woodland, but a seemingly endless one. Snows lay in the darker places, and here and there streams trickled out into the sunlight, whose only sources were these melting snows. It was a land of silence and loneliness--a land forgotten or unknown to record. The Hopi trail was stronger here and we followed it eagerly, but night overtook us early in the forest.

That evening we gathered about a huge fire of pine boughs beneath a low stone ridge covered with evergreen trees that sheltered us warmly from the sharp west winds. We heard the cries of night-roving beasts, and in the darkness, now and then, a pair of gleaming eyes, seen for an instant, and then the rush of feet, told us that some wild creature had looked for the first time on fire.

"To-morrow night will see our journey's end," Jondo declared. "The Hopi can't be far away, and I'm sure they are safe yet, and we shall reach them before the Apache does."

The Indian runner's face did not change its blankness, but I felt that he doubted Jondo's judgment. That night he slipped away and we never saw him again.

We were all hopeful that night, and hopeful the next morning when we broke camp early. A trail we had not seen the night before ran up the low ridge to the west of us. Eloise and I followed it up a little way, riding abreast. The ridge really was a narrow, rocky tableland, and beyond it was another higher slope, up which the same trail ran. The trees were growing smaller and the sky flowed broad and blue above their tops. The ground was only rock, with a thin veneer of soil here and there. Gnarled, stunted cedars and gray, twisted cypress clung for a roothold to these barren ledges. The morning breeze swept, sharp and invigorating, out of a broad open space beyond the edge of this rocky woodland height. Eloise and I pushed on a little farther, leaving the others still on the narrow shelf above our camping-place.

Suddenly, as we rode out of the closer timber to where the scattered growths were hardly higher than our heads, the first heaven and the first earth seemed to pass away--not in irreverence I write it--and we stood face to face with a new heaven and a new earth--where, in the Grand Cañon of the Colorado River, the sublimity of the Almighty Builder's beauty and omnipotence was voiced in one stupendous Word, wrought in enduring color in everlasting stone. Cleaving its way westward to some far-off sea, a wide abyss, a dozen miles across from lip to lip, yawned down to the very vitals of the earth. We stood upon the rim of it--a sheer cliff that dropped a thousand feet of solid limestone, in one plummet line, to other cliffs below, that dropped again through furlongs of black gneiss, red sandstone, and gray granite.

Beyond this mighty chasm great forest trees were, to our eyes, only as weeds along its rim. Between that rim and ours we could look down upon high mountain buttes and sloping red tablelands, and dizzy gorges with pinnacled walls and towers and domes--vast forms no pen will ever picture--not hurled in wild confusion by titan fury, but symmetrical and purposeful and calm.

Through slowly crawling millions of patiently wearing years, while stars grew old and perished from the firmament, with cloud, and frost, and wind, and water, and sharp cutting sands, these strata of the old earth's crust were chiseled into gigantic outlines, and all the worn-down, crumbled atoms of debris were swept through long, tortuous leagues of distance toward the sea by a mad river swirling through the lowest depths. A mile straight down, as the crow never flies here, it rushes, but to us the river was a mere creek, seen only where the lower gorges open to the channel.

In the early light of that October morning the weird, vast shapes that filled, the abyss were bathed in a bewildering opulence of color. Pale gold along the farther rim, with pink and amber, blue and gray, and heliotrope and rose--all blending softly, tone on tone. Deeper, the heart of every rift and chasm that flows into the one stupendous mother-rift was full of purple shadows. Not the thin lavender of the upper world where we must live, but tensely, richly regal, beyond words to paint; with silvery mists above, soft, filmy veils that draped the jutting rocks and rounded each harsh edge, melting pink to rose and gray to violet. Eternal silence brooded over all this symbol, wrought in visible form, of His Almightiness, to whom a thousand years are as a day, and in the hollow of whose hand He holds the universe. Measureless, motionless, voiceless, it seemed as if all the cañons of all the mountains of our great continent might have given to it here their awful depth and height and rugged strength; their picturesqueness, color, graceful outlines, dizzy steeps and awe-inspiring lengths and breadths. And fusing all these into itself, height on height, and breadth on breadth, entrancing charm on charm, with all the hues that the Great Alchemist can throw from His vast prism, it seemed to say:

"'Twas only in a vision that St. John saw the four-square city whose twelve gates are each a single pearl! whose walls are builded on foundation stones of jasper, sapphire, and chalcedony, emerald and topaz, chrysolite and amethyst; whose streets are of pure gold, like unto clear glass; whose light is ever like unto a stone most precious.

"To you who may not dream the vision beautiful, the Mighty Maker of all things sublime has given me a token here in finite stone and earthly coloring of that undreamed sublimity of all things omnipotent."

My companion and I sat on our horses speechless, gazing down at this overwhelming marvel below us. We forgot ourselves, each other, our companions of the journey, its purpose, Beverly, and his enemy Santan, the desert, the brown plains, green prairies, rivers, mountains, the earth itself, as we stood there in the shadow of the Infinite.

At last we turned and looked into each other's eyes for one long moment. In its space we read the old, old story through, and a great, up-leaping joy illumined our faces. God, who had let us know each other, had let us stand by *this* to feel the barrier of misunderstanding fall away.

* * * * *

A sound of horses' hoofs on the rocky slope below us, a weird Indian call, and a great shout from our calverymen drew us to earth again. The Hopis were coming. Father Josef knew the signal. Our Indian runner had found them in the night and sent them toward us. We dashed into the forest, keeping close together; and here, a mile away, under green pines, surrounded by a little group of a desert Hopi clan, was Beverly Clarenden-- big, strong, unhurt and joyful. And Little Blue Flower.

The years since that far night when I had seen two maidens in Grecian robes beside the Flat Rock in the "Moon of the Peach Blossom," had left no trace on Eloise St. Vrain, save to imprint the graces of womanliness on her girlish face. But the picturesque Indian maiden of that night looked aged and sorrowful in the pine forest of her native land, bent, as she was, with the dull existence of her own people; she, who had known and loved a different form of life. Only the big, luminous eyes held their old charm.

We came together in a little open space with pine-trees all about us. The minutes went swiftly then--and I must hurry to what came hurrying on, for much of it is lost in mist and wonder.

In the moment of glad reunion Aunty Boone suddenly gave a whoop the like of which I had never heard before, and, dashing wildly toward Eloise and Sister Gloria, she drove them in a fierce charge straight back into the shelter of the pine-trees.

At the same time a sudden rain of bullets, like a swift hail-storm, and a yell- -the Apache cry of vengeance--filled the air. Long afterward we learned that our Indian runner had met this band and tried to turn it back--and failed. He would have saved us if he could.

It was over soon--that encounter in the forest where each tree was a shield. The cavalrymen and maybe, too, we who had been plainsmen, knew how to drive back a villianous handful of Apaches. In any other moment since we had ridden out of Sante Fé we would have laughed at such a struggle. They took us in the most unguarded instant of that fortnight's journey.

The Hopis fled wildly out of sight. Here and there, from the defeated, scattered band, an Apache warrior sprang back and lost himself quickly in the shadows. But Santan, plunging into our very midst, seized Little Blue Flower in his iron grip, and the bullet from a cavalry carbine, meant for him, struck her.

He laughed and threw her back and, whirling, dashed--into the arms of Aunty Boone--and stopped.

We carried our wounded tenderly up the steep wooded slope and out into the sweet sunlight of its crest, where we laid them down beside that wondrous rift with its shimmering mist and velvet shadows, and colorings of splendor, folded all in the magnificence of its immensity and its eternal silence.

We knew that Jondo's wound was mortal, and Father Josef and Eloise and Rex Krane sat beside him, as the brave eyes looked out across the sublimity of earthly beauty toward the far land no eye hath seen, facing, unafraid, the outward-leading trail.

But Beverly was in the prime of young manhood, and we felt sure of him, as Esmond Clarenden and Sister Gloria; and I ministered to his wants.

"It's no use, Gail." My cousin lifted a pleading face to mine a moment, as on that day, years ago on the parade-ground at Fort Leavenworth. Then the bright smile came back to stay.

"Why, Bev, you have a life before you, and you aren't the only Eighteenth Kansas man who deserted. We can pull you through somehow--and people will forget. Even General Sheridan was willing to send a squad with us, on the possibility of a mistake somewhere."

"Deserted!" Beverly's voice was too strong for a dying man's. "Uncle Esmond, Jondo, Eloise--all of you--Gail calls me a deserter. Me! Knock him over that precipice, won't some of you?"

We listened eagerly as he went on:

"Why, don't you know that Charlie Bent and his renegade dogs crawled into camp like snakes and carried me out by force. They had a time of it, too, but never mind. Bent told me he left a note for you. I supposed he would say I was dead. And when Gail stirred, half awake, he went pacing around the camp, looking so near like me I thought it was myself and I was Charlie Bent. I was roped and gagged then, but I could see. Deserter! I'm glad I got that white horse of his on the Prairie Dog Creek, anyhow."

Beverly's face paled suddenly and he lay still a little while.

"I'd better hurry." The smile was winsome. "They didn't give me a ghost of a chance to escape, but they didn't harm a hair. They kept me for a meaner purpose, and, well, I was landed, finally, at Santan's door-step in the Apache-land. Santan offered to let me go free if I'd persuade Little Blue Flower--dead down there--to marry him. He had her come to me on pretense of my sending for her. She hated the brute, and she was a woman, if she was an Indian. I told him I'd see him in hell first, and I told her never to give in. Poor girl! It was a cruel test, but Santan knew how to be cruel. He said he'd fix me, and I guess he has done it."

"Oh no, Bev. You are good for a century," I declared, affectionately, holding his head on my knee.

"Little Blue Flower managed, somehow, to fool the Apache dog, and we escaped and got away to her people," Beverly continued, speaking more slowly, "then she sent word to Father Josef. But the Hopi folks were scared about the Apaches coming against them on account of harboring me, like a Jonah, among 'em; and they were going to make it hard for Little Blue Flower. I don't know heathen ethics in such things, but a handful of us had to cut for it. I'm no deserter, though. Don't forget that. As soon as I could be sure the little Indian woman's life was safe I was going to get away and come home. I could not leave her to be sacrificed after she had saved me from Santan's scalping-knife."

Beverly paused and looked at us. His voice seemed weaker when he spoke again:

"I thought, sometimes, that even if I wasn't to blame for it, I ought to take Little Blue Flower with me when I got away. Dear little girl! she gave me one smile and whispered '*Lolomi*' before she went just now. I told her long ago I was just everybody's friend. I never meant to spoil anybody's life, and I can meet her down at the end of the trail and never fear."

Just then a half-wailing, half-purring cry came from Aunty Boone, who was standing beside a gnarled cypress-tree.

"I knowed the morning we picked up Little Blue Flower, back at Pawnee Rock, we was pickin' up trouble for the rest of the trail. I see it then. You can trust a nigger 'cause they never no 'count, but you don't know what you gettin' when you trust an Indian. But, Cla'nden, that Apache Indian, Santan, ain't goin' to trouble you no more. When the world ain't no fit place for folks they needs helpin' out of it, and I sees to it they gets it, too. Whoo-ee!" She paused and leaned against the crooked cypress. Half turning her face toward us, she continued in a clear, soft voice:

"That man they call Ramero down in Santy Fee--I knowed him when he was just Fred Ramer back in the rice-fields country. His father, old man Ramer, tried to kill me once, 'cause he said I knowed too much. I helped him into kingdom come right then and saved a lot of misery. They blamed some other folks, I guess, but they never hunted me up at all. Good-by, Clan'den, and you, too, Felix, and Dick Verra. I've knowed you all these years, but nobody takes no 'count of niggers' knowin's. Good-by, Little Lees, and all you boys. I'll see you again pretty soon, I'm goin' back to my desset now. It's over yonder just a little way. Jondo--but you won't be John Doe then. Whoo-ee!"

Aunty Boone slowly settled down beside the cypress, with her face toward her beloved "desset," and when we went to her a little later, her eyes, still looking eastward, saw nothing earthly any more forever.

Jondo's face seemed glorified as he caught Aunty Boone's last words, and his voice was sweet and clear as he looked up at Eloise bending over him.

"Thank God! It is all made right at last. Eloise, the charge of murder against your father's name would have broken the heart of the woman that I always loved--your mother. One of us had to bear the shame. I took the guilt on myself for her sake--and for yours. I have walked the trails of my life a nameless man, but I have kept my soul clean in God's sight, and I know His name will soon be written on my forehead over there."

He gazed out toward the glorious beauty of the view beyond him, then closed his eyes, and, bravely as he had lived, so bravely he went forth on the Long Trail, leaving a name sweet with the perfume of self-sacrifice and love.

We did not speak of him to Beverly, for our boy had suddenly grown restless, and his blood was threshing furiously in his veins, and he was in pain, but only briefly.

Presently he said, "Let us be alone a little." The others drew away.

"Lean down, Gail. I want to tell you something." He smiled sweetly upon me as I bent over him.

"I tried to tell you back on the Smoky Hill, but I'd promised not to. And honor was something to me still. But I'm going pretty soon. So listen! I loved Eloise always--always. But she never cared for me. She was only my good chum. I've been too happy-hearted all my days, though, Gail, to make a cross of anything that would break me down. Men differ so, you know, and I never was a dreamer like you. Turn me a little, won't you, so that I can see that awful beauty down there."

I lifted his shoulders gently and placed him where his eyes could rest on the majestic scene spread out before him.

"Eloise loves you, but she thinks you would not marry her because they say her father was a murderer. I don't believe that, Gail. I told her that you didn't, either, not one little minute. You care for her, I know, and losing her will break your heart. I tried to tell you long ago, but Little Lees made me promise not to say a word that night at Burlingame when you had gone away and I thought maybe I had a half-chance with her. Tell me you'll make her happy, Gail."

"Oh, Beverly, I'll do my best," I murmured, softly.

"Come closer, Gail. Look at those colors there. Is it so far across, or only seeming so? And see the soft white clouds drop purple shadows down. Is that the way the trail runs? How beautiful it must be farther on. Good-by, old boy of my heart's heart, and don't forget, however long the years, and wide away your feet may go, to keep the old trail law. 'Hold fast.'"

We laid them away in the deep pine forest--Aunty Boone, of strange, prophetic vision; Santan, the cruel Indian; the loyal Hopi maiden; Jondo and Beverly. God made them all and in His heaven they will be rightly placed.

Beside the cañon's rim, in the soft twilight hour of that October day, Eloise St. Vrain and I plighted our troth, till death us do part--for just a little while. Plighted it not in happy, selfish affection, such as youth and maiden give, sometimes, each to each; but in the deep, marvelous love of man and woman pledged where, in sacred moments on that day, we had seen the mortal put on immortality. To us there could be no grander, richer, lovelier setting for life's best and holiest hour than here, where, upon things finite, there rests the beneficent uplifting beauty that shadows forth the Infinite.

IV

REMEMBERING THE TRAIL

XXII

THE GOLDEN WEDDING

The heart that's never old! Oh the heart that's never old!--
'Tis a vision of the lavender, the crimson and the gold
Of an airy, fairy morning, when the sky is all ablaze
With an ever-changing splendor, driving back the gloom and haze!

'Tis the vision of an orchard in the balmy month of May,
Where the birds are ever singing, and the leaves are ever gay;
Where the sun is ever shining with a glory never told,
And the trees are ever blooming--for the heart that's never old!

--JAMES E. HILKEY.

The summers and winters of fifty golden years have brought to the plains
their balmy breezes and blazing heat, their soft, life-giving showers, and
their fierce, blizzard anger. And down through these fifty years Eloise St.
Vrain and I have walked the love trails of the plains together.

In the early spring of this, our "golden-wedding" year, we sat on the
veranda of our suburban home in Kansas City, above the picturesque Cliff
Drive, rippling with automobiles. The same drive winds in its course
somewhere near the old, rough road that once led from the Clarenden
home, above the valley of the Kaw, down to the little city of great promise-
-now fulfilled.

"Eloise, youth may have a charm that is all its own," I said to my wife, "but
I wonder if it really matches the enduring charm of age when one looks
back on busy years of service."

Eloise smiled up at me--the same gracious smile that has lighted all my days
with her.

"You are a dreamer still, Gail. But dreams do so sweeten life and keep the
fires of romance forever burning."

"When did romance begin with you, Little Lees?" I asked.

"I think it was on that day when I came bounding up to the door of the old

San Miguel church," Eloise replied, "and saw you looking like a big, brown bob-cat, or something else, that might have slept in the Hondo 'Royo all your life. But withal a boy so loyal to the helpless that you were willing to fight for me against an assailant bigger than yourself. You became my prince in that hour, and all my dreams since then have been of you. When did romance begin with you, or have you forgotten in the busy years of a life swallowed up in mercantile pursuits?"

"My life may have been, as you say, swallowed up in building trade that builds empire, but I have never forgotten the things that make it fine to me," I answered her. "Romance for me began one day, long ago, out on the parade-ground at Fort Leavenworth. I've been a Vanguard of the Plains since then, bull-whacker for the ox-teams that hauled the commerce of the West; cavalryman in hard-wearing Indian campaigns that defended the frontier; and merchant, giving measure for measure always, like that grand man who taught me the worth of business--Esmond Clarenden."

"On the parade-ground? How there?" Eloise asked.

"It came the day that I first knew we were to go with Uncle Esmond to Santa Fé--for you. We didn't know that it was for you then. I think I was born again that day into a daring plainsman, who had been a sort of baby-boy before. I sat with Mat and Beverly on the edge of the parade-ground, when I looked up to see, with a boy's day-dreaming eyes, somewhere this side of misty mountain peaks, a vision of a cloud of golden hair about a sweet child face, with dark eyes looking into mine. That vision stayed with me until, one morning, fifty years ago, on the rim of the Grand Cañon--you looked into my eyes again and I knew my life dream had come true."

I rose and, bending over my wife's cloud of beautiful silvery hair, I kissed her gently on each fair cheek.

"Gail, why not take the old trail for our golden-wedding anniversary--a long journey, clear to the mountains?" Eloise suggested.

"There is no trail now; only its ghost haunting the way," I replied, "but, Little Lees, I don't believe that we who look back on so many happy years, after the stormy ones of early life, could find any other path half so dear to us as that long path we knew in childhood and early youth, and the one we followed together in our first years of mature womanhood and manhood."

And so we did not celebrate one October day with all of our children and grandchildren and friends coming to offer us gold coins, gold-headed canes--which I do not use--and gold-rimmed glasses for eyes that see farther and clearer than my spectacled grandsons at the university can see to-day. We made a golden summer of the thing and followed where, like a will-o'-the-wisp of memory, the Santa Fé Trail of threescore years ago reached from the raw frontier at Independence on to the Missouri bluffs, clear to the sunny valley of the Holy Faith.

Only a headstone at long intervals shows the way now--a stone that well might read:

Here ran the old Santa Fé Trail. This stone, set here, is sacred to the memory of the Vanguards of the Plains who followed it.

They stand, these "markers" now, on hilltops and in deep valleys; by country crossroads and where main streets cut each other in the towns and villages. They ornament the city parks, they show where splendid concrete bridges, re-enforced with structural steel, span streams that once the ox-teams doubled and trebled strength to ford. They gleam where corn grows tall and black on fertile prairies; where seas of wheat have flooded barren, burning plains, and perfumey alfalfa sweetens the air above what was once grassless desolation. They whisper of a day gone by among the silent mountains, where tunnels let the iron trail run easily under the old trail's dizzy path. They nestle in the shadows of gray-green cliffs and by red mesa heights; until the last monument, sacred to the memory of a day forgotten, speaks at the corner of the old Plaza in the heart of Santa Fé.

That was a journey long to be remembered--the long, golden-wedding journey of Gail Clarenden with his wife, Eloise St. Vrain, and all of it was sweet with memories of other days. Not in peril and privation and uncertainty did we follow the trail now. The Pullman has replaced the Conestoga wagon, dainty viands the coarse food smoke-blackened over camp-fires, and never fear of Kiowa nor Comanche broke our slumber. The long shriek that cuts the air of dawn was not from wild marauders on a daybreak raid down lonely cañons, but from the throats of splendid, steel-wrought engines swinging forth upon their solid, certain course.

The prairies still lap up to the edges of the little town of Burlingame, whose main street is still the old trail's path. The well has long since disappeared from the center of the place. Where once the thirsty gathered here to drink, there stands a monument sacred to the memory of the old trail days. And sacred, too, to the memory of the one far-visioned woman, Fannie Geiger Thompson, who first conceived the thought of marking for the coming generations the course of commerce that built up the West in years gone by.

We never lived in Burlingame, where once--a heart-hungry little boy--I longed to have a home. But the Krane children and their children's children still make it an abiding-place for us.

To Council Grove, and old Pawnee Rock, the Cimarron Crossing of the Arkansas River, the open plain about the site of old Fort Bent--where only ghosts of walls and the court remain, and on to Santa Fé, dreamy and picturesque--hoary with age, and sweet with sacred memories, we wandered on our golden-wedding trail.

The name of Narveo in New Mexico still stands for gentleman. The old church of San Miguel still shelters troubled hearts, and in the San Christobal valley the Pictured Rocks still build up a rude stair for feet that still may need the sanctuary rim of safety set about them. Along the length of the old trail a marvelous fifty years have enriched a history whose epic days record the deeds of vanguards, who foreran and builded for the softer days of golden-wedding years. The last lap of all that wondrous journey bore us in ease and comfort beyond the desert--the Africa, of Aunty Boone's weird fancy--to the Grand Cañon of the Colorado. Here, as of old, the riven crust, in its eternal silence, and sublimity, and beauty indescribable, calmly, year by year, reveals its mighty purpose:

To quarry the heart of earth,
Till, in the rock's red rise,
Its age and birth, through an awful girth
Of strata, should show the wonder-worth
Of patience to all eyes.

Amid luxurious surroundings we lived the October days upon the cañon's rim, where, half a century ago, we had gone in hardship and looked on tragedy. We crept down all the dizzy lengths to the very heart of it, and ate and slept in easy comfort, and gazed upward at the sky-cleaving edges thousands of feet above us; we stood beside the raging Colorado River, which no man had explored when we first looked upon it here. In the serene hours of our sunset years we went back in memory over the long way our feet had come. Life is easy for us now, made so by all the splendid, simple forces of those who, in justice, honesty, and broad human sympathy build enduring empire. Not empire gained by bomb and liquid fire, defended by sharp entanglement and cross-trenched to shut out enemies; but empire builded on the commerce of the land, value for value; empire of bridged rivers, quick transportation on steel-marked trails that girdle harvest fields and fruitful pastures; empire of homes and schools and sacred shrines.

Our fifty golden years have seen such empire rise and grow before our eyes, made great by thrift and business sense, swayed by the Golden Rule. An empire rich in love and sweet romance and thrilling deeds of courage and self-sacrifice. Glad am I to have been a vanguard of its trails upon the Kansas prairies and the far Western plains, sure now, as always down the years, that its old law is still a righteous one: To that which is good--

"HOLD FAST."

THE END